Along the Mabole:

Two Years in Sierra Leone

Daemion Lee

Along the Mabole: Two Years in Sierra Leone

Copyright © 2024 Daemion Lee

Published by: Daemion Lee

All rights reserved. No part of this book may be used or reproduced or transmitted in any form by any means, electronic or mechanical, including photocopying and recording, or by any information storage and retrieval system, except as may be expressly permitted by the 1976 Copyright Act or in writing from the publisher.

This is a work on nonfiction. Names have been changed to protect privacy.

Editor: Brooke Goode
Cover design and page layout: Daemion Lee
Cover image: original watercolor by Daemion Lee

ISBN: 979-8-9917836-0-6

Along the Mabole

7	Introduction
11	Someday I Will Speak Krio
29	Almost Like a Dream
40	Of Cassava Farms and Kola Nuts
48	Come Let Us Eat Rice
69	Not-o Monkey-o
84	African Bicycles
89	Uses of the Banga Tik
93	Kamasiki
97	You De Suck Boobie
107	Islam in Waridala
113	Snake Bites and Witch Guns
120	Donki Sali
124	Ramadan in Waridala
131	The Hippopotami in Sierra Leone

135	Lake Sonfon
143	Cow vs Farmer
155	Mount Bintumani
171	River No 2
179	The School in a House
196	We Haven't Had a Riot
203	A Wula Ka Jan
208	Teaching Africa English
217	From The Village to the City
224	Lick Your Palm Three Times
230	Schools for Africa
247	Study the Koran with the Maninka
252	Election 2012
263	Towards Tiwai
295	Afterword

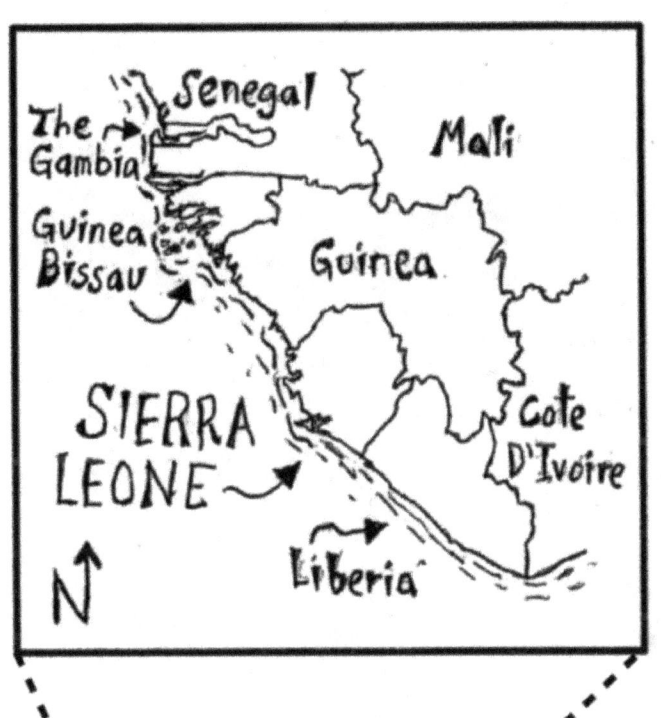

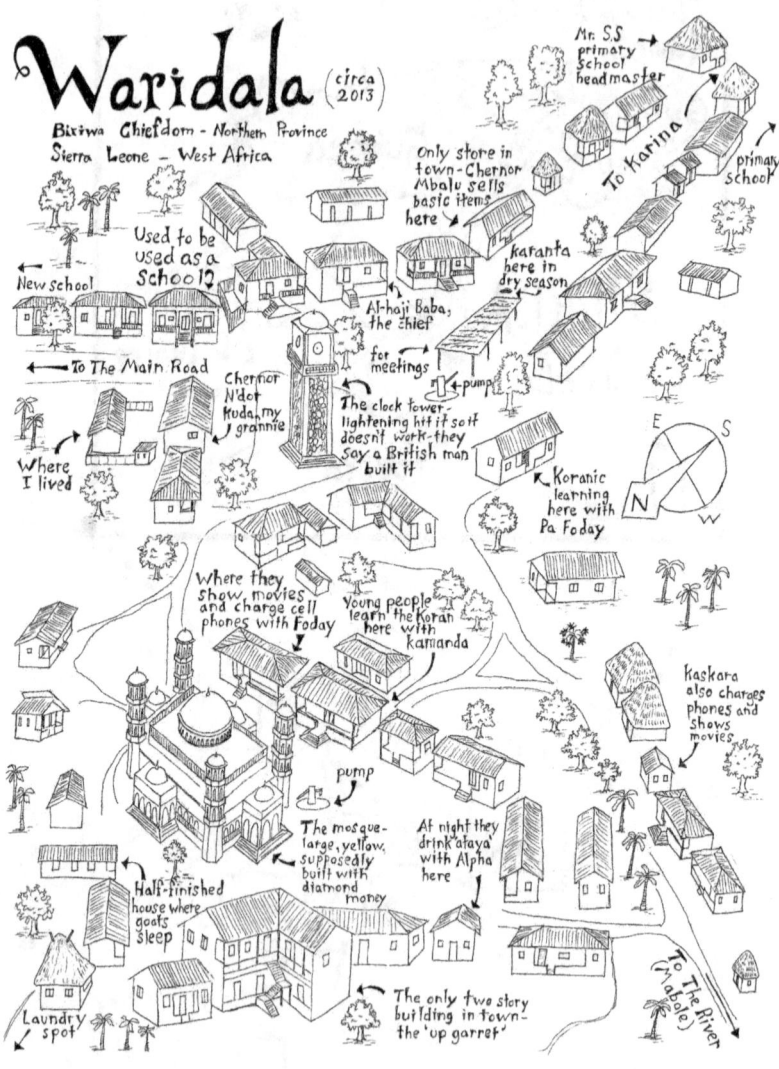

Introduction

In 2011, I left the U.S. and my home state of Oregon, where I had grown up in a small town on the coast and I moved to Sierra Leone, West Africa. It was a dizzying transition. I had graduated university a few years previously and was still exploring. In the midst of the 2008 Great Recession, and a lackluster job market, I decided to apply to the Peace Corps, although, truth be told, I probably would have made the same decision in better economic circumstances as well. I wanted to see the world, not just to travel but to live somewhere new and different and do something positive while I was at it. Like many, I wanted to leave my small-town upbringing and get as far away as possible. The Peace Corps seemed like a good way to do that.

I almost didn't make it through the paperwork phase. This was back when Peace Corps applicants could only pick a region of preference, rather than a specific country. I indicated an interest in going to Africa if no other reason than it seemed as far away as I could imagine. As part of the application process, I had to get a physical and even get checked out by a dentist, and send all the forms and reports back to Peace Corps headquarters in Washington D.C.

I was living in Providence, Rhode Island at the time, without a regular doctor or dentist. Out of convenience if nothing else I made an appointment with a dentist who had a little office downtown right off Kennedy Plaza. I remember the dentist charging me extra to take the x-rays of my teeth home with me – so I could mail them off – and I was so annoyed about the extra charge. In retrospect, this exchange presaged the extensive "talking price" that I would have to do in Sierra Leone, the land of bargaining and flexible prices.

I also had to get a series of extra vaccines. I dutifully made an appointment at a local urgent care, where I had been once previously when I was sick. This is where I got stuck. It turned out that the clinic did not have one of the vaccines I needed, a required polio booster vaccine. I remember being a little surprised about the polio one – was that even a thing anymore? I understood the need for vaccines for infamous tropic diseases like yellow fever, but polio was unexpected to me. At that time, though, polio still did persist in isolated cases around the world, including in Sierra Leone. The need for a polio vaccine was, unfortunately, also unexpected for whoever oversaw the stocking the vaccine refrigerator at the clinic. I was told that they could order it, but it would take a week. In the meantime, I had had a cross country trip planned – a bicycle trip to Oregon in fact – which is its own separate, rather long story. I had no choice, I felt, but to pause the search for the booster vaccine.

By this time, I had even advanced far enough in the application process to be assigned a general region – Francophone West Africa – and the recruiter I worked with thought it probably meant Cameroon. I was likely going to be working in the education sector, given that my main qualification was being a somewhat-recent college graduate. But I spent that summer traveling, and I missed a deadline for completing some of the paperwork, including being injected with the appropriate number, and type, of vaccines.

However, I was persistent and once I was back in Oregon, I resumed the search for a polio booster. As I recall, some of the medical stuff I had to redo, including the physical, and I think I had to call the Peace Corps office a couple of times to get everything straightened out. It is worth mentioning that this was before the price of college tuition really took off – I had graduated in 2008 -- and I had been able to graduate student-loan free from a state college. This meant I had the freedom to work odd jobs and sort out Peace Corps paperwork in the meantime without much concern for paying bills. Among other things, I worked at a cranberry farm that winter, a major crop in the little corner of coastal Oregon where I grew up.

Finally, I checked off all the boxes in the application process and I received the packet in the mail: I had been accepted to the Peace Corps and I was going to Sierra Leone. I didn't even know where Sierra Leone was, at the time, and I thought for a moment that I was heading to South America, given the rather Latin-sounding ring to the county's name. There is, in fact, a Romance-language connection: the Portuguese had been the first European explorers along the West African coast. But at the time I knew next to nothing of West African history or geography.

    The packet included a small pamphlet titled "Your Assignment" which included my start dates – June 1-2, 2011 -- and a warning that I had only seven days to respond to the offer. It was exciting. The pamphlet was written in a friendly second person – "Congratulations on your selection to serve in our friendly and peace-loving county" and I was informed that "Your assignment will be to teach English at the junior or senior secondary level." I could see the pamphlet attempted to present realistic picture of Sierra Leone. The text balanced the positive – Peace Corps is "well-loved in Sierra Leone" – with the difficulties – "you will be challenged by social norms and school systems that differ from your experience in the US." The pamphlet acknowledged the history of war in the country: "In April 1992, a coup d'état necessitated that the 82 Peace Corps Volunteers in Sierra Leone leave the country" and noted that Peace Corps operations had only recommenced the previous year, in 2010. Conditions sounded a bit grim – "Your school may be small, overcrowded and poorly lit" – although some attempt was made to leaven the grit with some humor: "Some of your best and worst Peace Corps memories will involve transportation!" I was assured, at least, of cell phone connectivity – "Almost all calls are made by cell phone" and was told the Peace Corps would be providing me with a phone.

    Certainly, I had access to books to read and websites to browse, to learn more about the country, and I did so. I learned that Sierra Leone is located on the Atlantic coast, a former British colony, though the Portuguese originally explored the area, naming the mountainous peninsula along the coast "Lion Mountains." It was a bit of poetic license, perhaps, given the area is not known for lions. Perhaps it earned the name instead for the way the mountains crouched on the horizon. Freetown, the capital, was originally founded as a settlement for former slaves and was ruled as a British colony until independence. The mixture of ethnic groups in Freetown gave rise to Krio – both the name of a group of people and their language. With time, Krio became the language that, in the present time, is spoken by people across the country. The country is a mixture of various ethnic groups – mostly Themne in the north and Mende in the south – with religion a mixture of Muslim and Christian. Independence took place in 1962 and worsening corruption, in part, lead to the country's civil war, thirty years later, in 1992.

But even as I tried to learn more, it was hard to know where to start, or where to finish. Quite simply, moving to this new place was hard to imagine. "Expect a slower pace of life," the pamphlet warned. "Managing these differences in a socially acceptable way will also be part of your challenge." Good luck; don't lose your mind, in other words. I didn't really know what I had gotten myself into until arrived in Freetown, Sierra Leone in June of 2011. Over the next 27 months of my Peace Corps service, I sketched and wrote like I never had before. I had plenty of free time, that was part of it, but it was also a way to make sense of the new world that I was living in. At first, I kept a journal, noting my observations, but somehow, I felt this approach didn't quite capture the place. Instead of writing a chronological record, I started taking a thematic approach, writing about the people around me, routines I observed, and events I took part in. I drew with what I had available: mostly printer paper and ball point pens. Now, ten years later, I put together those writings and drawings into a narrative. My sketches were at times simple, but they captured a certain immediacy, the thrill of putting pen to paper to capture something interesting. I edited my text, where warranted, with the benefit of hindsight, but I also tried to keep the original spirit of what I wrote as much as I could.

Someday I Will Speak Krio

Our arrival in Sierra Leone was how you might imagine it would be in a tropical county. We all got off the plane, stepped into the humidity and walked across the hot tarmac towards the airport building. The sign on top read Freetown International Airport in slightly crooked letters, an ambitious claim for this quiet, rundown building. We hadn't quite arrived though. We still had to load up into the Peace Corps vehicles and drive to the ferry that takes passengers across the bay to the city of Freetown, about a 30-minute boat trip. On the ferry ride over, the Peace Corps doctor gave us a talk about malaria, then we all were given our first dose of anti-malaria pills, a medicine called Lariam. The large white pills had a strange bitter taste and it felt like I had just joined a cult. The ferry ride, although less than an hour, didn't end until well after dark, and then it was still necessary to navigate throngs of motorcycles, stalled cars, and overloaded flatbed trucks.

We reached our destination, the Stadium Hostel and, along with the rest of the new Sierra Leone Peace Corps Volunteers, I went to sleep that night in Africa. I had a roommate, but I was so tired, and the moment was so intense, I hardly interacted with him. In the darkness, the tropical rain poured down, rustling the leaves and slapping the ground.

In the morning the rain had stopped, and I woke to the sound of the news from BBC Africa blaring on a radio from somewhere outside. It was June in 2011, the beginning of the rainy season, and I was now a Peace Corps volunteer-in-training. The rain came that day in fits and starts, alternating between sudden downpours and blazing sun.

For the next few days, we were all in effect under house arrest at the Stadium Hostel, the lodgings adjacent to Sierra Leone's National Stadium. The rooms were dirty and worn, the building wrapped by walls and barbed wire. The house arrest was for our own safety, we were told. And I didn't doubt it. I didn't know what kinds of mistakes were possible to make in this new place. We were given cell phones, at least, simple but functional, and I was able to call home to say I'd made it.

Perhaps this was the most remarkable thing—that I was able to call home so easily. I had heard stories from Peace Corps volunteers who served decades ago who were only able to phone home once every three months, or not at all. But cell phones were ubiquitous in Sierra Leone in 2011, the wireless technology meaning that little infrastructure was needed to spread coverage around the region. As I would later learn, in some ways nothing changes in Sierra Leone, especially in the small villages. But in 2011 everyone, it seemed, had a cell phone. Charging them was difficult at times, and coverage spotty in rural areas, but calling home was as easy as pressing a button. By the time I would leave, two years later, internet-connected cell phones were becoming common as well.

From the window of my room, it was possible to see the ocean; that was my favorite view, the jumble of buildings and vegetation that gradually sloped down to the placid blue of the Atlantic, the sea often dotted with small, colorful fishing boats. Freetown, at least from a distance, was beautiful. From the window I also caught glimpses of street scenes, chaotic, vibrating with a strange intensity. In the alley visible out my window, people trickled by, dressed in bright colors, many balancing bags and buckets on their heads, their black skin sweating in the sun. The massive graveyard across the street, with lush rainy-season vegetation surrounding the gravestones, imparted a somber air to this experience of house arrest.

One day a soccer game took place at the National Stadium, throngs spilling out into the streets, people inside and outside the stadium yelling and cheering. Police officers in blue camouflage waded through the chaos, directing traffic, while a local marching band, complete with bells, drums, shakers and a wooden box as a bass drum, wove through the crowd. The tension in the atmosphere seemed to suggest some kind of mounting crisis and I wasn't sure what was coming next, but after the game the crowds dispersed, and I felt an odd sense of relief.

It was a strange experience to suddenly land in the middle of this country, this new world. I had experienced a

The view of the Atlantic from the hostel

geographic relocation but also an abstract and conceptual change: a change in culture. My familiar sources of meaning, family, friends, media, consumer products, social customs, were thousands of miles away. As a white person, I was now a minority in a majority black country. For a while when I first arrived it was like I couldn't quite think right: My thoughts were curiously empty. My disorientation was perhaps heightened by the fact that I was going to have to stay here for two years. I was both excited and terrified.

After a few days, all the volunteers were brought to the north central city of Makeni for ten weeks of training, where the Peace Corps had arranged for each of us to stay with a host family. We again took the Peace Corps vehicles through the chaos of Freetown, and then continued onto the relatively wide, well paved road that cut through the low rolling hills that stretch inland from the Freetown peninsula. After the bustle of Freetown, the land suddenly seemed empty, just brush and scattered palm trees. We passed occasional villages with grass roofs, traders trying to sell snacks to the passengers in the vehicles that stop, mangos and guavas and roasted corn and other food I didn't recognize. It was a three-hour drive, although my own sense of the passage of time had long since been distorted, and the trip felt like anything from one hour to one day.

Makeni is a hot, flat city spread out on the central plateau of Sierra Leone, and, like Freetown, growth outstripped the infrastructure, giving the town a ragged, unfinished look. When we arrived at the hall where training was to be held, the sun was out and the heat fierce. A group of drummers was performing as we arrived and a couple of men traded off as lead dancer, athletically demonstrating acrobatic dance moves. All the volunteers shook hands with the new Peace Corps staff and we wiped away sweat to the beat of the drums. I remember being surprised at how dirty the inside of my shirt collar was by the end of the day, a spectacular brown-black streak, created by a potent mixture of sweat and dust.

Being white, like the majority of Peace Corps volunteers, I was highly visible in this nation of black people. The tropical sun was particularly brutal on the white volunteers, giving many a reddened, wilted look, but the black locals seemed to glow in the sunshine. I soon learned that I was automatically given a degree of respect and deference that was based on my skin color. It was strange and unsettling to see how people deferred to me, how assumptions were made based only on my skin color.

Spectators at Wussom field watching a football game, i.e. soccer

That afternoon, we had an Adoption Ceremony, where we were introduced to our host families. All the volunteers were new to the Peace Corps and the Peace Corps was new to Sierra Leone—it was in its second year after re-opening in 2010—and everyone was excited on that day: volunteers, staff, and host families. "Adoption" seems like a strong term, but I really felt like a child, still learning about the basic routines of life, so perhaps it was fitting. After each of the new family arrangements were announced, we ate rice together — Sierra Leone's staple food — and then everyone dispersed into various corners of Makeni for the first night with a Sierra Leonean family.

That night, my host father, Alhaji Sorie Koroma, took me for a walk around town in the darkness, along roads without sidewalks as motorcycle taxis whizzed by. *Okada*, I later learned, was the local term for these ubiquitous two-wheel forms of transportation. The night was thick and hot and in the glare of headlights, I felt disoriented and confused. I could see that shacks lined the road, built from sticks and tin roofing – structures used by traders and other people with small businesses

– and pedestrians flooded the edges of the roadway. Some larger buildings – shadows and silhouettes in the darkness – were visible, too, set off from the chaos of the street. I didn't see sidewalks at the edge of the street, only the broken edge of the pavement.

The TVS Star motorcycle: small and cheap.

What people take to get around in Makeni

Le 1,000 to go anywhere in town

We came to a roundabout, the center of town I later learned, and the buzz of *okada* traffic increased. I thought, for perhaps the third time on that walk, that I might die. In the darkness, I felt my host father grab my hand, his palm and rough fingers gently touching mine. It was a shock at first, for one accustomed to American ideas about what men should do with their hands when they are together, but I found his touch strangely comforting in this new place. Men holding hands in this gentle, casual way, I later learned, is a common sign of affection. We safely crossed the road and he released my hand, but the feeling stayed with me.

The next couple of weeks was difficult. I became suddenly very ill, and I made frequent use of the night "soil bucket" that the Peace Corps provided to volunteers— a small, lidded plastic bucket that made it possible to avoid outdoor latrines at night. I puked and shit into that bucket constantly for several days before somehow the stomach bug turned into a respiratory infection, and I began wondering if I had malaria.

Bananas from a tree, not a boat

That wasn't all. Soon after my illness developed, an even stranger thing happened to my body. One evening I was casually sitting on Alhaji's veranda with one ankle over my knee, and when I stood up my lower leg was tingly and numb. Some sensation quickly returned, but my right toe remained without any feeling. Inexplicably, my toe was numb. I had no ability to move it. I was terrified. I didn't know what was happening and it seemed an inopportune time to experience a neurological disease. I was able to walk, but I had to adjust my gait to accommodate the numbness.

Somehow, though, my body gradually became used to this new place. My respiratory and gastrointestinal infection cleared up over time; it was not malaria after all. The Peace Corps doctor helpfully suggested that my numb toe was possibly related to my malaria prophylaxis, Lariam, also known as mefloquine, which is widely known to have severe side effects such as vivid nightmares. Extremity numbness, though not as well documented, seemed to be a side effect as well. A month later, after changing malaria medications, to doxycycline, sensation returned to my foot.

Eventually, I became healthy enough to begin learning. The Peace Corps provided us training about Sierra Leone culture and Peace Corps policies and provided local language trainings. We were all education volunteers, destined to be assigned to teach in local secondary schools, so we were also trained in pedagogical techniques, such as how to create effective lesson plans. These trainings were led by Americans and Sierra Leoneans. Sessions lasted all day; it was a bit grueling and tedious at times, but information gradually soaked in.

We learned more about the state of education in the country and how in 2002, President Tejan Kabbah instituted universal primary education in the wake of the civil war. The country was faced with the tremendous task of finding enough qualified teachers to teach and enough money to pay them. By 2010, when the Peace Corps returned to the country, huge numbers of primary students were graduating into secondary schools and the country didn't have enough people to teach them. Teaching, especially in secondary schools, became the primary focus for the Peace Corps as it reopened. Peace Corps volunteers were providing much needed staffing for the schools and our arrival provided much positive symbolism as the country was rebuilding.

But before we could head out to teach, there was a lot to learn first, starting with new languages. Language courses were the most interesting; we all learned Krio—an English creole and the national language of Sierra Leone—and we also learned a local language, depending on our placements. It was overwhelming and exciting at the same time, a whole-body learning experience and I did my best to take in all that I could.

One of the first things one learns about Krio is it sounds like English until suddenly it doesn't. The sound of familiar English words used in Krio, like "go" and "come" and "eat" and "sleep," can obscure deeper cultural differences built into the language. With an English lexicon combined with various words from West African languages and grammar rules more like West African languages, the linguists say Krio is its own language. But Sierra Leoneans seem to think Krio is English with a Sierra Leonean accent. They are both right in their own way, but the Sierra Leonean view seems like a more accurate description. As I began learning it, at times I couldn't quite tell if I was speaking Krio or English. But language is culture, they say, and Krio really does seem like English that has been adapted to fit a different culture. The language gives Sierra Leone a surprising national unity. With 16 different ethnic groups speaking as many languages in the country, the Krio language provides an easy way for everyone to communicate.

It was straightforward to pick up the basics, but more complex topics were immediately opaque. Interestingly, Krio gets pulled in the direction of one's native language; I found people whom I knew spoke English to be easier to understand when they were speaking Krio, compared to those who didn't speak English. Krio was a fun language to learn, and an easy window into Sierra Leone culture, as we were continuously reminded by the Peace Corps staff. Sierra Leoneans were delighted to hear Americans speak Krio, even if at first, I could only say a few basic phrases.

I will always remember one of the Sierra Leonean trainers telling us, when we were first learning Krio, about how important it was to greet people. *"Aw di bodi? "Aw yu slip?" "Aw di time?" "Aw di work?" "Kushe-o."* "That's the culture," she said, "and never forget it." She told us a story about a man who was walking along a footpath during the time of Sierra Leone's civil war and he passed some people sitting under a tree. The man greeted them and the people told the man to turn back because rebels were ahead. He gratefully followed their advice. Sometime later another man was walking along the same path and he failed to greet the people under the tree. As a result, the people offered no warning and the man walked into a trap set by the rebels. It was a chilling story, and from the way she told it, I couldn't tell if it was a tale told for the sake of illustration, or something that had truly happened. But I never forgot to greet after that.

For the most part during training, references to the civil war were brief and off hand, such as the cautionary tale about greeting. But I do remember one training session in which the Sierra Leone staff members addressed the legacy of the war directly. They chose to perform a skit, to explain the origins of the war as they saw it. I remember some silly costumes and some laughter, as they attempted to address the unspeakable legacy of war and violence. They chose to emphasize the Organization of African Unity summit, in 1980, as a turning point.

In the 70's and 80's, a politician named Siaka Stevens took power in Sierra Leone and he ran the country by means of one-party rule for nearly 20 years. Stevens built up an informal system of patron-client relationships with himself at the pinnacle. The government was slowly starved of funding. Teachers weren't paid. Roads crumbled. Opposition leaders were hanged or simply disappeared. Stevens spent lavishly to host the Organization of African Unity summit in 1980, diverting already limited public funds towards the event.

This was the moment that the Sierra Leonean Peace Corps staff portrayed in their skit. I recall that the staff person who portrayed Stevens made him pompous yet sinister. The upshot of their skit was that the grift and mismanagement that characterized the OAU summit in 1980 helped push Sierra Leone towards chaos and war.

By the 1990's, fighting broke out. No one knows exactly why, but it did. Conflict had been raging in Liberia and then it spilled over into Sierra Leone, and the weakened national government could do nothing. Political corruption, poverty, and widespread frustration were factors that many cited as reasons for the conflict. Ethnic divisions or religion did not play a major role. On March 23rd, 1991, the rebels entered the town of Bomaru near the Sierra Leone-Liberia border. The rebel forces called themselves the Rebel United Front and began a campaign of looting and violence, initially in the southern and eastern parts of the country. At the time few people realized how serious the conflict would prove to be. The military's efforts to end the fighting were ineffective and the violence escalated. The conflict

Pineapple, widely available in the rainy season

was fueled, in part, by the illicit diamond sales from the mineral-rich areas in the eastern part of the country. An estimated 50,000 people were killed and even more fled as refugees to Liberia and Guinea. Krio, the language of Freetown, spread more widely. During the conflict, huge population shifts occurred, as people fled the violence seeping into their communities. Krio became a last resort for communication for many people. A UN peacekeeping force eventually intervened in the conflict, but it wasn't until the arrival of British forces that the conflict was finally put to an end in 2002.

    It may be that the civil war is what Sierra Leone is most known for. But I took to heart the skit the staff performed about the OAU summit in 1980 – that the real story of the war wasn't the violence and the killing, but deep-seated corruption and the use of public institutions for private gain. It had been a problem long before the civil war, and the fighting, if anything, had perhaps made the corruption worse. In those first weeks in

Sierra Leone, I think all the volunteers had a sort of morbid curiosity about the war and what had happened. But I learned later that it was the corruption, in the school systems, in the government, in the working of local communities, that had a much greater impact on day-to-day life.

    Staying with a host family, where we learned about culture firsthand, was perhaps the most educational part of training. My host father lived with his wife and three young children. But the boundaries of his family didn't stop there. The compound Alhaji's family lived in belonged to his cousin, who owned a large cluster of houses, one of which he lived in. A steady flow of people circulated through the compound, borrowing things, sharing food, talking, all of whom were in some sense part of the family.

    This communal living came with a new set of standards for privacy that I had to get used to. People are together, all the time, and being alone was not common, not normal. Even when I first arrived and was so sick I could hardly move, my host father stayed home from school to keep me company. The solitary habits of this introverted American were something my hosts would have had difficulty understanding. I didn't know how to explain my need for privacy, though the luxury of having my own room, which the Peace Corps required of the host families, made it easier to manage.

    But whether I was ready or not, immediately I was a part of this community. I was involved in the family's daily routines, even matters of life and death, as I learned about halfway through the training. When I first moved in with my host family, my host mother was quite pregnant. And while I was still living with them, she delivered the baby. They decided to name the baby after my father, Alan, and the baby only lived for about a week. I do not know the details of exactly what happened, but the child was weak and ill from birth and had to stay at the hospital. He never came home. Alhaji visited his wife and child frequently and brought meals. I came along on one of these visits and they let me hold the baby. He was so small, nestled in his swaddle, and he hardly moved. I had little experience with infants, and I was afraid I would break him. It was unexpected that they had named him after my father, although I later learned that babies are almost always named after a relative or other important person in the parents' lives. Among other things, it's a way to curry favor.

The view of the street from my host family's veranda

When the infant passed away, I was mortified. I had no idea what to say, other than "*Osh ya*," as they say in Krio, meaning something like "sorry." The funeral and burial happened on the same day the child passed away, in accordance with Muslim practices, and the family appeared to move on quickly. I could only imagine how they felt, the sadness of losing a child, compounded by the fact that their ordeal was witnessed by this visitor from the U.S. whom they deeply wanted to impress. The experience framed my stay in Sierra Leone. I felt involved in the infant's passing; they had named it after my dad, after all. Death seemed closer, in this place with little infrastructure, nonexistent safety precautions, and rudimentary health care. Life seemed simpler and more precarious here.

Fortunately, the other lessons I learned during my time with the host family were more mundane. Infrastructure is rudimentary, to put it mildly, requiring a lot of extra work. During my stay in Makeni, bathing involved a bucket, using the toilet involved going to a communal latrine, and access to water involved going to a well. The easier way to get water was by placing buckets under the eaves to catch the rain; usually there was a scramble in the compound at the beginning of a big downpour as people positioned their empty buckets in the necessary places.

Buckets for laundry a.k.a. brooking

Clothes were washed by hand, using several buckets of water, soap, and the heel of your palm. They call it to "brook" in Krio. Small plastic kettle-like containers, called "coolers" in Krio, were ubiquitous, used for pouring, rinsing, and washing—a substitute for a faucet in a place without plumbing. At night, the town was plunged into darkness, with battery-powered LED flashlights providing feeble light in the darkness. My host father put a special LED light in my room and with great ceremony he would insist on installing the batteries and turning it on once it got dark, even if I wasn't in the room. Some of the wealthier families had generators to turn on in the evenings, though they rarely did so due to the cost of fuel. An important part of many people's evening routines involved charging their cell phones, which meant going to one of the many charging booths that lined the streets, with generators roaring, and leaving it to charge for a few hours for a small fee.

The bench on the veranda, all purpose social tool

    Entertainment options were few, at least compared to what I was used to. Sitting on the veranda was common. The veranda is the most important area of the house, where cooking, eating, cleaning, and relaxing takes place, where children play, chickens peck, and people nap. My host family's veranda was simple, with a concrete floor, low concrete walls, a roof. On their veranda was perhaps the prize possession of the household: a wooden bench. It was a simple wooden bench, able to seat three men intimately, small enough to be easily carried around the house or yard. At first I thought veranda-sitting was boring, but eventually I came to appreciate it —"keep time" they call it in Krio, when people sit together and talk or listen to the radio or simply sit in silence.

    From the veranda, I spent a lot of time watching people going by. The passersby would usually be carrying something they had just purchased, or items they were selling. Whatever they had, often it was balanced on their heads. They call it to "tote" in Krio. Usually, it is the women and children who were carrying things, but men do it too. I was filled with wonder at this method of carrying. Buckets of water, tubs of sandals, bundles of sticks, trays of peanuts, boxes of bread, all were balanced on the head carefully and seemingly without effort.

A coal pot, handmade from scrap metal, with a pot balanced on top

The other part of veranda-sitting involved greeting people who stopped by to visit. Greetings were in Krio, English, or Themne, the language of Makeni—sometimes a little bit of all the three together—and also involved handshaking, but not the firm grip-and-release handshake common among white males in the U.S. These were more like "hand hugs" and it took a while for me to get used to them. They involved squeezing, but not too firmly, sometimes adding a few pulses of pressure to convey feeling. Some people would touch their chest after shaking hands; others supported the right elbow with the left hand, a gesture of respect. Often the handshakes were quite prolonged, especially when meeting someone for the first time, and sometimes I found that the other person just held on and wouldn't let go. Usually, if I was unsure of the exact handshaking protocol, I would just smile widely, in order to make my intentions unmistakable.

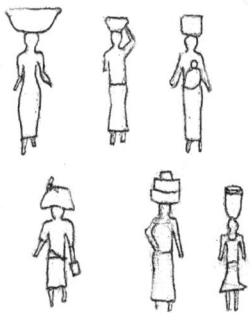

Women toting items to and from the market

Petty theft is one of the most common crimes, largely because almost everyone is extremely poor. It is an interesting tension that such hospitable people could be so prone to theft, but some take advantage of the anonymity granted by the growing populations in urban areas. My host family's house had three different rooms, a so-called parlor, i.e., a living room, and two bedrooms, one of which was mine.

One volunteer told a chilling story about someone trying to force down her bedroom door during the night—with her inside—and how the door frame was beginning to split before the intruder gave up. The windows in my room had no glass, only screens to discourage the mosquitos and metal bars to discourage the thieves or "tif men" during the night. The conventional wisdom was to close the shutters at night—no matter how hot it might be—and I felt I had no choice but to obey this suggestion. And, fortunately, I had no problems with tif men during my time in Makeni.

A mato odo, *the wooden mortar and pestle, a key part of any house*

Almost Like a Dream

The clock tower in Waridala - the view from my new house.

A colony of sparrows inhabits the tower.

Soon enough, training was over, and it was time to move out to our sites and start teaching. I was assigned to a small village about 25 miles north of Makeni called Waridala. Although it wasn't too far, these 25 miles seemed like a much longer distance, mostly due to the poor state of the roads and rudimentary forms of transportation. In Waridala, I taught English at the small junior secondary school in town.

My first visit to Waridala came about halfway through training when we all went on site visits. The school principals came to Makeni to meet the new Peace Corps volunteers, whom they had applied for, and to learn more about what they were supposed to do to host a Peace Corps Volunteer. The Peace Corps trainees traveled to their schools with their respective principals for a few days to visit the school they were going to be posted to.

My principal was Gibrilla Sesay, a relatively young man for a principal. He had helped build the school from scratch, he told me, and he was eager to involve me in the ongoing process of improving the school. I had no idea how tenuous the school really was in Waridala, although he did admit to me that classes were conducted, as he put it, "in a house." Nor did I have much grasp of the complicated dynamics between Mr. Sesay, a well-educated Themne from Makeni, and the local leaders of Waridala. In short, I was clueless. All I was able to do at that point was do what people told me and pretend I could speak Krio.

The first part of the adventure was just getting to Waridala, about 25 miles north of Makeni. Public transportation involves no tickets, no stations, and no schedules. A traveler goes to the "lorry park," the area of town where you find intra-city transport and looks for a vehicle going in the desired direction. Generally, all the drivers have a helper, usually a younger man, called an apprentice, who calls out the vehicle's destination in the lorry park, helps load the people and their luggage, and collects the fare. All sorts of vehicles serve as transportation; a lorry park contains a wide assortment of cars and vans, usually in various states of disrepair and subject to a variety of modifications.

Mr. Sesay and I found a car going north, in the direction of Waridala. It was a worn-out passenger car probably of 80's vintage, with seats for five. Or at least so I thought. By the time we had finished loading, the driver had put three people in the hatchback, four in the back seat, and one in the front seat, for a total of nine, not including the driver. Only two of the doors worked, so it was a puzzle to figure out how everyone would fit in. Once we were packed in, the overloaded car began its journey, although, of course, we stopped about 100 feet down the road to add another passenger who shared the seat with the driver. That was a total of ten passengers. Later we stopped to let someone onto the roof—his feet hung over the window I was peering out of—putting the count at eleven.

The whole thing was like a comedy routine, yet everyone kept a straight face, for this was the typical procedure. The car itself was falling apart. The starter was a button wired onto the dash; the speedometer's needle was still; the windshield wipers didn't work so when it rained the driver leaned out with a cloth to wipe the windshield. I felt a combination of astonishment, fear, and amusement to be riding in such a contraption.

As this overloaded car sputtered northward, we left behind the crowds of Makeni and the toot of the motorcycle taxi horns. As the road followed the undulations of the land, I watched the landscape go by through the window: It was flat and green and thick with vegetation at that time of year, during the rainy season. A few high rocky outcroppings stood against the horizon like sculptures. Dark clouds gathered in the sky, threatening rain, until the storm passed and the blazing sun returned. Here and there among the palm trees, farms were hacked into the undergrowth, bearing the signature of work done entirely by hand: small plots and irregular rows. On occasion I glimpsed the bright shirt of a person in the fields, the small blot of color soon overwhelmed by the green of the trees. Villages flashed by, with houses of mud walls and conical grass roofs, naked children and menageries of goats, dogs, cats and chickens in the bare dirt yards. Some farmers could afford a tin roof on top of the mud walls. Gradually the undulations of the land deepened and turned into hills. This was the edge of the Guinea Highlands, a mountainous plateau that stretches across Senegal, Guina, Sierra Leone, and Liberia.

At one point, we stopped at a village to drop off one of the passengers; then the car wouldn't start again. The driver enlisted the help of some young men who appeared out of nowhere. They helped push the car, so the driver could pop the car into gear and turn the engine over, thus bump starting it.

Soon, we stopped in Kamabai, a town of about 3,000 near Waridala, and here we had to switch vehicles. It is difficult to get a vehicle that goes directly to Waridala, Mr. Sesay told me, because it is about four miles off the main highway at the end of a dirt road. Eventually an empty van came by out of nowhere and Mr. Sesay arranged for the driver to take us "inside," that is, away from the main road and into the bush. This vehicle was another piece of mechanical artwork, the sliding door on the side wired on, and it also required a few bump starts. Finally, we reached the turnoff to Waridala, which at first I thought was only a wide spot in the road The junction is easy to miss as it blends in with the adjacent bare dirt yard. But a few faded white signs announced the presence of a school, and a few other signs heralded a forgotten international development project, hinting at the presence of a community somewhere nearby.

We rattled down the dirt road. At times thick bush and grasses touched the van on both sides, and in places runoff had cut its own path across the road. The driver followed this thin line scratched into the vegetation, as the soil changed in color from red to brown to black and back again. We passed by small villages, the mud and grass houses gradually decomposing back into the vegetation. Sleepy dogs raised their heads and the more adventurous children called out and yelled at the vehicle while chickens scrambled to get off the road. We crossed over more ruts and rocks and soon we were there: Waridala. My arrival was a little anticlimactic. Everyone in the village was busy with the peanut harvest and since everyone is a farmer, the town was almost empty.

    Mr. Sesay showed me my house—the first one on the right as soon as you come into town—and then he left, to where I wasn't sure. My house was a newer structure, small, with three rooms and a tin roof, concrete walls and floor. It was right across from the school, which, I noted, was indeed a house, an old crumbling concrete house like the others in the village. Inside my house I found a wooden bed with a foam mattress, a mosquito net, a few rough wooden tables made by the local carpenters, and a metal lock box where I was to put my valuables. I checked my phone and, remarkably, I had faint service.

    I felt fresh and free and light. And I had no idea what to do or what would come next. A few curious neighbors visited me, Mr. Sesay checked on me later, but mostly I was on my own. None of the teachers at the school, I later learned, actually lived in Waridala, but it was a while before I understood the implications of this, that Western-style education was new to the area, and that anyone who knew English well enough to potentially teach it no longer lived in the village but had moved elsewhere for other opportunities. Most of the teachers in town were Themnes from Makeni.

    Daylight, when I woke that first morning there, seemed to come suddenly. I could hear people's voices as they prepared for the day, the routines that many had followed their whole lives, which for me were utterly strange and new. I watched as women and children walked to collect water for the day, carrying brightly colored plastic buckets on their head. A group of three cows passed by on the road, trailing behind long ropes, while a man followed behind with a stick. They were wild, tough-looking creatures and I could hear their snorts from inside my house. These mundane routines were fascinating to me.

    Later, some of the young people – my soon-to-be students -- showed me around town, like the Mabole River, a short walk away, almost invisible due to the relatively flat terrain, until you are almost upon it. Along the bank, women washed clothes, beating them against rocks, while children frolicked in the shallows. The origins of the Mabole – like all the rivers in Sierra Leone -- are in the highlands to the northeast, and as the river crosses the flat lowlands it begins to meander before it joins the Little Scarcies River and empties into the Atlantic. In some cases rivers may serve a connecting function for people, but the Mabole seemed more like a boundary. Some rivers in Sierra Leone in fact have different names along their courses, suggesting isolation rather than connection; for example the Rokel River is called the Seli in its upstream reaches. The Mabole only has one name, as far as I could tell, but crossing it was a production, requiring paddling in a wooden vessel carved from a tree trunk. "Over side" people said in Krio when they were going to cross the river, as in "I am going over side." Social division was evident in ethnic composition of the villages: on the Waridala side, a mixture of Maninka, Limba and Fula, while on the other side of the Mabole, the villages were almost exclusively Loko.

Apart from the nearby Mabole, a broken clock tower marked the center of Waridala, a stone structure 50 feet tall, which had been hit by lightning and had to be rung manually. No one in town could give anything other than vague explanations for why the clock tower existed in this village. The houses in town seemed to be more elegant than would be expected for a village, many made of concrete with wide verandas. One house even had two stories, the "up garret" they called it. However, all these structures were built a long time ago, and they were now crumbling and stained. I was told around 500 people lived in Waridala, although it felt smaller than that, perhaps 200. Even so, Waridala was a mid-sized village for the area; many villages' populations consisted of only a handful of families.

Folks in Waridala were especially eager to show me the huge mosque, disproportionate to the size of the village, which people had been telling me about for weeks before I arrived. It was worn, but elegant, a relic from some forgotten time. Later, when I had lived in Waridala for some time, I was told various stories about the mosque. Some said that the mosque was funded by profits from raising cattle, but others said one of the founding brothers of Waridala discovered a diamond in the eastern part of the country, sold it, became rich, and built the Waridala mosque. Some said that the architect who designed the mosque received his inspiration from a devil who would come out of the river at night and communicate to the architect. At night, the man would draw up the plan on paper and by morning he would have the next phase of the construction planned out. It is said that as soon as the construction of the mosque was completed, the man died and the plans were lost. The village elders favored the version about cattle profits.

Even the founding story of Waridala was surrounded by suggestions of the involvement of magic. Everyone agreed that seven brothers of the Fofana surname, lived in Karina, a nearby town. These seven brothers had a large herd of cattle, and they took them to the bush every day to look for grass. Some said there was conflict with the neighbors when the cows destroyed others' farms, and people in town began to argue. So they started their own village. They called it Waridala, which means something like "the place where the cattle are reared." Some said that the brothers had a special connection with the cows, that the brothers and cows could talk with each other. Some even said the cattle could sing. In this version, the brothers told the cows that they needed a new place to live, and the cattle led the brothers to the site where Waridala sits to this day. These stories bordered on the fantastical. But in a place without a written tradition, everyone tells slightly different versions of the same the story, with magic often referred to in this matter-of-fact way. It was not clear if the storyteller believed the fantastical elements of their story, or if it was simply added to make a good tale.

Much of the fighting during the civil war had been concentrated in the southern part of the country, sparing more northern places like Waridala of the brunt of the damage. Even so, the violence had spilled into the north during the latter part of the conflict. The rebels went as far as the northern regional capital of Kabala, well north of Waridala, inflicting a trail of violence and chaos. During this time, people in Waridala told me, they stayed away from main roads, cautiously following bush trails. In the neighboring village of Karina, the rebels entered the town, massacring people as they filed out of the mosque. The violence seemed random, irrational, inspired by nothing more than deep frustration among disenfranchised young men. Later, after I had moved to Waridala, someone showed me a broken window in town, webbed with cracks, a small rectangular hole at the center. The rebels had come through town, I was told, and a rebel had stabbed a machete through the window. They also destroyed the mosque's generator. This damage was slight compared to what was inflicted on other areas, although it seemed no less consequential. The damage to the mosque in particular seemed like a potent symbol of loss to the locals.

Over the course of three days, I was gradually introduced to the people in town. Mr. Sesay introduced me to Foday Sheriff, a teacher at the primary school, who served as my informal guide for the next few days. The people were almost all Maninka, also called Mandingo, with a few other ethnic groups, mostly those who married into the town, and almost all were Muslim. One evening during this visit, Mr. Sesay organized an introduction for me. People gathered around the mango tree in the middle of town, sitting on benches and standing. Formal public introductions are a standard part of the local culture, and Mr. Sesay was sure to give me a proper one, describing where I had come from and what I would be doing in Waridala. Then he introduced the various important community members to me. Almost everyone's last name seemed to be Fofana, and I soon lost track of the names.

Then it was my turn to speak, and I did my best in Krio. I told them, "*Wey I apply fo di Peace Corps, I no know usai ah go go fo tich. Maybe I go enisai na di world. But now, I know usai a de go.*" I was telling them that I didn't know where I was going to go, when I decided to join the Peace Corps, but now I did know. In response, everyone laughed. Then I told them, "*I go de ya fo tu years en a wan fo be insay una family.*" I'll be here for two years and I am ready to join your family, I said. They laughed again and the town chief, Alhaji Baba, told everyone that, if I wanted to be a part of Waridala, I needed to have the right name. So he renamed me Ali Fofana, giving me the surname of three-quarters of the people in Waridala. Perhaps in other contexts, someone giving you a new name would be strange, even awkward, but foreigners receiving new names is the custom across the region, and I took it for what it was: a gesture of hospitality.

My visit to Waridala was an abrupt contrast to Makeni with its bustle, motorcycle horns, constant shouts of "*Opoto!*" — "white person" in Themne — the chant the children in Makeni directed at me constantly. In Waridala, the only sounds were of women cooking, the chickens, and the radio. The children looked at me with great curiosity, but they only watched and did not shout greetings; some were afraid. While white people are rare in Makeni, they are almost unheard of in Waridala, and the children didn't know what to do. While I was there, a couple of young boys even greeted me in Arabic, assuming my white skin indicated a Middle Eastern origin. The residents were poor but generous—for the three days I was there, they provided copious food, and some of it contained chicken, a luxury.

At the end of the site visit, it proved just as challenging to return as it had been to arrive. No vehicles regularly left directly from Waridala, so it was necessary to travel by foot, bicycle, or motorcycle to the highway before one could get transportation. The Peace Corps didn't allow volunteers to ride motorcycles, so that wasn't an option. I didn't have a bicycle yet, so I couldn't ride.

That left only the first option, so I left on foot early in the morning, escorted by Foday Sheriff, one of the only Maninka teachers in Waridala. We headed in the direction of the highway. Along the way we took a detour onto a forest path—I didn't know where we were going but I followed dutifully along. After winding through brush and trees and crossing over a small river on a fallen log, we reached a small village, a Limba village, consisting of a total of about three grass houses. Limbas, I learned later, are known for their isolated villages, and their places of habitation are sometimes called Limba Corners.

Limbas are also famous for tapping palm wine, and, as Mr. Sheriff told me after a rapid Krio conversation, the man who taps the palm trees was coming soon. So this was the reason for the detour: Here, away from the eyes of the Waridala Muslims, we were free to sample some palm wine.

We found a seat behind a grass house and waited for a long time, chatting but mostly just sitting, watching the activity in the village, which was basically nonexistent because it was almost entirely empty. Eventually, the guy showed up with a plastic gallon jug of fresh palm wine, a worn-looking middle-aged man with a bright smile. Over his shoulder he carried what looked like a crude hoop made from dried palm fronds, the only tool he needed to climb the palm trees. It was a wonder that it would ever support the weight of a man.

With great ceremony, Mr. Sheriff poured me a cup and handed it to me. I peered cautiously at the whitish liquid. A bug was floating in my beverage. Several in fact. A fly and a bee, to be precise, and what looked like a couple small grubs. But that was a good sign, Mr. Sheriff told me—that meant that it was fresh. I took a sip of the sweet, mildly alcoholic beverage. It had a sort of fruity taste, almost like the watery remains of a slowly fermenting fruit salad, a taste I didn't learn to appreciate until later. "From God to man," people liked to say about palm wine, a humorous comment about how easily the beverage is made; you just have to climb the tree. The cup Mr. Sheriff had given me was quite large, but it wasn't until I was done drinking that I realized we were going to drink the whole gallon.

After a couple hours of slightly drunken walking, I finally made it to Kamabai, where I caught a ride to Makeni. I felt overwhelmed, confused, but also exhilarated. Waridala was so peaceful, so different from all that I was used to, it seemed like a relic from another time, or a dream even.

About a month later, the Peace Corps Land Rover dropped me back in Waridala and I was there for good. At first, I had no idea what to do in this new town, what to think, what to feel. I sat on my veranda in the green plastic lawn chair someone gave me, at once curious and wary and confused. I didn't yet understand that a large portion of my time would be spent sitting on verandas. I hadn't yet sunk into this world, I hadn't been lulled by its timelessness. I didn't understand that almost nothing happens here, nothing changes, except for the passing of the seasons. In the rainy season, the tin roofs are rained on; in the dry season, they reflect the sun, year after year. Even the chaos of the civil war, ten years old at that point, seemed far away. I didn't yet understand that anything that does happen occurs according to its own obscure timeline.

Of Cassava Farms and Kola Nuts

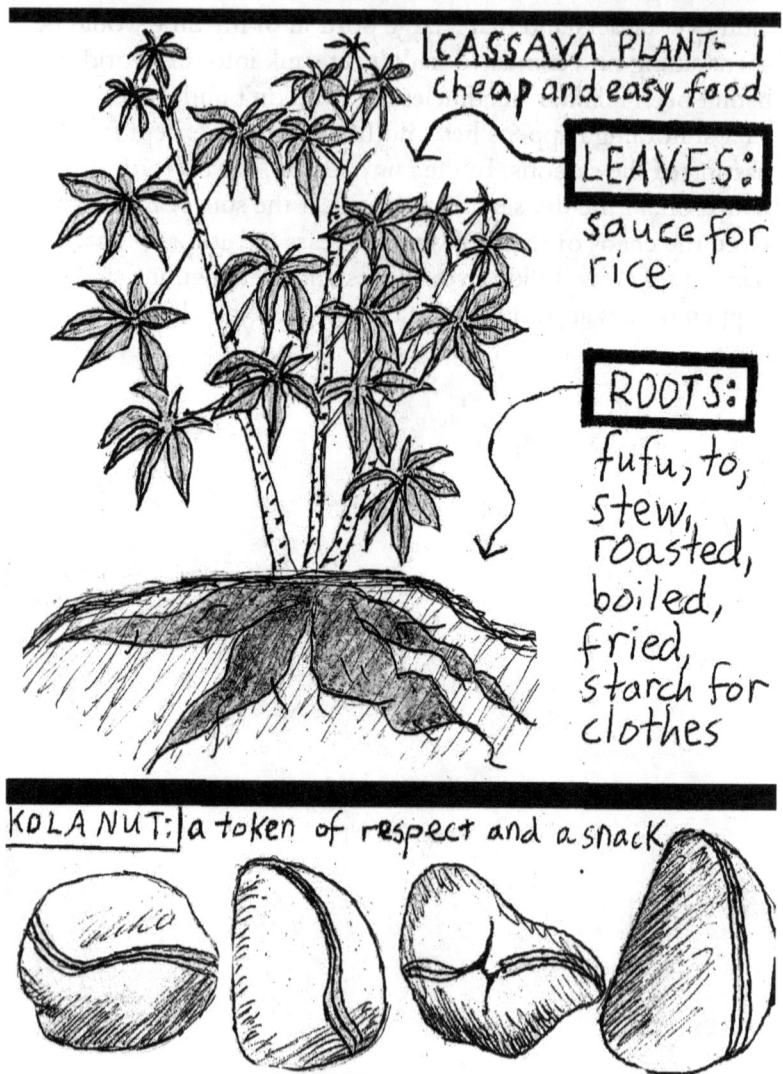

How to plant cassava: 19 Easy Steps.

Soon after I moved to Waridala, I decided to start a "garden" in order to have a source of produce and get to know the community. It quickly became more complicated than I expected. I was assigned a small plot of land, perhaps 100 feet on each side, according to the informal village methods that I didn't quite understand, other than it operated according to verbal agreement. Groundnuts, a.k.a. peanuts, had just been harvested from this plot, I was told, and it is usual to plant cassava after the groundnut harvest. Cassava goes by many names globally — manioc, tapioca, among others — and in Waridala the tuber was a supplement to the usual meals of rice. It was eaten boiled or fried, or pounded into mush and shaped into balls of fufu, or *to*, a dish similar to fufu. During mango season, people would make a stew of cassava and mango called *yebe*. The leaves of the cassava plant are used to make a sauce for rice; it quickly became my favorite variety of sauce.

1. **Get some help.** People told me some farmers in the village could help me get it started. Not seeing any problem with this plan, I agreed. I had little idea about what I'd agreed to. I was "given" some land according local customs that no one really explained to me – perhaps my race helped make it possible.
2. **Give the farmers a kola so they help me.** I was told I had to give a kola nut to formally request their assistance. Kola nuts grow on trees in the bush and appear in two hues: a rich purple and white with yellow highlights. When the nuts are fresh, they almost seemed to glow.
3. **Feel confused about why people make a big deal out of kola nuts because they are so horribly bitter.** A kola nut has different uses. It is a snack, with a sharp, bitter taste followed by a slight buzz from the caffeine content. It is also used as a dye: People use it to make a type of brown tie-dyed-like cloth. Giving a kola nut is considered a sign of respect, often used in meetings between chiefs or elders, or for marriage proposals or religious sacrifices. Or it may be a sign of friendship: The kola nut is broken into pieces and shared among the group.

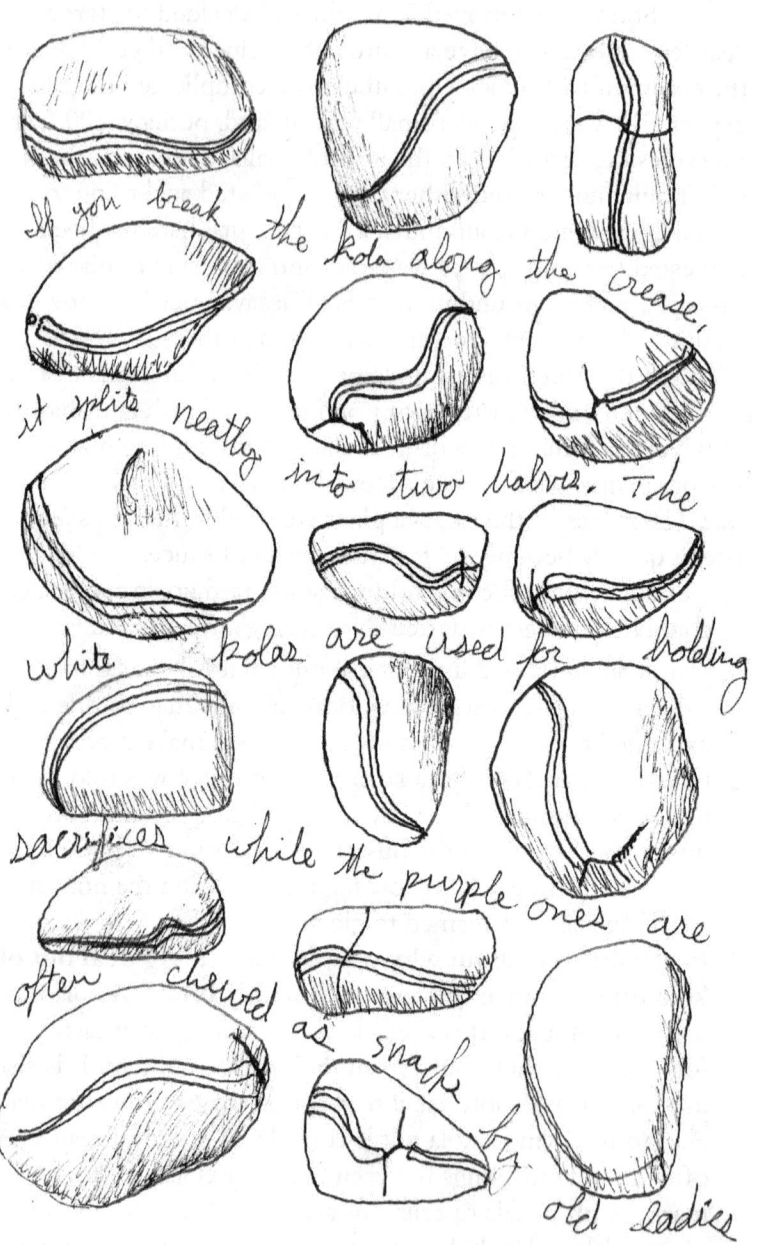

If you break the kola along the crease, it splits neatly into two halves. The white kolas are used for holding sacrifices while the purple ones are often chewed as snacks by old ladies

4. **Realize that "kola" does not always mean "kola nut."** Actually "kola" often really just means money. So when I asked the farmers to help me, I soon realized that I was expected to give them, not a kola nut, but a "kola" of money.
5. **On the day of the work, give the farmers another "kola."** This is not exactly a payment, since prices or rates were never discussed. Rather I was expected to give an amount of money based on the amount of respect I wanted to show the recipient, in accordance with what I was financially capable of. The exchange was not based on a market price, but relationships, the personal and particular terms of the transaction: who is giving, who is receiving, and how much the giver wants to impress the receivers.
6. **Feel confused and humbled because I am no longer in the orderly world of a wealthy capitalistic society.** The exchange took place on the level of the group. The leader of the group of farmers received the kola from me and distributed it. Presumably the leader takes the largest portion of the money and the chief of the town receives a portion as well (i.e., those with higher status get a bigger cut; that's what counts as fair).
7. **Try to help the farmers make "heaps,"** i.e., piles of dirt, for planting the cassava.
8. **Realize that the tool they call a hoe looks different from anything I had seen before, and I am not even sure how to hold it.** A local blacksmith makes a broad, thin blade, curved, with a spike on one end. Meanwhile a tree branch is cut and trimmed, with a thick knot on one end for strength. Then the spike end is heated and driven through the thick knot end of the handle. The hot metal burns a hole into the wood, thus connecting it to the handle.
9. **Receive impromptu lessons about how to use a hoe.** It was harder than it looked. You first select a spot on the ground, then scrape the top layer of soil into a mound, leaving a slight depression around the perimeter of the mound.

10. **Fail at using a hoe.** It was a challenging task but it looks deceptively easy. It was even harder because all the farmers were doing it without gloves and in flip-flops. I tried this bare-hand approach but I did not last long—to be honest, I had blisters almost instantly and my feet hurt.

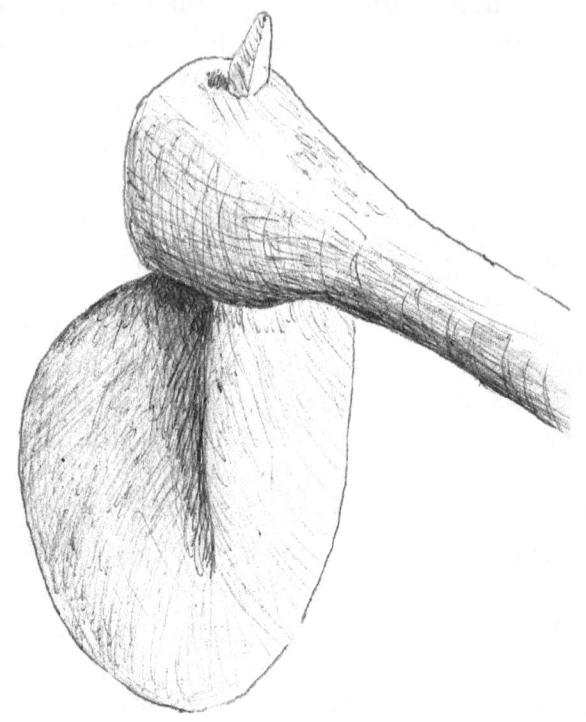

11. **Find someone who will give you their cassava stalks.** This is not too hard: Whenever the roots are harvested, it is necessary to remove the stalks, which are then ready for replanting.
12. **Carry the stalks to my new farm with newly constructed heaps.** One of the boys in the village helped me. He insisted. He rolled up a rag to use as a pad for his head and balanced the cassava stalks on top.

13. **Try to carry cassava stalks on my own head.** I managed to stagger the rest of the way to the farm with stalks on my head. I was the opposite of graceful.
14. **Plant the stalks.** This part is actually very simple. Cut the stalks into short lengths and stick one end into a heap. When a heap has a stalk protruding all over it, every 18 inches or so, move on to the next one.

15. **Wait for the magic to happen.** After a few weeks, the ostensibly dead sticks begin to sprout. It was necessary to weed a few times before I would have a nice harvest. Easy!
16. **Watch helplessly as hordes of green grasshoppers arrive with the dry season.** I believe this was in fact the infamous locust swarm, although it did not engulf any nations, only my farm it seemed. They perched on my cassava plants for weeks until the leaves disappeared and even the bare stalks grew shorter.
17. **Watch in amazement as the dead stalks resprout.** Eventually the rains returned, the grasshoppers departed, and then the plants started growing again. Cassava seems to have an indomitable capacity to grow. The plant is in fact poisonous, although this did not seem to discourage the grasshoppers. The leaves and the skin of the root contain cyanide. That is why you must peel the root and boil the leaves before you can eat them (the grasshoppers did not).
18. **Pick leaves for your neighbor to cook for me and be ridiculed.** You have to pick only the newly sprouted leaves, or it tastes horrible, apparently.
19. **Acknowledge that farming is much harder than I ever imagined it would be.** Growing cassava was physically challenging, extremely time consuming, and unexpectedly involved lots of grasshoppers. The amount of energy that I and others spent on growing the cassava seemed out-of-proportion to the end product, although, as I would learn, this is entirely typical of any farming enterprise.

Epilogue. As it turned out, someone dug up all my tubers and took them before I was able to harvest. So the whole cassava farm project was more or less a disaster. I suppose whoever took them no doubt needed them more than I did.

Come, Let Us Eat Rice
A Story About Cooking

Illustrations by children in Waridala

She had the most beautiful hands I had ever seen. When she spoke, her long, slender fingers would escape from the fist on her lap and unfold gracefully, floating up into the air and making slow pirouettes. When she smiled, her white teeth were radiant against her black skin. She was my cook, my own personal cook, and her name was Haja. The town chief had sent for her; she had been living in Freetown. He called upon her to come to the village to cook for me, the newly arrived foreigner who had come to teach at the village school. I sat, mesmerized by her hands. I think they wanted me to marry her.

Acquiring food in Waridala can be a challenge. There are no supermarkets, or restaurants because people do not buy their food: They grow it. In a place where everyone is a subsistence farmer, the family forms a tight economic unit, growing their food and making it into meals. So, of course I needed to marry, at least according to local custom. How else would I eat?

The arrangement with Haja, however, did not last long. After reaching an agreement with her and the school principal, I gave Haja a month's worth of money to buy ingredients to put in the *plasas*, the Krio word for the sauce that you put on rice. Less than a week passed before she came to me to ask for more money. Clearly some misunderstanding had taken place.

We certainly could have worked out this misunderstanding. However, the situation, I soon learned, was more complicated. Some of the other teachers were telling me a rumor: that Haja was cooking meals of rice for me, but also for her secret lover, too. This man, I was told, also happened to be one of the teachers at my school. I had no idea if these rumors were true but the cooking situation was quickly becoming complicated. I hadn't been living in Waridala for more than a couple weeks or so and I had no idea what to do, or even what was really happening.

The lack of options for food is what made the situation challenging—either I had to learn to cook using local ingredients, or someone had to cook for me. I tried the former option and I only lasted one day. The results were almost inedible. It was difficult to make a single serving of rice and sauce, just for me, because rice and sauce lends itself to family cooking. During my short-lived efforts at cooking, I ended up with leftovers, which went bad overnight, spoiling quickly and viciously in the tropical climate with no refrigeration. I could have purchased harder-to-find ingredients in a larger town and stocked up, in order to broaden my potential menu of recipes.

mortar and pestle
(mata odo and
mata pensil in Krio)

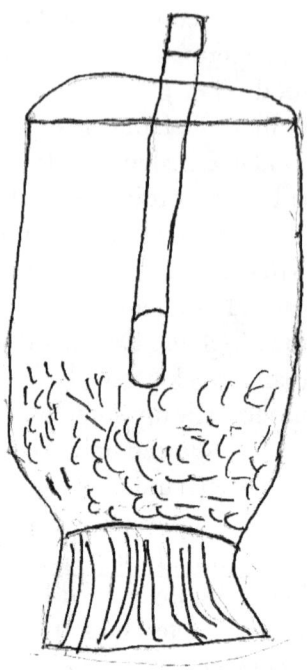
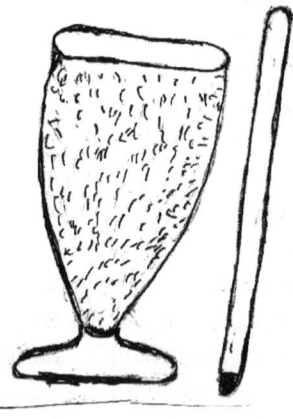

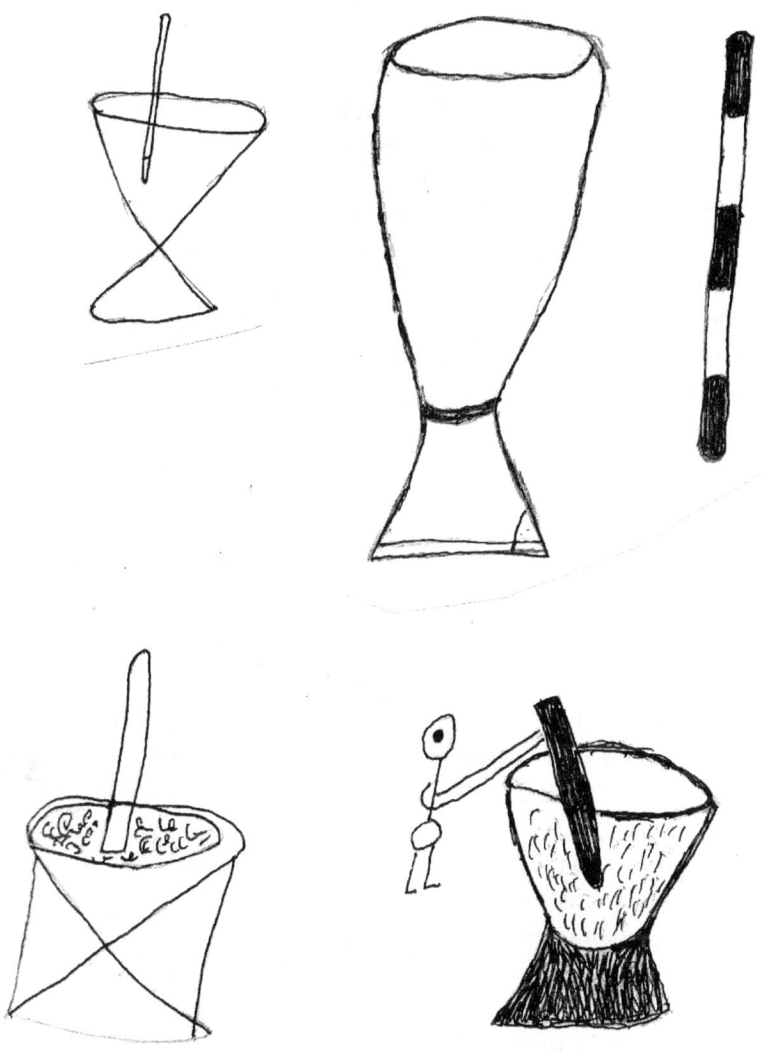

But this would be difficult and time consuming. Also, I knew that it was important to try to integrate with the community—this was one of the main lessons I took from the Peace Corps training, after all. Getting meals from a local person seemed like a simple way to meet people.

The principal at my school quickly heard about the situation with Haja and he went to talk to her. When he came back, he told me that I had a new cook. Unfortunately, this was only the beginning of a series of people who cooked for me, in a complicated saga that lasted almost a year. I did not know how hard it was going to be to find a reliable way to eat, a task that I had taken for granted my whole life up to now.

In the aftermath of the fiasco with Haja and her rumored lover, a new cooking arrangement was set up for me. The wife of one of the teachers at the primary school, a woman named Sadan Fofana, was going to cook for me. This seemed like a better plan because it was not a special arrangement: She was already living in the village and cooking for her husband and family. I hoped her marital status meant surreptitious delivery of extra rice to a boyfriend would be less likely. The plan was this: I would buy rice by the bag and give it to Sadan to cook—for me and her family. Her family would provide the sauce ingredients.

The arrangement seemed fair enough and for a while it worked out. Sadan was a short, no-nonsense woman with a friendly, round face, who had a hardly concealed hatred for her husband for some reason but was otherwise very cordial to me during our brief interactions. She cooked the usual repertoire of rice dishes, mostly village staples like rice with potato leaf or *kren kren* sauce, the latter made from the leaves of a plant called jute in other parts of the world. Just like every other cook in Sierra Leone, she used plenty of palm oil, while dried fish provided flavor and some crunchy bones.

Cooking rice was a difficult and time consuming, as I learned from watching the routines around me. The first step was perhaps the most challenging, pounding rice in the *mata odo*, the locally made mortar and pestle carved from a tree trunk. Women and children take turns bending their backs to lift the long stick that serves as the pestle, then slamming it into the rice-filled *mata odo* as hard as they can. With each blow, more of the kernels break, separating the rice hull from the inner kernel. Then the rice is scooped out of the *mata odo* and put it into the *fana*, the winnowing basket. The women toss the rice in the air repeatedly and every time it falls back into the basket, some of the chaff separates from the rice and falls to the ground. This is country rice, the rice that people grow on their own farms. It is easy to identify because the rice grains are not whole, like the machine-processed rice from the store, but are broken into pieces due to the pounding they received in the *mata odo*.

Every day a little girl, who was somehow related to the family, would come to my house in the afternoon carrying two lidded pots—a larger one for the rice, and a smaller one for the sauce, or *plasas* in Krio. She was hardly big enough to carry the pots and she seemed terrified of me, but she continued to come every day. She went by the nickname Grannie because, I was told, she has the same name as her grandmother.

However, this arrangement with Sadan soon began to go awry. The thing is, I needed to go to Makeni to buy rice, then transport the rice back to the village because there was no easy way to buy a bag of rice in Waridala. Everyone else just eats the country rice they grow on their farms. The problem began like this: Sadan's husband, the teacher, told me he knew a person going to Makeni on a motorcycle who could buy the rice; I just needed to give him money and he would arrange the rest. I agreed. However, even after I gave him the money, Sadan continued to cook country rice, as was quite clear from the contents of my plate.

I kept waiting for the machine-milled rice to show up in my daily meals. Maybe the man who had gone to Makeni had been delayed, I told myself. But the country rice continued. Gradually, I became suspicious, and it became increasingly clear that Foday never bought rice from Makeni and there was probably never any motorcycle either. He was still getting the rice locally and pocketing the money I gave him.

To be sure, it was a small lie he told. And I was hesitant to let money affairs tarnish any relationships. But I was learning quickly that not only single women would be scrambling to get a deal from the clueless white person in the village. I felt disappointed. But more than that, the teacher's behavior was strange. Why create this elaborate ruse? I told myself school teachers, who are not paid well, have to look for creative ways to make ends meet. But I really wasn't sure what was going on.

I began looking for someone else to cook for me. It so happened that Sadan was pregnant and decided to move to Freetown, which gave me reason to find a new cooking arrangement. So, soon a third person began cooking for me, a woman named Seray. I shared a compound with her, as well as her aging mother. A tall, thin woman, she seemed like a logical person to cook for me. Every day I had been watching her, from my porch, do the job with business-like efficiency, so now she started adding a little extra for me. I wasn't quite sure why I hadn't had Seray cooking for me before; it seemed so convenient. Unfortunately, this new arrangement did not last longer than a week. Without warning, she disappeared. Later I learned that she went to Freetown and did not tell anyone.

In time, I came to understand that she had a rather volatile personality, given to ferocious yelling matches with her relatives that echoed through her house, and I thought that perhaps it had been purposeful that no one had recommended Seray to be my cook in the first place.

But I was again left without a reliable source of food. I felt disappointed, but more than that, I felt a little embarrassed to be put in such a vulnerable situation. When Seray left, so did my daily meals. I had no backup plan or alternative way to get food. The experience made me acutely aware of the web of interdependence and mutual aid in a small community like Waridala—and what it was like to be left out. The cooking routines were hard work, going into the bush to collect firewood, splitting the firewood with an axe, collecting water from the well. The women worked together, along with squads of children, to do this daily hard work, and everyone had to help out. I remember the women and children walking back to town by my house, everyone balancing a bundle of sticks on their head, the size of each bundle in proportion to the size of the laborer. Even the little ones helped.

pumps for getting water

The fourth person to cook for me was the Mamie Queen of the village, Chernor Mbalu Fofana. She soon learned about my situation and offered to help. The Mamie Queen of the village is a ceremonial role, something like the chief of the women in the village, usually an elderly woman whose responsibilities, among other things, include cooking for guests who come to the village. The Mamie Queen had been hoping to cook for me for some time. Ever since I first moved to the village, she would periodically reassure me that I was her child. Usually she would cup her breast to emphasize her point, a particularly graphic gesture if she happened to be shirtless at the time, as old women in the village often are. The Mamie Queen lived next door to me with her family and, soon after we made a deal, one of her grandchildren came every day with my food, rice pot and sauce pot balanced on a big plate on their head.

Again, it seemed like a good arrangement. The Mamie Queen was very generous to me, and I thought it might work out. However, from the beginning we had trouble understanding each other. She did not speak Krio well, and my Maninka skills were limited to saying hello and goodbye. But deeper than that, we had different understandings of the terms of our arrangement. The agreement I was hoping for was this: She would cook for me on every weekday; on weekends I would make other arrangements, as I often left the village to visit somewhere else. Every day, I would contribute 2,000 leones for the sauce, meaning I would pay 10,000 leones per week. I intended to give her the money every Sunday.

In retrospect, this was a ridiculous plan. I was trying to be more formal and structured in the arrangement, because the three previous cooking arrangements had ended so poorly. But this was the wrong approach. Mamie Queen didn't understand this arrangement I tried to set up. I think in her world, the only reason a person would not cook every day would be due to lack of food. To skip a day of providing food would imply she was not doing her job properly. And the village just didn't operate according to a weekday-weekend schedule. Time was measured by the seasons, by Muslim holidays, by sunrises and sunsets. The school held classes five days a week, but the school and the village, I was learning, were quite separate. I needed to follow the village model: let her cook every day and give her money sporadically, without trying to adhere to a schedule.

However, before I could make any adjustments, the Mamie Queen became sick and left the village to live with her daughter. Once again, I had to find someone else to cook for me. By now I had been in Waridala for over six months and still had not managed to secure a steady cook. I had gone through four different people cooking for me. It seemed I needed to start to cook for myself. I wasn't sure what else to do. However, I felt confident enough with how things worked in the village that I thought I would enlist the help of a *borbor*. *Borbor* in Krio means boy, but in the communal, hierarchical culture, a *borbor* is like an adult male's assistant. The *borbor* does various chores and, in exchange, the man takes care of the boy, such as providing clothing, school fees, etc. The *borbor* also earns social capital, due to his association with the older man.

So, having been left again without a cook, I decided to have a *borbor* help me do the cooking. I still had a coal pot—a metal, clay-lined cylinder which burns locally made charcoal—from when I tried to cook for myself. All I had to get was a rice pot, a *plasas* pot, and a big bag of charcoal, which they made locally by cutting down small trees and burning the wood in earthen heaps for several days. I also had to find the usual ingredients: onion, salt, fish, Maggi, rice.

Finally, I needed the *borbor*. I asked for the opinions of my friends in the village before picking one. He was the top student in Form I at the time, Mohamed Turay. It was tempting to try to enlist the help of a wayward student who seemed to be in need of some adult guidance, rather than a star student. However, I was weary of cooking fiascoes and wanted to find someone reliable. One afternoon, I called the kid over to talk on my veranda. Foday Sheriff, another teacher, was there, too, to facilitate the discussion. We made him the offer and he agreed. Later we talked on the phone with his father, who lived in Freetown, and he also agreed. The deal was set.

This is my Pots

pots with a tripod of three rocks

I quickly learned all about cooking. Even though cooking is considered a woman's job, Mohamed had helped his female relatives often, so he knew enough to give plenty of pointers. I learned how to time the cooking right, so the rice would be done at the appropriate time of day.

I learned how Loko women would come across the river in the morning to sell leaves like *kren kren* and potato leaf to cook for the afternoon *plasas*. I learned how if the Loko women don't come with the leaves, you have to cook groundnut soup instead. I learned how to talk about cooking in Maninka: add salt, take the pot off the fire, names of different kinds of leaves that go in the *plasas*. I learned to add Maggi and then palm oil, which coagulates into deep red-orange circles that float in the water. I tried to cut the leaves to put in the *plasas*. The women grab a handful and by increments cut the stems and leaves that protrude from their fist into tiny pieces. I utterly failed to do this with any approximation of the grace and efficiency with which the women executed this task. And so I learned how much work cooking is: the daily chore of finding ingredients, watching pots as they cook, cleaning up.

But gradually I realized that the relationship with Mohamed was not working out. Quite simply, we didn't get along. He bothered me; and our personalities just didn't mesh. He told the other children who would hang out on my veranda what to do. He started not just helping me, but doing the cooking himself. He began criticizing my meager skills in speaking Maninka. We seemed to have different expectations about what our relationship meant. The fact that I am white had something to do with. But the real problem, I think, is that American culture is not very hierarchical. I didn't keep enough distance between me and him. But for Sierra Leoneans, who is the "elder one" is something they are always aware of, always careful to respect. My informal style did not provide enough guidance for Mohamed. He didn't know how to behave outside of the social models he grew up with, and I didn't show him.

The school year came to an end and I used it as an opportunity to find a new person to cook for me. I was exhausted by the day-to-day work and hassle of cooking; it required constant effort and attention—and I wasn't even using the *mato odo* to pound country rice, or gathering firewood, or carrying water from the well. School was on vacation and I had things I hoped to do—travel, meet people, read, write, and draw. I had gone through five different cooking arrangements. But my travails of finding regular meals in Waridala were not over yet.

    I asked some people in town about a new cook and they suggested the chair lady of the parent association at my school, a middle-aged woman named Mariama Sheriff. This new arrangement seemed off from the beginning. A few days after the arrangement had been made, Mariama began cooking for me. But I soon realized it was actually Mariama's daughter who was cooking for me, a young woman named Sadan, who was not Mariama's biological daughter, but her *"men pikin"* as they say in Krio, the daughter of a relative, whom she was raising.

    I should have known this was going to be trouble from the beginning. I should have known, especially after my experience with Haja. Man. Woman. Cook. Love. Money. Etc. But I wanted badly for this arrangement to work out. And I felt pretty experienced with how the village worked. I thought I could navigate the situation. I learned from the Mamie Queen that people in Waridala prefer to operate according to an economy of informal favors.

    Having someone cook for me is not a business relationship, but a personal relationship. I needed to give the person money and buy them things to keep them happy. I gave Mariama and Sadan the coal pot I had used when I tried cooking with Mohamed, a bucket, a thermos to keep tea water hot. Every once in a while, I bought them something small, like a new pair of sandals, and occasionally I would go over to the old woman's place just to talk, even though it was awkward.

Kitchens — outdoor with thatch roof

This is my Chisen

Kichen

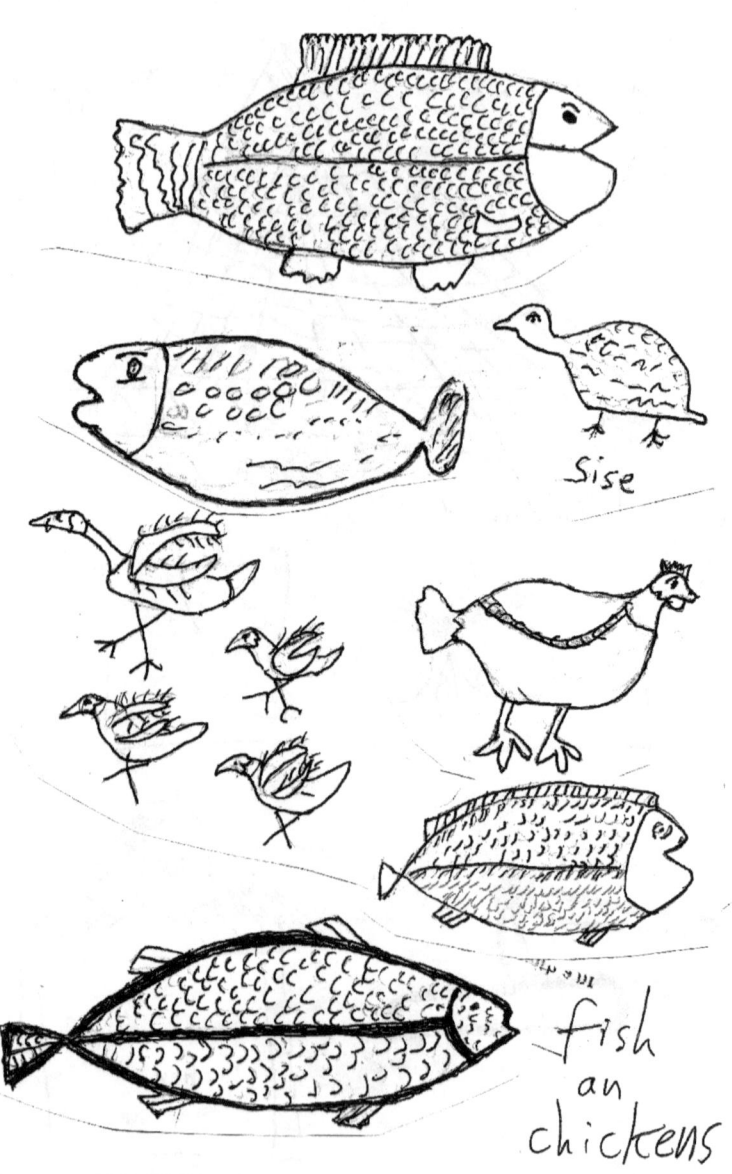

I realized there were problems almost immediately. When Sadan was done cooking, she would put on nice clothes and bring the rice and *plasas* to me. Personal delivery is a sure sign of romantic interest. Of course, my interest was finding a reliable source of food. But it really seemed like Mariama was conspiring to get her *men pikin* involved with the white man. I really wasn't sure why she thought that that would work out. Perhaps they thought I would be unable to resist her amazing cooking.

At the same time, Mariama was trying to get me involved with intrigues about money. For example, she sent a message to me one day through Sadan telling me someone in town was selling cloth and that she wanted me to buy some. I agreed but I asked to talk to the person directly. However, no one could tell me who was actually selling the cloth until I eventually figured out that it was Mariama Sheriff herself who was selling the cloth.

The end of this cooking arrangement came rather suddenly. I bought some country rice from a local farmer that needed to be put in the *mato odo* and have the husks beaten off it. When I gave Sadan this rice to cook, she said no, that she wanted me to buy milled rice. I think we could have reached an agreement; perhaps I could have purchased country rice that had already been pounded as a compromise. But I was feeling frustrated with Sadan and Mariama already. So I told her that we wouldn't cook that day and sent her home. And I never saw her again.

I know it wasn't fair of me to buy country rice with husks on it, and to ask Sadan to pound it in a *mato odo*, especially since it is such hard work, especially when I could afford rice without husks. But at the same time, I think that Mariama and Sadan thought they could take advantage of me. I think I was right to push back; however, in an ideal world, I would have ended things more diplomatically.

After that, I didn't have anyone to cook for me and I was reluctant to find a new cook as all my other arrangements had been such disasters. So I just didn't cook. For a couple weeks, the only meals I ate were those I shared with others, on verandas, during celebrations. Sierra Leoneans, after all, love to share food and not a day goes by when someone didn't call me to come eat.

I didn't necessarily blame the villagers for my cooking difficulties. In fact, my experience with cooking shows how much they accepted a foreigner like me into their community. They were ready to command their children to work for me and eager to let their women be with me. It was I who didn't accept the terms of their hospitality. Perhaps what the cooking fiasco really revealed was the depth of the divide between the school and the village. If another teacher at my school lived in the village – they would have been in a better position to help me out, giving advice, explaining the culture, sharing food. However, not one of the teachers at the school actually lived in Waridala.

Eventually, I gave in and accepted the fact that I needed someone to cook for me. And a new arrangement just seemed to happen. I finally figured it out. My neighbor across the road, Nyima Daramy, cooked for me every day. She had a big family—Usu her husband, Foday her oldest son, and a host of other relatives living in the house. I bought all the ingredients to cook African-style food: the salt, onions, fish, palm oil, etc. I bought rice from people in the village: already-pounded country rice. And every day I gave the ingredients for the day to Nyima and she cooked for me. It was a simple and effective relationship.

Part of it, perhaps, was that I had finally figured out how to appropriately manage this sort of relationship. But also, I think, Nyima and Usu had never offered to cook for me earlier because they did not expect to get anything from me, nor did they want to get anything from me. They were kind people who minded their own business and, after all I had been through, I was deeply grateful for Nyima and her family's help.

concrete houses, like those in Waridala

No longer directly involved with the cooking, I still caught glimpses of my neighbor and the cooking routines she followed with her female relatives and friends. An important part was doing the dishes: a female from the house would squat in front of a bucket to wash an assortment of plastic and metal containers. Every family is a complicated net of relationships, which was reflected by this confusing mess of containers. Each segment of the family will have its own set of containers: one set for the husband and older male children; another set for the younger children; one for the co-wife; one for the elderly parent; one for the cousin who has moved in for a little while; one to keep as reserve to eat later. And I, too, had my own set of containers, to be washed, and then filled with that day's portions of rice and sauce.

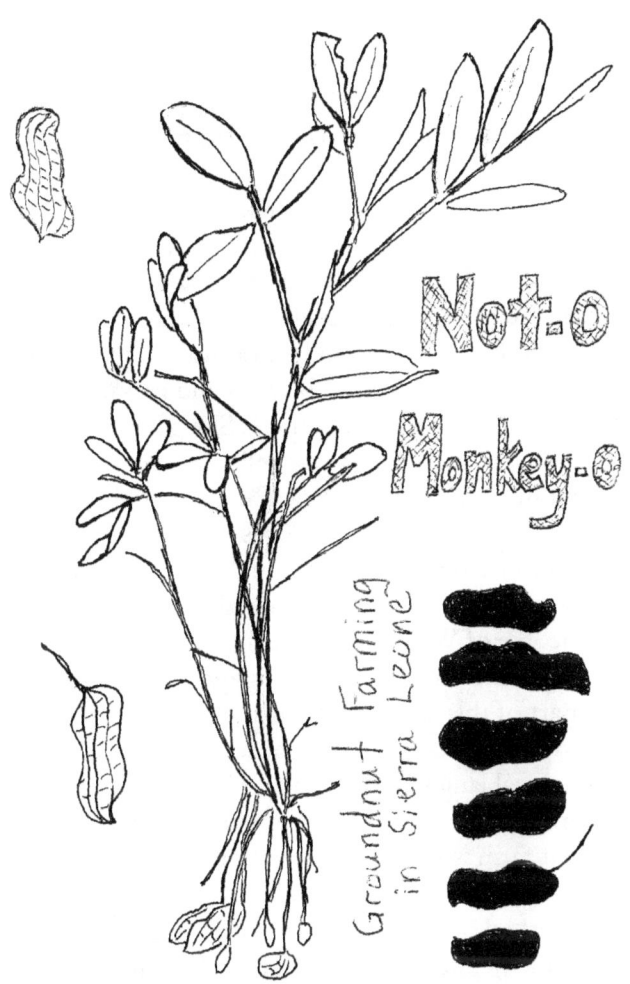

Not-o Monkey-o

Groundnut Farming in Sierra Leone

A s the dry season ends and the first storms of the rainy season approach, the people in the village of Waridala prepare to plant groundnuts. The surpluses and the leisure of the dry season begin to slip away and the people have to go back to work. My main job was to be a teacher, but as a foreigner in the village, I decided to plant my own groundnut farm along with rest of the village, as a sort of experiment, to understand the community.

In December, when the prices were low, I bought two bags of groundnuts, perhaps forty pounds worth, from a farmer in a nearby village. This is the time of year when the rains stopped coming, the dry season arrived, and the green land dried up. After I bought them, the two bags of groundnuts sat in my spare room, unused and nearly forgotten.

However, soon enough, even though there were still no clouds in the sky, the people knew the rains would be returning. It was time. So I went with the chief's wife to her farm, following the winding bush trail. The heat was sweltering and the land was still dried up and raw, all browns and grays. My lips became parched just from walking there. She gave me the piece of land in Mankarika, as the area was called, and gave me a place in Waridala's unwritten farm registry. Here it was, the place for my farm, all ten-foot-tall brush and grass. She asked me what I thought of it, and I did not know what to think. The brush seems to grow well at least. I said it looked fine.

The people of Waridala were delighted that I was making a farm. Every person I met began asking me about my farm. Becoming a part of this community of subsistence farmers had an unexpected side effect: It helped me learn how to talk about farming in the local language, Maninka. The first phrase I had to learn in Maninka was: *n'na tiya du mansa la musu torfe le*, meaning "My groundnut farm is near the chief's wife's farm." For a while I just would repeat this phrase no matter what people said to me, and usually it turned out to be an appropriate response.

But one day, Alhaji Fofana, Foday Daramy, and Mohammed Fofana, three boisterous students from school, came to help. I was grateful because I had no idea what to do next. I didn't even know the boundaries of my new plot of land. Granted, the brush was well over our heads, but even when they pointed out the boundaries based on a line of sight to that tree with a split trunk in the distance, I still didn't understand. They also pointed out the small piles of worm castings on the ground, hopeful signs that point towards fertile soil. We only had three machetes between the four of us, but I insisted on using one of them and together we began chopping at the robust brush.

Machetes are called "cutlasses" in Sierra Leone. They're made by the local blacksmith. The handles are wrapped with old inner tubes. The stick is used to hook the vegetation to be cut with the cutlass.

The most unpleasant residents of this ocean of brush were the tall, spiky bushes with thorns about two inches long. These thorns were able to pierce right through the bottom of my shoes. The only footwear that could resist the thorns, I eventually found, was my locally made flip-flops with soles fashioned from car tires. It was brutal work. The end of the dry season is perhaps the most searing weather of the year, the land not having seen rain in five months, and we were shielded from the raw sun only by the haze of dust and smoke hanging in the air. Quickly we were all exhausted.

Despite putting in several hours of work with the help of my students, the brushing was still not done until another of my students, Jeramiah Koroma, came to help me. Granted, it was not entirely on his own volition that he came. He wanted me to work on his bike and I helped him to fix it, on the condition that he would come help me brush my farm. He did his best and I was impressed. He showed up before seven in the morning with his machete and wearing his rubber boots, and he worked until soaked in sweat. As we attacked the brush together, I watched him out of the corner of my eye, and I finally began to learn the proper technique for cutting brush with a machete, after having endured criticism from my other students. Now when I cut, I was learning how to leave all the brush lying neatly on the ground in the same direction. Sun-cooked water in a plastic bottle never tasted so good.

After cutting the brush it was necessary to burn everything that we had cut. The idea is to let the cut brush dry in the sun for a few days, and then set fire to it all. However, the man who had the farm adjacent to mine made a mistake: He set a fire at the wrong time. He was not patient, I was told. The wind was blowing in the wrong direction, resulting in a patchy burn. The brush on his farm and the adjacent farms did not burn cleanly. It was now necessary to drag and carry all of the debris on my farm into piles. I am lucky that two teachers from school, Mr. Sanja and Mr. Sheriff, came to help me. One by one we dragged the limbs into piles by hand and watched as the orange flames devoured them.

Where once the brush stood ten feet tall, now there was only flat ground spotted with piles of gray ash and blackened twigs and stumps. It was time to turn over the topsoil. In Maninka they call it *du bukandia*, "turning the ground." For this task, I needed more help than a few friends—or a few students who wanted bicycle repairs. I had to turn to a cherished tradition among schools in rural Sierra Leone, that of students providing free labor on their teachers' farms.

Everyone works at subsistence farming, even the teachers, for the government does not pay them very well or very regularly. Sometimes teachers may use their position to provide extra encouragement: In exchange for work, the teacher will give the student a passing grade. They call it a "practical," as in "Today after school we are having a practical for language arts." The use of these practicals, especially to inflate students' grades, bothered me, and the thought of students working on my farm made me uncomfortable. It didn't seem quite right. But what else could I do? I had already started the farm and it was too late to turn back. I needed their help.

Digging, like cutting brush, is one of the tasks in groundnut farming that is assigned to the boys. A group of them, from Form I and II, came after school one day, and they were quite pleased to work for me. Thus I learned the word for "help" in Maninka: *madema*. Mohamed B. Fofana and Kanda Kallon and Alpha Sawaneh and others, too, were all there. It was hard work, swinging their hoes into the dry soil, and the dust rose around them like a low fog as they dug. They divided the ground into sections. Each section they called a *bara* in Krio. One person was responsible for turning the soil in one *bara*; when the *bara* is finished, the person must claim a new one to work on. It was one boy's job to mark out the *baras* by making marks on the ground with a hoe. Due to their large numbers, the work didn't take long. Their reward came, perhaps, when I gave them the opportunity to pose for my camera when done.

Now, at last, it was time to use the bag of groundnuts I had stashed away in December. Before I could plant, however, it would be necessary to shell the groundnuts. By hand. For weeks

I had been seeing people shelling on their verandas, during the day and at night by the light of flashlights. I had a late start and the thought of shelling thousands of groundnuts was daunting. However, one night, Mohamed Fofana, Foday Daramy and another Muhamed Fofana, came over to my house, and young Osman was there, too. They all helped me to get started.

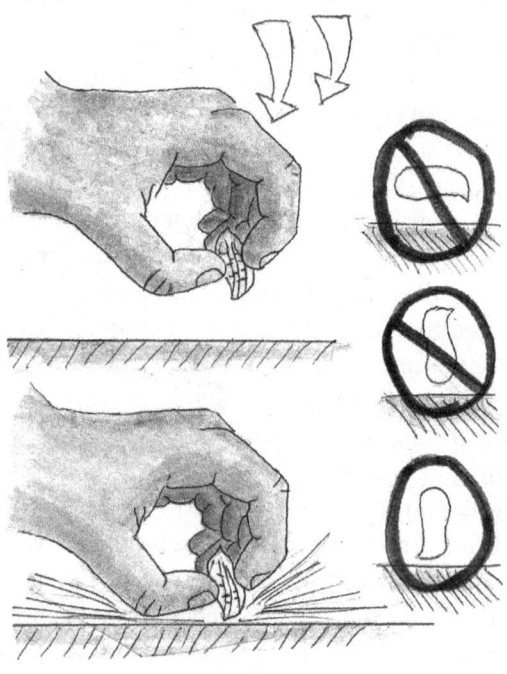

That night I lit a candle and turned on the radio and they dumped a big pile of the groundnuts onto the floor in my parlor. Arranging the benches around the perimeter of the pile, they sat down to begin shelling. My rudimentary technique of shelling paled in comparison with their mastery. Holding a groundnut in each hand, they slammed the pointy end of the shell against the bench top, cracking it open. Then, they removed the contents, in a single motion. The process made a sort of alternating rhythm— pop-pop... pop-pop—as the right hand then the left hand broke a groundnut open. Soon they were all cracking groundnuts in unison to the rhythm of the songs on the radio.

Around this time some of the old women in town began to criticize me. No doubt they are the undisputed authority on groundnuts, having grown them for most of their lives. They would ask me, *I ma tiya lan budu?*: "Have you not planted your groundnuts yet?" When I told them I hadn't, I would usually receive a look of scorn and disgust. However, their criticism mostly served to rile me, rather than guide me. I was new to the work, and teaching is my main job, not groundnuts. Saidou Sanou – known to everyone as Mr. SS -- gave me more helpful comments. He may have been the principal at the primary school, but I think he was truly an agriculturalist at heart. He explained to me that there is a narrow window for planting groundnuts. May 15th, he told me, is the deadline by which groundnuts had to be in the ground. By the time June comes around, it is too late; groundnuts planted in June will grow leaves but not produce groundnuts.

The time for planting was quickly approaching. It was May, the rains had been coming since the end of April, and the once-dry landscape was beginning to explode with wild green growth. But I still wasn't quite ready to plant; one more step was necessary. When people shell groundnuts for planting, the empty shells and the nuts get mixed together. In order to separate them, it is necessary to use what they call a *"fana"* in Krio, a wide, shallow basket made from woven cane cut from the raffia palm. Put the mixture of nuts and shells in the *fana*, and then use a flick of the wrist to toss it all about a foot into the air. As the nuts and shells fall back down, the nuts, which are heavier, fall back into the *fana*, and the shells, which are lighter, drift wide of the *fana* and fall onto the ground. Of course, my wrists had not been trained in the precise angle at which one must flick the *fana* in order to separate the shells and seeds. My *fana*-ing was awkward at best. Fortunately, some girls from Form III came to help me and they soon had the shells and nuts separated.

At last, I was ready to plant, but now I had a problem. At this time of the year labor was scarce in the village as everyone was working hard to get their groundnuts in the ground on time.

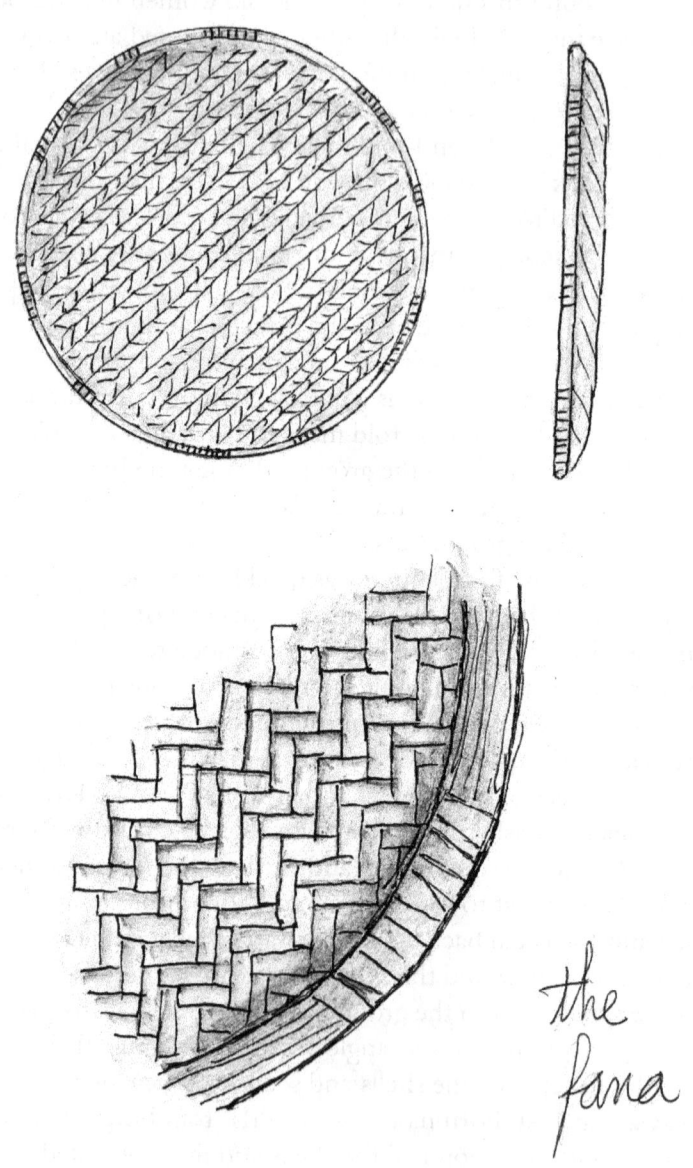

the fana

All the people in town were organized into small work groups of their peers that they call a *katee*. A *katee*, around ten people in size, rotates from farm to farm. Everyone in the *katee* goes to the farm of one of the members and does the necessary work. When that work is done, they go to the farm of another one of the members, and so on, until the *katee* has gone to each member's farm. Even my students were organized into *katees*, helping each other do work on their parents' farms. At dusk, I would watch the villagers come back from planting with their *katee*; they were tired but laughing as they talked with their friends, their hoes dangling from their hands.

    I also had another problem, in addition to the scarcity of labor: I had delayed too long before planting. Now the brown, freshly turned soil at my farm had received a fresh mat of green from the rain. Several people told me I simply could not plant groundnuts like that. The ground had to be clean of all weeds and grass when the groundnuts are planted, thus giving the groundnuts a much-needed head start. That meant the place had to be re-dug. I was discouraged.

    During this time of urgent work, Mr. Kamara, the vice principal, was taking full advantage of the students' labor: every week during the planting season it seems, he was taking the students to his farm in the bush for work. On one particular weekend, he had arranged for the boys at school to work; that particular weekend, however, was also my last chance to get my groundnuts in.

    Finally the town chief got involved. One of his main responsibilities is helping to mediate the various disputes and conflicts of interest that occur in the community. The chief did not deliberate long. He said Mr. Kamara had worked with the students enough and he authorized the cancellation of Mr. Kamara's workday, allowing the students to come work for me. Thus, it was determined that the following day the male students would re-dig my farm and then the female students would plant.

    Sisters Haja Barrie and Isata Barrie were the first students to come, and gradually more came; soon even some students from the primary school were released to come help me. By mid-morning it was a show. The boys began digging, while one boy, Mohamad Turay, marked out the *bara* for the boys to work on. The girls followed, planting the groundnuts. It was interesting to see how students assumed leadership on the farm, often taking on much different roles than they do in the classroom. Some who struggled to read at school were very skilled on the farm.

Each took a pile of groundnuts and put it in a pouch made by tying the loose end of their *lappa*, the long, durable bolts of cloth that women and girls wear as skirts. Then, taking a short hoe with a small blade, they would make a line of divots in front of them, and with the other hand drop a single groundnut into each divot. Taking a step forward, they would make a new line of divots, and each new strike of the hoe would kick dirt back to cover the groundnut. That morning, I decided to arrange to have rice cooked for the kids who were working for me. Some of them politely objected, telling me, "Don't cook rice for us!" However, no rice was left over when they were done eating.

Finally, the groundnuts were planted. It was May 18th, only three days after the May 15th deadline that Mr. SS had suggested. Once the groundnuts sprouted and began to grow, it was necessary to weed after about a month. The work was not difficult, only time consuming. Fortunately, another one of my students, Mohamed Barrie, came with me, and he was helpful on the farm as well as at school. He pointed out to me the scattering of other crops sprouting among the groundnuts, like *kren kren* plants and okra. These plants were the remains of crops that had been planted on this same ground in past seasons; the dormant seeds had been exposed by the turning of the ground.

Unfortunately, a newly weeded patch of groundnuts attracts monkeys. They love to pull up the groundnut plants and crack open the nuts growing among the roots. The monkeys living around Waridala were small and dark colored, with long tails. *Tulafen* they call them in Maninka, literally "forest thing." It is said that when a person happens to catch some of them uprooting groundnuts on the farm, the monkeys will put their hands up over their heads, as if declaring their innocence, while they run away. Most families station their young boys at the groundnut farm to drive away the monkeys. The boys make little huts from palm fronds, start small fires to keep warm in the rain, and spend the days yelling and banging on pots.

I did not have any children to drive the monkeys away for me. Plus, a grove of trees bordered my farm. Despite the yelling and yodeling of the boys at the nearby farms, the monkeys visited my farm frequently and although I never spotted them myself, they left piles of uprooted groundnut plants as evidence. The best way to get rid of monkeys, the people told me, is to enlist the help of the town hunter. If the hunter shoots a monkey on your farm, they will never dare to come back. However, I did not resort to this measure, and the monkeys continued to come.

At last, the groundnuts began to mature. It takes three months for the groundnuts to be ready for harvesting. I had planted in mid-May and now it was mid-August. When the people in the village started harvesting their groundnuts, the village was empty during the daytime. The entire family would go out in the bush to help uproot groundnuts—men, women, and children. I had planted my own a little bit later than most people, so my groundnuts still had some time left. For two weeks, everyone was asking me, *I la tiya bara kor?*, "Have your groundnuts become strong yet?" I would have to tell everyone, *A ma kor budu*, meaning "They are not strong yet." When the groundnuts become mature, I was told, their leaves begin to get black spots; when nearly all the leaves have darkened, the groundnuts are ready to be harvested.

Sorie Fofana showed me the final test. He had one of the farms next to mine, and he was happy to demonstrate. He pulled up one of my groundnut plants, took a groundnut from among the roots, and squeezed it between his thumb and forefinger. If the shell cracks, it means the shell is hard and mature; if the groundnut pops like a pea, it is not mature yet. It cracked. But then, Sorie looked on the inside of the shell. In immature groundnuts, he explained to me, the inside of the shell will be velvety white; when the groundnuts have matured, the inside of the shell will begin to turn black. Sure enough, as he displayed the shell in his calloused palm, it was apparent that the inside was beginning to turn black.

Now that my groundnuts had matured, everyone was asking me in Maninka: *a den ni?* This means something like "Did your plants produce a lot of groundnuts?" The appropriate response, of course, is "I praise God," *Ni Allah tanto*. Eventually, I brought some of my groundnuts into town, since everyone was asking me about them, so that I could show some examples of my crop. The village people seemed fascinated by the groundnuts' capacity to reproduce. Everyone made the same observation: They all noted how the five or ten groundnuts dangling from a plant come from one seed. They would say, "From one seed, ten more! Isn't God great?" Almost everyone I talked to made the same comment.

Finally, the time came to harvest my own groundnuts. I tried to find some people to help me, but everyone was busy with their own harvest and planting rice, the next crop to go into the ground. I felt embarrassed to ask for help as my meals didn't depend on the success of this harvest, unlike everyone else in town. Also, this was the middle of a school holiday, so there was no school full of kids to help me work.

So I decided to go by myself. Harvesting the groundnuts is simple—you just grab the plant and pull it out of the ground and shake off the dirt. Simple work, but time consuming and incredibly boring. There were a lot of weeds among the groundnuts, too, so it was necessary to search among the weeds to find the groundnuts. I didn't last much longer than a couple of hours. As I discussed the groundnut work with people, I learned another phrase in Maninka, *sene ke a ka'gbele!*, which means "farm work is hard!" I became adept at saying this with a slight bitter tone in my voice.

Mariama Sheriff was the chairwoman of the school where I taught. That is why they told me to go to her to ask for help. However, her role with the school was mostly ceremonial, I learned. She was first and foremost a farmer. I asked her for help, she agreed.

 However, I had to leave town before the job was finished in order to attend a workshop regarding my job as a teacher; I didn't have enough time to finish the harvest. Mariama Sheriff said she would send people to finish it. I gave her some money. I wasn't sure how to get her to finish the work for me, but I thought the money might help.
 When I came back to Waridala, Mariama Sheriff's daughter brought me my groundnut harvest. It was one bag. Her daughter said to me, "It was the monkeys," by way of explanation. Originally in May I planted thirty pans of groundnuts—about one full bag—and now in August I had harvested one bag. Great. When I told the people in the village that I had planted one bag of groundnuts and harvested one bag, they all laughed. They thought it was hilarious. They told me, *allah tanto, nye?*, that is "Thanks to God, right?" Like the punch line in a joke. And what could I do except laugh with them? It could have been worse. I heard stories about people planting

more groundnuts than me and getting nothing at all come harvest time, due to poor soil or untimely planting.

Just like every other household was doing at the time, I spread my meager harvest out to dry in the sun, on top of an old mosquito net that someone gave me. One day, my neighbor Siri offered to *fana* my harvest -- to remove the dirt and leaves and rotten groundnuts-- and measure it. Quickly she did the job and told me the final tally: 13 pans! That was worse than I thought: The one bag I had planted contained thirty pans; the entire harvest only amounted to thirteen.

I decided to confront you, Mariama Sheriff. I walked across the village and shared my suspicions with you and your daughter and everyone else on your veranda at the time. I talked in Krio because I was mad; "Not-o monkey-o," I told them, "Na you!" I added, as a sort of threat, and because I didn't know what else to say: "I will take it to the chief!" But Mariama Sheriff folded her arms across her chest and told me quite simply that no, I was wrong, it was indeed the monkeys. I suddenly felt sheepish. Was she lying? I didn't know, and there wasn't anything I could do about it. Eventually my friend the teacher, Foday Sheriff, did insist on brining the matter to the chief. But after the chief had heard both sides, he asked me, in an apologetic tone, *i di mu ke*? that is, "What can you do?" It was a rhetorical question, because there wasn't anything I could do.

Now, finally, I saw the reason that they call groundnuts the woman's crop. This designation is not the result of a peaceful division of labor in order to maximize productivity. In the rural household in Sierra Leone, the man and the woman in the family negotiate for control of resources, and the battle over the groundnuts is the one that the women always win. They are patient and through all the tedious uprooting and picking they simply outlast the men. By the traditional rules of the game, Mariama Sheriff had won her fair share.

So in the end, learned all I needed to know and more about planting groundnuts. I am grateful for the generosity the people of Waridala showed me, for them letting me into their community, and I am no longer angry about the so-called monkeys. People have been farming in their way for generations, perhaps thousands of years and the harvests happen the way they always do, sometimes good and sometimes bad. The real lesson I learned was about work, about the tremendous labor of farming, and about how relationships make farming possible, and, for brief moments, even fun. Waridala, I learned, is a community reduced to its essentials. Among these farmers, who have almost nothing, it was possible for me to see what is most important, not food or water or shelter, but a group of people to belong to, who will help you when you need it most.

African Bicycles

They used to regularly arrive at my house after school, pushing their bicycles and seeking repairs. Their machines had been tortured: bald tires, bent rims, spent bearings. Although I came to Waridala to be a teacher, word spread quickly that I knew how to repair bicycles. So my students started coming to me every day with their mournful, broken bicycles.

Their bicycles looked something like the following. They were a haphazard mix of old mountain bikes and road bikes from twenty years ago. Few had more than one gear, due to broken cables, etc., and the derailleurs served mostly as a means to take up slack in the chain. Functional brakes were rare, a crucial safety feature whose absence made me feel nervous. All these bikes seemed to have chronic flat tires.

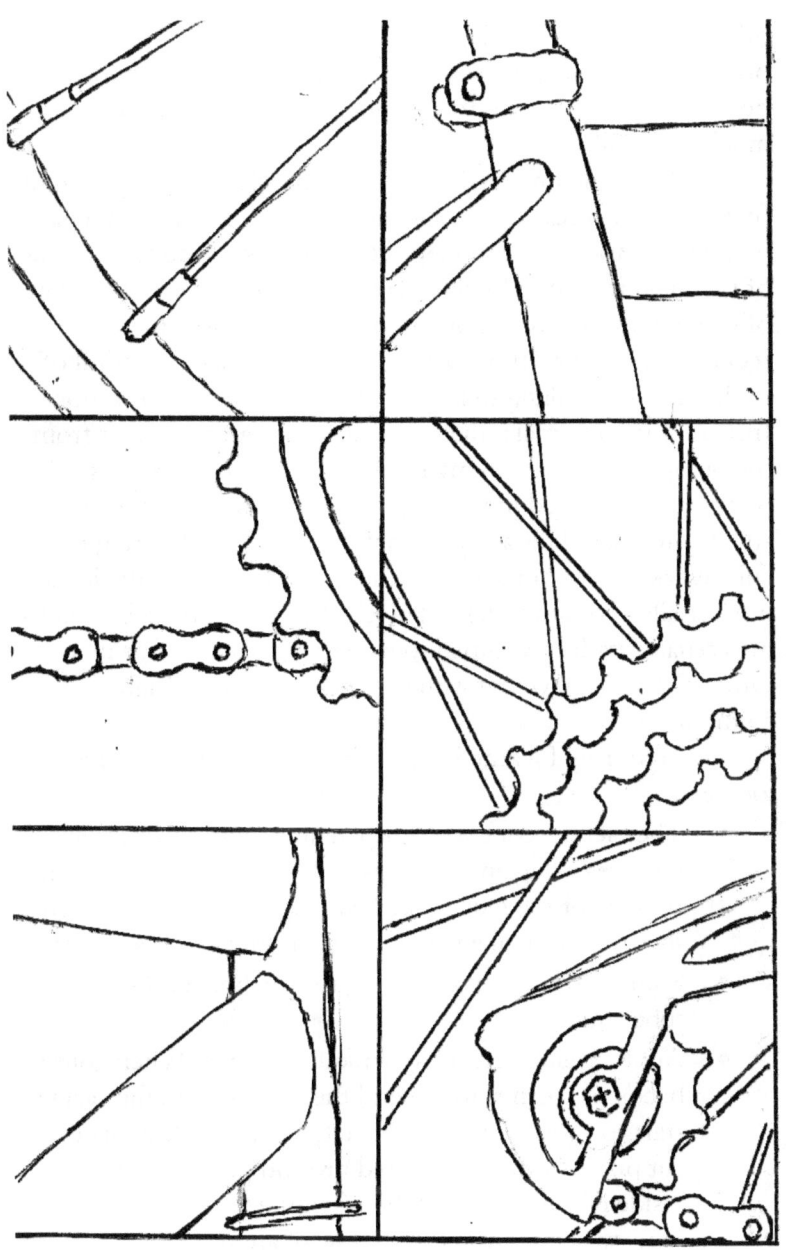

Why were these bicycles so worn out? The main reason seemed to be that people don't have enough money to fix them. The other problem was gaining access to replacement parts and tools, both of which are quite scarce. Even when tools and parts can be found, they are often too cheap and poorly made to be of much use at all.

I became involved with fixing bicycles gradually. I enjoy fixing bicycles occasionally and, at first, I would offer to repair a bicycle and not ask for money. After all, lack of money was one of the main reasons why these bicycles were in such a dire state of disrepair. However, soon people began to assail me with requests for repairs. It was easy to see why. I had a handful of tools and I was willing to help them and I didn't ask for money. Instead, I tried to make the kids deals: like carrying water from the pump or working on my farm, in exchange for repairs. This barter system helped me manage requests, but on some days, I still had to chase kids away. Sometimes a kid would bring me a chicken as a form of payment, a half-grown one that the kid's mother allowed him to take. The chicken would be delivered to me casually, its feet wrapped together with a strip of palm leaf. Other times the payment would be a container of bright red palm oil.

Gradually I learned interesting techniques from the locals:

- The Sierra Leone way for patching inner tubes always involves using an old hacksaw blade to roughen up the rubber for the glue to stick and literally hammering on the patch to make it stick after the glue has been applied.
- Some people even use string to tie a hole in the inner tube shut.
- Another Sierra Leone technique: packing. When your tire becomes worn through and the strings from the casing start to show, you don't have to get a new tire. Instead, cut pieces from another old tire and put them on the inside of your own tire, between the tire and the inner tube, which reinforces the threadbare tire.
- Some add packing before the tire wears out, to prevent flats.

- If the sidewall of a tire begins to tear, a popular solution is simply to sew it back up using heavy thread.
- If you are replacing spokes and replacement spokes are too long, take a pair of pliers and bend the end of the spoke where it fits into the hub. If you make the bend sharp enough, it will effectively make the spoke shorter.

All these techniques are examples of what they call "managing" in Krio. You can often hear people say: "I go manage am" or "I de manage." This means something like to cope or deal with or even to figure out how to keep something going without actually fixing the problem. People are always managing: They manage their lack of money, they manage their leaky roofs during the rainy season, and they manage their rickety bicycles.

Occasionally I would see a few quality bikes ridden around the region with multiple gears and functioning brakes. The owners would ride them proudly and adorn them with extra reflectors on the wheels and wrap the frame in colorful tape. But wealthy people in Sierra Leone—with few exceptions—do not ride bikes. The people who have enough money for a nice bike usually choose to spend their money on other things; the bicycle remains the vehicle of the rural poor. (The male rural poor, I should add. Females are rarely seen on a bike and it is only the male students who would come pester me for repairs.)

Bicycles, in this context, are strictly functional: going to the market, traveling to a funeral, or riding to a distant village to visit a friend. Often people use a bicycle to carry jugs of palm wine out of the bush to town where they can be sold. Some petty traders use bicycles to travel from village to village selling their wares. One trader I used to see had a cardboard box strapped to the back of his bike to carry his supplies.

Perhaps these bicycles could be seen as signs of poverty. And that is true. But these bicycles also have a rough sort of beauty, with their polished bearings, worn sprockets, and patched inner tubes, and there is a gritty creativity in the techniques that people use to fix them.

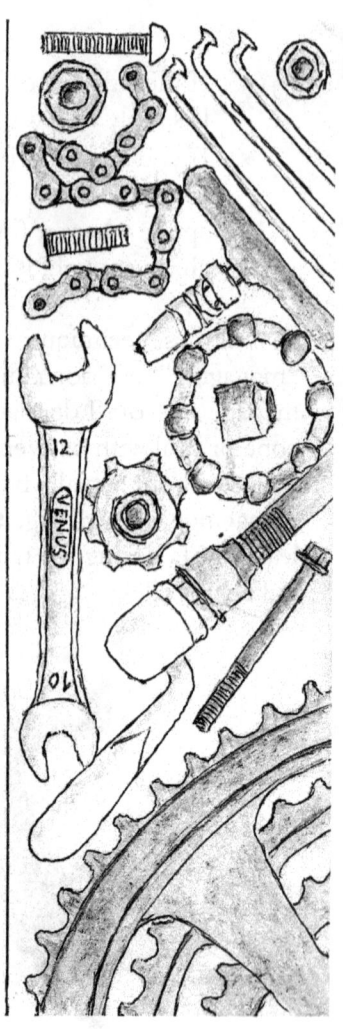

Bicycle terms in Krio

American English	Krio
rim	cant
patch	patcha
inner tube	inna
tire	outa
valve stem	tube
bearing	beads
freewheel	ratchet
air	breeze
wrench	spanna
to fix	make
to hammer	knock

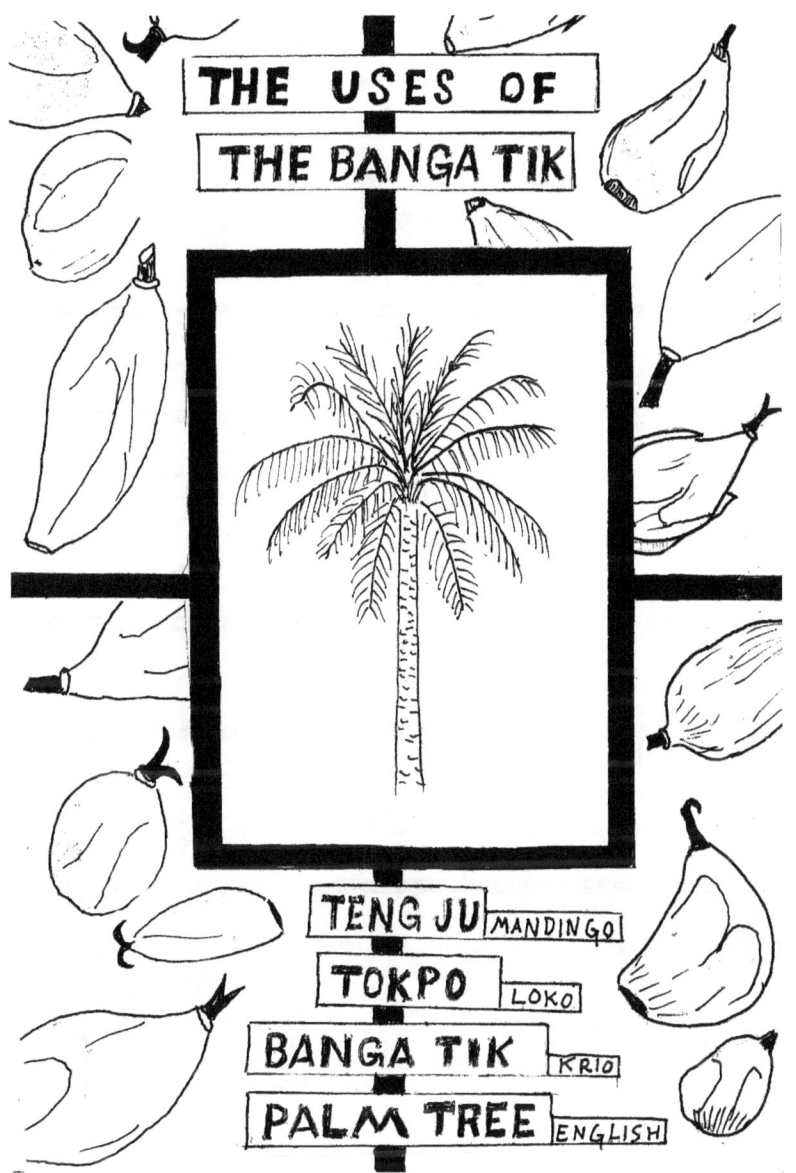

1. **PALM OIL** Men climb up the palm trees using hoops made of vines to harvest the bright red-orange palm kernals, where they grow in spiny bunches. Then the women make palm oil from the oily outer skin of the palm kernal, in a labor intensive process: huge pots bubbling over fires and mortar and pestles filled with steaming palm kernals, resulting in a pot of deep red palm oil.

2. **GBONTO SOAP** Leftover brown sludge from making palm oil is used for gbonto soap, for doing laundry.

3. **NUT OIL** Once the red outer skin is removed from the palm kernal, a hard dark seed is left behind. Women break these seeds open with rocks, exposing an oily seed from which they make nut oil, used in cooking and soap making.

4. **A SNACK** People boil the palm kernals or fry them to make sugar banga.

5. **FIRE STARTER** One byproduct from making palm oil is a fluffy fiber used to start a fire. Also, the leftover shells from making nut oil help start a fire too.

6. **BROOM** The individual leaves of a palm tree each have a long stiff center vein. When the leafy part is removed, a bundle of these makes a good broom.

7. FISHING NET In the dry season currents and water levels reduce and people fish with small hand held nets. Women pull the fibery part out of individual palm leaves and twist it into a string. Then they knot these strings together to make a net.

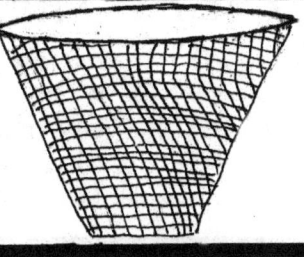

8. HAMMOCK A hammock can also be made in a process similar to making a fishing net. They can be found swinging on verandas or from two forked sticks buried in the ground.

9. ROPE AND KATA Palm tree leaves also provide an impromptue source of rope. Just pull off a few leaves to tie a bundle of wood or the feet of a chicken. A few fist fulls of leaves, wrapped into a disk and tied, makes a "kata," a pad you put on the top of the head to carry loads.

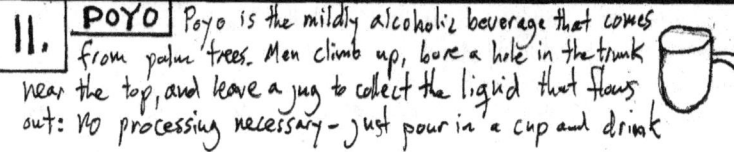

10. BUILDING MATERIALS Palm tree trunks make good bridges over streams on bush trails. Palm tree fronds are used to make the roof and walls of temporary structures, such as a farm hut or a pavilion for an outdoor event. Some tribes use the leaves in making the roof of their home.

11. POYO Poyo is the mildly alcoholic beverage that comes from palm trees. Men climb up, bore a hole in the trunk near the top, and leave a jug to collect the liquid that flows out. No processing necessary - just pour in a cup and drink.

PALM TREES

are everywhere in Sierra Leone, and there are many different species: the most common one, and the most useful, is the one they call the 'banga tik'. People use it for many things - most ubiquitous is palm oil. It is in everything: it is in the sauce that goes over the rice, it is used to fry, it serves as a lubricant

for rusty bolts, and goes on a cut to keep the flies off. The women bending over the pots making palm oil did not learn how to do it in school or from a book - they learned it from their mothers, in a tradition that stretches back to the first people to figure out how to turn palm kernals into palm oil. With these women making palm oil, we can see the conservatism that is at the heart of African society: life doesn't depend on innovation and progress, but on adherence to an ancient tradition which makes everything else possible. (Drawings by students at CJSS Waridala) 30 May 2013

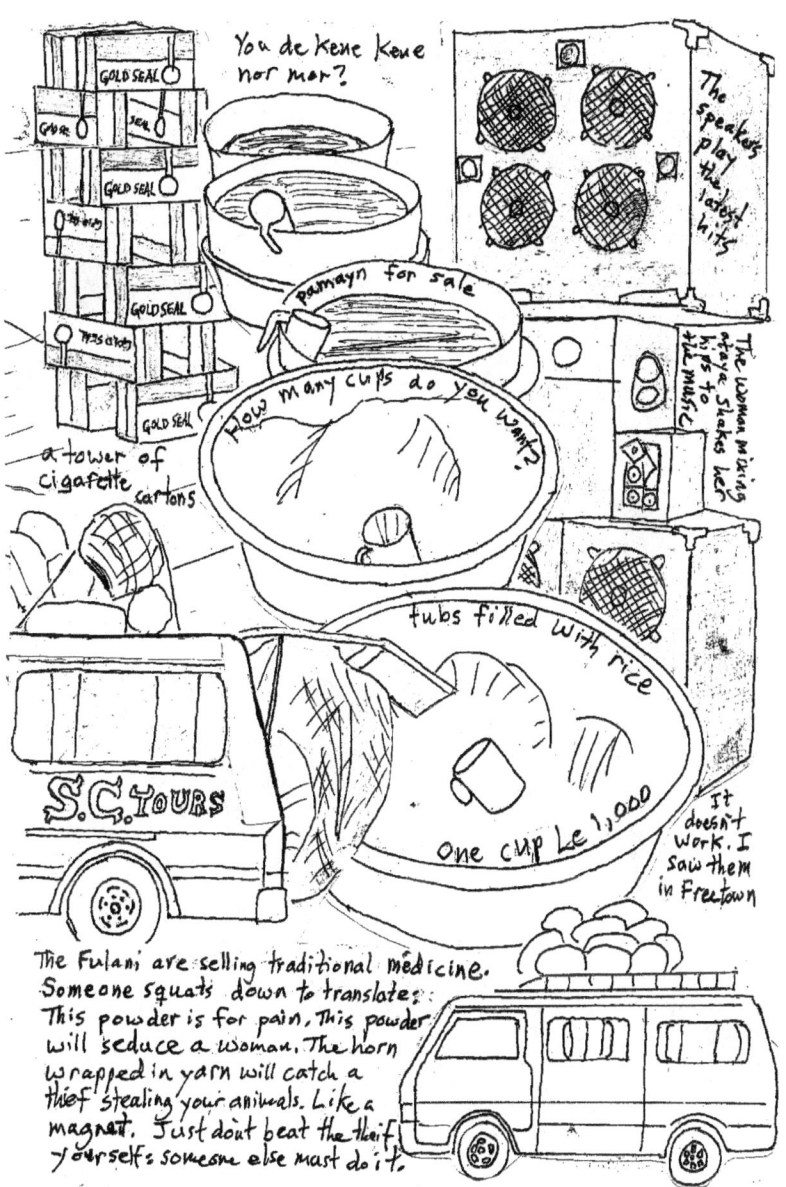

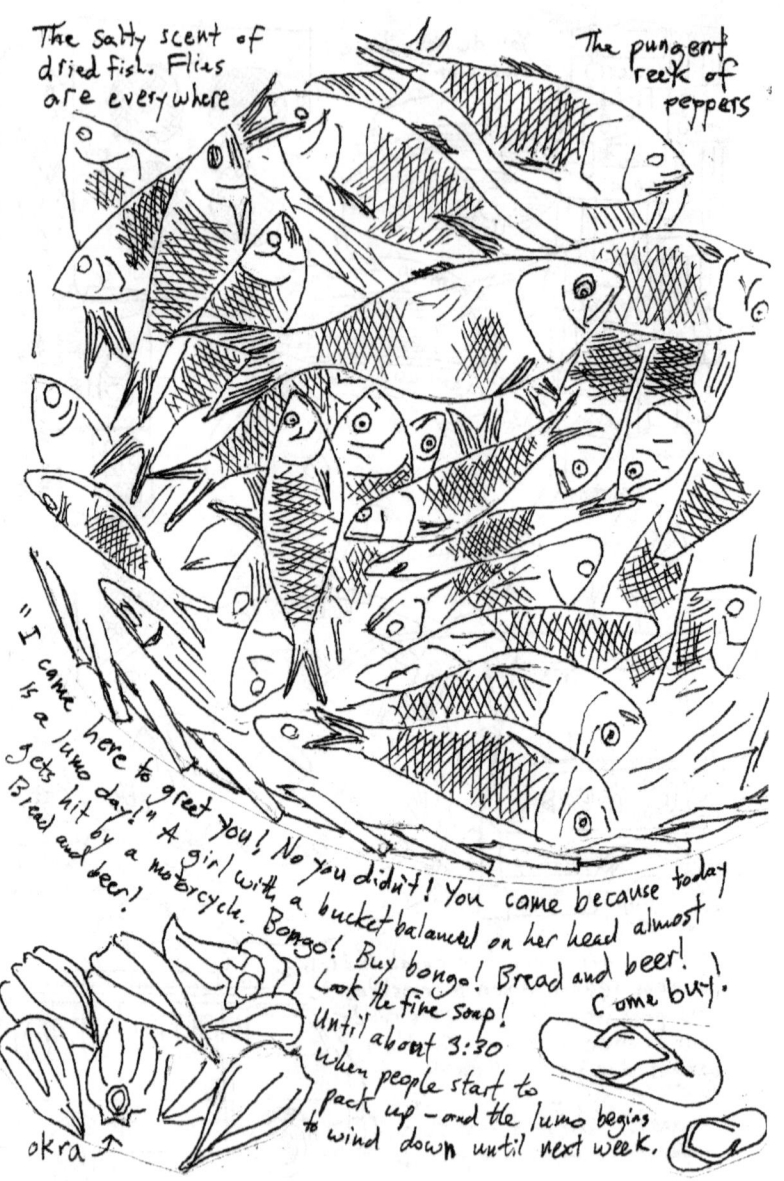

HEY MR LEE YOU de SUCK BOOBIE NOW![1]

When my mother came to visit, everywhere we went people told us in Krio, "Mr. Lee, your mama done come! You de suck boobie now!" That is to say, they were teasing me, telling me that my mother had come to nurse me. As was often the case, I wasn't sure what else to do except laugh along with them. "*Den ko*" was the other thing people said, in Maninka, in a sentimental tone of voice, that is, "child business"—for the mother-son bond is viewed with particular affection. "See how far she traveled to check on her son?" was the implication.

It was late afternoon by the time my mother and I reached the small junction branching off from the main road, the dirt track that leads to Waridala. We got out of the motorcar and unloaded our luggage. This was the last hurdle: Somehow, we had to get two people, five pieces of luggage, and four bags of rice these last four miles down the bush road to Waridala. Motorcycle taxi was the only option. One of the teachers, Francis Kamara, owned a motorcycle and he was happy to give us a ride. My mother and I and a few of our bags squeezed onto the seat behind Francis; another driver took the bags of rice.

With the three of us perched on top of the 125cc motorcycle, we sped down the unmaintained bumpy road, guided by Francis's expert hand. At one point, the road crossed a steep, rough patch of exposed bedrock. As we bounced up to the top, Francis looked back over his shoulder with a grin and cackled, "This is Africa."

It was only the day before that my mother had set foot on the continent, walking out of the crowd gathered around the exit door at the Freetown airport, the culmination of 36 hours of plane travel. After a year and a half of separation, she was the same mother I had always known, rolling a bag of luggage on the concrete behind her and wearing a smile on her face. On the ferry trip across the bay from the airport, it was night, the scattered lights of Freetown reflected on the black water. The ferry was filled with Sierra Leoneans, all well dressed and in festive moods. Going abroad is a sort of Sierra Leonean national dream, after all, and the folks on the ferry from the airport were those few for whom the dream was a reality, either for themselves or their family members. Once the boat was underway, the first thing my mom did, ever the navigator, was ask what direction was north.

That night we stayed in the Stadium Hostel, a rundown place, a poor choice in retrospect, due to its general state of disrepair and filth, but it was where I had first stayed as a Peace Corps volunteer, so perhaps I thought it was fitting. Early the next morning, we left for Waridala. Before we left Freetown, my mother had to change money. It was too early for the official exchange bureau to be open, and to be fair, I had never actually used one. I changed some of my mom's one-hundred-dollar bills on the street. As I squatted on the sidewalk, filling a black plastic bag with bundles of leones, it felt like I was doing something illegal, and technically perhaps I was, but the truth was, many routine things felt slightly illegal in this place. Soon we were on our way.

The 140-mile trip from Freetown to Waridala was a bit of an adventure, as usual. We squeezed into the back small motor car and I paid for an extra seat to allow for a little extra leg room. Soon after our departure, the driver had his license confiscated by the police because he had picked up a passenger in a restricted area. The driver then had to chase down the officer and pay a bribe in order to get the license back. Once we were finally on our way again, the driver picked up another person in the same restricted area. Mom, ever the good sport, commented that at least he seemed like a competent driver.

In Makeni we changed cars to continue north. My mom and I shared the front seat of a tiny passenger vehicle so overloaded with people and bags that the rear hatch door couldn't close. The driver lashed it down with a piece of rope. However, the potholes that we encountered on the road were so bad that the window of the rear hatch shattered, spraying glass on the luggage and the rear seat. Finally, we arrived at the junction to Waridala, where we dusted the broken glass off of our bags and rode on the motorcycle with Francis down the bush road. Later, reflecting on the trip to Waridala, my mom wrote:

> The journey out to Waridala is a story unto itself, but the gradual leaving behind of the stench and filth (piles of garbage just filling the streets) and despairing conditions (sewer running down ditches beside the streets, skinny stray dogs skittering about, hawkers descending upon the white man—"*Opoto! Opoto!*") gave way to the gentle countryside of palm and mango and banana trees.

It was a relief, to say the least, to finally reach Waridala. On that first evening, no sooner had we arrived, than a group of village women came to greet my mother, clapping and singing and dressed in their best lappa suits. Everyone wanted to greet my mother. They crowded around her, took turns embracing her, and delivered hot bowls of rice and sauce.

The next morning, we visited the school where I teach, and my mom introduced herself to the students and answered all their questions. The students were used to calling their teachers "sir" as a sign of respect, so they called my mother "sir," also, until they remembered they are supposed to call female teachers "ma," and they laughed nervously at themselves. My mom, retired teacher and ever the educator, read them a story and did a writing activity.

After school I took her on a tour of the village, the primary school, the river, the big mosque. Along the way, we greeted people, and everyone gave use an enthusiastic welcome. "Mr. Lee na we own pikin," they said in Krio, meaning, I was "their own child." Some even went so far as to say "Na we born Mr. Lee" – or -- "We were the ones who gave birth to Mr. Lee" – a special jest for the one who actually did the birthing. Others said "Mr. Lee na we Maninka brother," or "Mr. Lee speaks Maninka," or even "He no de return again to America." They were trying to show my mother that I was welcome in their community, that I "had people" there, who were willing to help me out, or at least, tease me. And of course, there were many sentimental mentions of *"den ko,"* that is "child things," in Maninka. For Maninka people, the bond between a son and a mother is considered to be especially close. In a large polygamous family, where often resources may not be plentiful enough to go around, a grown son is expected to help take care of his mother.

Taking my role as son and guide seriously, I brought her to sample palm wine – locally known as poyo. The beverage is layered with taboo – alcohol in a Muslim community, an uncouth drink reserved for poor, rural males -- but as long as we were discreet, our status as visiting white people insulated us from judgement. As my mother later recalled:

> One of the young teachers took Daemion and me (yes, three of us) on his motorcycle about 10 miles down a dirt, then paved road to a village that serves palm wine, the sweet, white, almost effervescent and slightly alcoholic juice that comes from palm trees. None is available in Waridala, since it's a Muslim village, so this served as the neighborhood tavern: benches under the

mango trees, one made of a large worn plank of wood perched on two rocks.

On the night of the second day, after evening prayer, the two traditional Maninka musicians, whom I had invited, began playing, welcoming my mother. The two musicians – called *yeliba* in Maninka -- were a man and a woman, drummer and a singer, and they led the crowd in call-and-response songs, with lyrics everyone knew by heart. One song's chorus included the line "*jama i bolo!*" – that is, "You have a crowd!" Since the *yeliba* came specifically to welcome my mother, many of the songs were about us; and according to custom, after a song sang about you, you have to give the *yeliba* money. One of the old women would give me a look when the time was right and I would throw down a bill in front of the *yeliba*. Then someone would shine a flashlight on the bill and everyone would cheer, before the female *yeliba* snatched it up and stuffed it into her purse.

The next morning the *yeliba* came again to lead everyone in dancing, again, and to summon everyone for a community meeting, where my mother was formally introduced and welcomed. It was a classic West African meeting, which basically meant everyone takes turns giving speeches, beginning with the most senior person. When it was my mom's turn, she told them that people in America may be rich, but they don't have the warmth and hospitality of the people in Waridala. Once her speech and been translated for the crowd, her words were met with cheers. When it was my turn, I tried to speak in Maninka. I began improvising a halting speech, but when I told them "*N'ti maliya ka n'na kili ka na yan,*" that is, "I am not ashamed to call my mother to come here," the crowd again broke out in cheers. They were delighted, even if I had to finish the rest of the speech in Krio.

At times like this it felt that even though my mom and I shared in this public space together with the Sierra Leoneans, sitting close together, my mom and I remained a world apart, and the Americans and Sierra Leoneans would never be able to quite explain ourselves to each other no matter how we tried.

The cultural gulf between ancient rural West African community practices, and the modern industrialized, individualized American mentality seemed vast. I was glad that my mother took the same approach I did in the face of this difference and aspired only to be kind and generous.

On Friday, I wanted to make sure my mother visited the mosque for Friday prayers. It is a big event in Waridala: Even if people miss all the other calls to prayer for the week, everyone must make an appearance for Friday prayer. People don't usually go to their farms on Friday mornings; instead they rest until about noon, when they get ready to go to the mosque. It was strange, that week, to see my mother among the crowd of colorfully dressed people entering the mosque. Later, my mom wrote:

> In the mosque, as we waited for the ceremonies to begin, I looked down the row of women in front of me and was so moved by how beautiful they were in their bright and patterned clothing, yards of gorgeous fabric draped over them, each one unique. As the imam spoke, I noticed many of the women nodded off, and I thought how it must just be a nice little break for them from the long days of work, work, work, and visiting the mosque seemed like a comforting experience rather than a deeply spiritual one.

During the week she was there, we spent a lot of time greeting people, the cherished African tradition. One afternoon we went across the Mabole river to a one-house village, called Foday Bockaria. At the riverside, as we prepared to cross, a group of women from Waridala had brought their dirty clothes and their children to the waterside for a washing. Everyone was half naked, or nearly so, the adults and children alike, playing and splashing in the water. Mom and I got into the wooden boat and one of my students paddled us across. At Foday Bockaria, we met a couple of Loko women without shirts behind the house in the shade of a tree. They were cooking and one of them was making a mat out of twisted grass. Although I had never met them before, they were delighted to see me and my visitor and the women took out some of the palm kernels boiling in the pot for us to eat as a snack, and one woman gave us a huge papaya as a gift.

On another evening we walked down the road that leads back to the main road, stopping occasionally to greet people. As my mom recalled later:

> Often, they just brush off a bench and move it to the shade and gesture for you to come sit. Then you sit, exchanging very few words, but just sit companionably under the mango tree for a bit, until it seems time to go, and you stand up and say "*i ni wali*" (meaning thank you and hello and good bye in Maninka) and shake hands and smile and nod and move on down the road.

One of the more challenging parts of my mother's visit, however, had to do with gift giving. Sierra Leone has a strong culture of gift giving, so nearly everyone I met during my mother's visit asked me at one point or another, "Will you not give me some of the money that your mother has brought for you?" My mother, of course, had not brought me money, nor could I ever imagine expecting such a gift in such circumstances. But I did, in fact, choose to give some people money. On the one hand, it was a poor choice to perpetuate stereotypes of wealthy white foreigners coming to Sierra Leone and handing out money. But on the other hand, there was nothing I could say that could convince people that my mother hadn't given me money, which I was withholding from my Sierra Leone friends. *Fadagbe a ti mor sor* – a phrase in Maninka meaning "Whites don't give to people" --- that was the other stereotype. And it was true to an extent: the white American culture I grew up in encouraged gifts on birthdays and Christmas and that was about it. But I had lived in Sierra Leone for nearly two years and people had been generous to me and I wanted to help them out. To not give a gift, that seemed like its own sort of cultural *faux pas*. What I gave was not a lot. But in the abysmal poverty of Sierra Leone, this is how subsistence farmers survive: on handouts from wealthier friends and family.

I gave some money to the woman who cooked for me, one of the teachers at the school, a few of my friends, and the Mamie Queen. My visit to the Mamie Queen was particularly interesting. Mamie Queen, as the head of the women in the village, had been cooking rice for my mother, since it is her responsibility to cook for guests who come to town. She was getting old and usually she was cross and sour, but when I gave her the money, she became very sentimental and talked to me for a long time, saying that all mothers are crazy because they think that their children are still small even when they grow up. Sierra Leone culture was so different and strange to me, yet there were always moments like these of unexpected similarity.

Soon enough, it was my mom's last day in Waridala. The town chief had been out of town this whole time attending a funeral. Only on the last day of my mother's visit did he arrive back in the village. Like everyone else, he happily welcomed my mother. We sat with him on his veranda, exchanging niceties and silences and we arranged to deliver to his house the three 50-pound bags of rice that my mom's school donated. Later, the chief delivered his own gift to my mom. As she later recalled:

> A half hour later, here comes this strapping beautiful 18-year-old young man across the yard, holding what appeared to be a rolled-up ball of fabric, cinnamon- and black-colored with some flashes of red. Then he was upon me, and handed over to my arms, "This gift, from my father, the chief." And he held out for me a live chicken.

We asked the neighbor if she would cook it for us. A few hours later, she delivered two pans to us, one of rice and another with this chicken immersed in a red sauce made of palm oil and peppers. The tiny breast meat, a quarter the size of a fattened American chicken, was delicious, spicy with peppers and clear and clean tasting. We couldn't eat it all, so we let two teenage boys finish off the stew and rice, which they ate in complete silence, so enamored they were with their good fortune. The rinsed the pans for us and tossed the bones out into the yard. For the goats.

It was time to head back to Freetown, but on the way, we stopped at the beach at Bureh. We had to changed vehicles in the town of Waterloo, a crowded market town just outside of Freetown. As soon as my mother and I arrived, someone asked us where we were going and immediately a few young men hustled us over to a ramshackle van painted bright blue, where we crunched in with the other passengers onto the flat steel benches. Now the van was full. The sliding door was slammed shut, the van coughed to life, and we bounced through the pot holes onto the main road.

I had made reservations for a place to stay at Bureh Beach, but I didn't know where it was located, only the name of the man who ran it, Prince. When we arrived in Bureh town, I approached a crowd of people and told a young man, loitering nearby, that "I am looking for Prince." It felt, for a moment, like I was getting involved with some sort of mafia. But sure enough, the young man knew who I was talking about. "Come," he said and put my mother's bag on his head and led us down the beach to the beach house where we were to spend a day and two nights. Bureh Beach, famous among locals and Peace Corps volunteers alike, was beautiful, lined with palm trees and a long stretch of white sand against the tropical-colored Atlantic Ocean.

We walked on the beach and later reclined in the hammocks, not doing a thing except rocking back and forth to the rhythm of the gentle waves, which were perhaps 25 yards away. After dark, the beach got a bit loud. A giant party going on at a bar a down the beach, with Sierra Leonean music blasting from loudspeakers and hundreds of young people from Freetown dancing. The music kept us up me up until probably 4:30am, when it finally quieted enough to go back to hearing only the waves. We both woke at 7am anyway, strangely rested, and we had tea on a tray, British style, then a giant breakfast of an omelet, beans and bread and Laughing Cow cheese.

Finally, it was time for my mom's flight back to the U.S. On the way back through Freetown, we stopped to visit a Maninka teacher whom I had previously met. Later, my mom commented,

> I'd assumed the visit with the teacher would be a somber, serious affair, looking at an alphabet and books I couldn't decipher; instead, his teacher turned the whole thing into a huge joke about how I was going to be his wife and stay in Freetown, or else I'd take him to America with me, that my husband wouldn't mind, and on and on. I think this made five marriage proposals I got while there.

We boarded the ferry and crossed the bay to go to the airport and then it was time for my mom to say goodbye, to me and to Sierra Leone. A visit from one's mother carries a host of emotions, nostalgia, nervousness and more. Since I was living in a village thousands of miles from home, the situation was even more complicated. My mother had never been to another country before; Sierra Leone lacks rudimentary infrastructure; an entire village of peasant farmers watched her every move. But there were no mishaps and people received us warmly. "Mr. Lee, you de suck boobie now!" This jest was an unexpected reminder that in some ways everyone all over the word is the same: everyone has a mother and sooner or later she might come to visit. My mom, for her part, found the trip to be a memorable and moving experience. Later she wrote,

> Muslim and Catholic and Evangelical Christians all mix, all the tribes and languages mix and overlap, the races mix, the ages mix—and I think their harmony is a result of seeing themselves as part of a much larger world, even from inside their tiny villages of mud brick houses.

A glimpse of one of the minarets on the mosque in Waridala

Every morning at 5 a.m., I heard the boom of a drum, at least if I was awake. The beat started out slowly and gradually increased tempo. Then with one last boom, the village would be silent again, locked in the pre-dawn darkness. Soon, however, the glimmer of a few flashlights would appear on darkened verandas. People had heard the drum, the summons to prayer, and they were preparing to go to the mosque. The Maninkas in town were well known for being proudly Muslim. The large and elaborate mosque was central to the town, and Islamic traditions were central to the community.

The most important thing is to pray—five times a day. Before leaving the house to go to the mosque, it is necessary to wash your hands and feet in a particular sequence, called "holding ablution."

The drum used to summon people to prayer. It is called the "tabali" in Mandingo and in order to beat it, they use a flexible strip of rubber cut from an old automobile tire.

the tabali

the first step in praying like a Muslim

In Sierra Leone, ablution is usually performed using what they call a cooler, the plastic kettle-shaped container filled with water.

To go to the mosque, the men usually wore a simple ankle-length robe and a round hat. Sometimes they would go in their ordinary clothes, although this was usually the younger men. The old men seemed to be perpetually clothed in their prayer robes. The women wore layers of colorful shawls to the mosque. The female area of the mosque was usually not as full as the male area as women are encouraged to pray in their husbands' homes. There, it is believed, they will get the most blessings.

The pulpit where the imam delivers sermons

In the early morning the mosque is dark except for the glow of flashlights. At the entrance of the mosque an old man—usually Pa Lamine, my neighbor—used to sit, reciting suras from the Koran. The recitation was a cross between singing and chanting and his voice floats through the darkened village, plaintive yet hopeful. Pa Lamine was usually gruff and stoic, but his voiced seemed transformed during the early morning call to prayer. Before entering the mosque, shoes are removed. Inside, the area for men as up front, and the area in back was reserved for women, separated by blankets hanging from a string. The mosque had no furniture, except rows of mats on the floor.

Prayer involves very specific procedures, divided into units called a *rakat*. A combination of standing, kneeling, and prostration makes up one *rakat*. The number of required *rakats* varies depending on the time of day: The morning is two; the evening is three; the other prayer times are four. Almost all praying takes place in Arabic, and many Maninka learn to read and write Arabic and recite suras from a young age. The first verse of the Koran, the al-Fatiha, is recited every time you pray, although other suras may be included as well.

    Soon a man would go outside of the mosque and do the official call to prayer, a cross between shouting, singing, and words of praise to God. The call to prayer announces that the main prayer is about to begin, and once the call has been completed, the imam leads the group prayer; everyone completes *rakats* simultaneously, standing shoulder to shoulder. As the group does *rakats* together, it gives the quiet room a charged atmosphere as everyone moves in unison. Waridala had four different imams when I lived there, who took turns leading prayer on different days. When the imam recites the prayers, his voice is a hybrid between singing and chanting. Each imam had his own style, and it was interesting to hear different interpretations of the same prayers. The melodies they chose were different, emphasizing different words or syllables. Some spoke quickly, others slowly. Given that I couldn't understand the words, all I could notice were these stylistic elements.

    After this, more prayers would be recited as a group, then everyone silently would recite—Allah is perfect; Thanks to Allah; Allah is the Greatest—33 times each. As they did this, the sound of beads clacking was audible as they counted. Those who did not have prayer beads would count by touching their thumb to each join on each hand, three per finger, times five fingers, equals 15 per hand. The al-Fatiha is recited one more time, after which you symbolically rub your face, as if washing. Then everyone greets each other, saying *Salam-Walekum* (peace be with you) and responding *Walekum-Salam* (and also with you) while shaking hands.

    I found Islam to be an interesting mix of influences. On the one hand, monotheistic metaphors about God's power and sovereignty are familiar to anyone from a Christian background. On the other hand, the bowing and prostrations resemble something much different, evocative perhaps of the spiritual tradition associated with yoga.

The alcove at the front of the mosque from which the imam leads prayer

It suggested that correct posture is on the path to God, as much as right belief or right action. Islam seemed to be a simple and practical religion, at least as practiced in Waridala: no singing, no outward displays of religious fervor, no proselytizing, no obtuse theological doctrines; just praying and reciting.

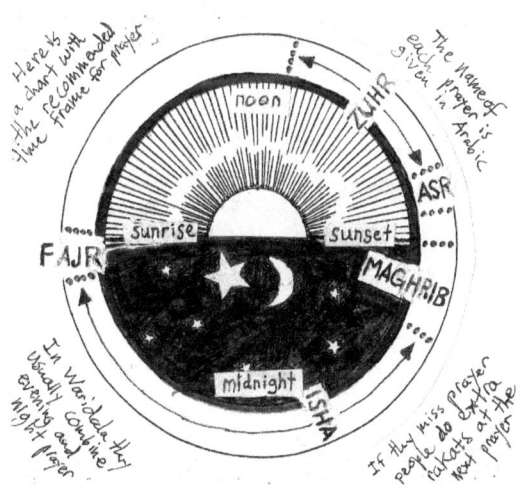

One of the minarets on the mosque in Waridala

 # SNAKE BITES

AND

WITCH GUNS

The traditional worldview in Sierra Leone can be divided into two realms: the town and the bush. This is an ancient division, with Muslim beliefs (or Christian, depending on the community) only layered on top. The town is the realm of civilization and order; the bush is the realm of disorder and chaos, ruled by spirits and devils. A witch is a person, male or female, who is in touch with these spirits and attempts to tap into their power. The bush sustains the town, after all, providing fertile ground for growing crops and being a source of other food. However, witchcraft is a dark art, which can be used for good or ill. Snakes have a special role in this world. Many people seem to regard them as an incarnation of a spirit; some suggest that witches take the form of a snake. To be bitten by a snake is akin to being afflicted by dark powers.

A common example of witchcraft is what they call a swear in Krio. A swear is often used by farmers to protect a crop and promote a good harvest. While the word swear in English suggests something spoken, these swears involve physical objects, usually consisting of little more than leaves and twigs, natural objects easily found in the bush. Perhaps it is words that imbue them with their secret power. *Swears* can be seen along a trail, perhaps hanging from a branch, used to promote a good harvest and protect crops from those with evil intentions. How they work is obscure—that's part of the point—but somehow the maker of the *swear* uses it to channel forces of the spirit world.

A more potent and fearsome example is the witch gun. I never saw a witch gun, but from what I understood, it operates in a similar manner as a *swear*. Ordinary objects, rather than actual guns, are somehow imbued with extraordinary powers. A witch gun may be held in the hand or set as a trap and it is used by one person to inflict harm on someone else. Although spiritual in mechanism, witch guns, I was told, shoot physical or physical-like objects, simply called bullets.

The Maninka in Waridala did not actively participate in witchcraft, they told me, and had no secret society, like the Poro society, which other groups in the region participated in. But that didn't mean that they didn't believe in witchcraft. They just usually got people from other ethnic groups to do it, especially the Loko, who live across the river. For example, many young boys in Waridala had vertical scars on their chests from a procedure, I was told, that was intended to release the devil that was stunting their growth.

When I first moved to Waridala, my friend Mr. Sheriff brought me, with his wife and child, to visit a traditional doctor who promised to help keep away the devils that were tormenting the child. We traveled for what seemed like hours along bush trails, and when we arrived, the doctor performed a serious ritual involving a chicken. Waridala had many devils around it, people told me, partly because it is right next to a river, the Mabole, and devils have close relationships with rivers.

The methods to combat these devils, or harness their power, were various, although invariably secret. The most public display I witnessed in the village came one day when I came across a group gathered around the veranda of a young man, who, people told me, had been suffering from a mysterious chronic illness. The young man was sitting shirtless on the steps of the veranda, holding a goat kid on his head as he gripped the front and back legs tightly. A woman stood above him on the steps, making pronouncements in a language I didn't understand, though guessed to be Loko. Then, someone slit the goat's throat and the blood poured over the young man's head and bare torso. I was told the ceremony was an attempt to rid the boy of the devil that was making him sick.

Witchcraft played an important role in people's worldview, even the most devout Muslims in Waridala. At the very least, it gives people whose lives were precarious and vulnerable a powerful way to explain and rationalize. A farmer's life, already, is at the whim of a thousand natural processes, seen and unseen. The lack of infrastructure or reliable health care further complicates things.

One day during my first year of teaching in Waridala, an accident happened on the river, as students were coming to school. Of course, for the students who lived across the river, there was no bridge, but they used a boat to cross the river, a large dugout-style canoe, carved from a large tree. The group of about ten students came staggering through town, soaking wet, and the people in town became riled up. Everyone was yelling at once, the students and teachers spilling out of the school to see what had happened. Eventually the students were able to convey that everyone was okay, just shook up, though some had lost their exercise books in the water. A few of the students didn't know how to swim and had to be rescued. It turned out the accident had been caused by one of the students, who was playing around and started rocking the boat, causing it to capsize.

The town elders became involved and made promises about improving safety for the students crossing the river. But underneath this public response to the accident, some people whispered that witchcraft was involved, that a devil had somehow influenced or inhabited the boy who rocked the boat. This whispered response to the accident illustrates how pervasive beliefs about witchcraft can be: It can be anything, it can be anywhere. Witchcraft is secret and it is magic, so that means it is impossible to escape.

Many secrets were certainly hidden in the shadows. Intermittently during the dry season, I would be warned to stay inside after dark, for the secret society from across the river would be coming through town. What would happen if I didn't stay inside, no one said, but the warning was sinister enough for me to take it seriously. At night, all I would hear was the sound of drums in the night.

People were terrified of witchcraft. I remember when a rumor swirled among my students that someone across the river was killing young girls and using their body parts in some sort of ceremony. Many didn't come to school at all for some time.

I didn't know quite what to think. I was circumspect of witchcraft, but at the same time, I saw how real it was for people. My identity as a white person also meant I was somehow immune. Quite simply, witchcraft does not work on white people. Everyone seemed to know this. This meant that I could never really know what the locals knew. In the dry season I used to bathe in the river with the men and boys, as was custom, right before dusk, and I remember one time I was the last one still in the river, as darkness began to settle. The others on the bank told me: Get out, there are devils in the water at night. I didn't quite take it seriously, but I immediately complied. As I moved through the black water towards the shore, I was perhaps the closest I ever was to knowing the terror of witchcraft. I saw how impossible it is to know what inhabits the dark, and how all I could do was stick close to those I knew and hope for the best.

White people's immunity to witchcraft meant the white Peace Corps volunteers in Sierra Leone were in this strange liminal space, both belonging to the communities where they lived and taught and being utter outsiders. One way this curious relationship manifested, it seemed, is that some volunteers elected to have snake bite medicine administered. The procedure, I was told, involves a series of small cuts made with a

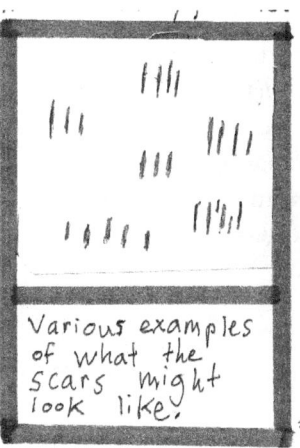

Various examples of what the scars might look like.

razor blade on various parts of the body. A poultice is rubbed into the cuts and when they heal, a residue of the medicine remains in the small scars left behind. On white people, the look is dramatic, as the dark color of the poultice stands out again pale skin. The volunteers I knew did it for fun, in a way, but at the same time it seemed difficult to entirely discount the possibility that the medicine is effective in ways we didn't quite understand.

One Peace Corps volunteer who lived near me was preparing to leave the country and decided to have a traditional doctor give him the medicinal marks on his arm to protect against snake bites and witches (which, in fact, may be the same thing). He was a friendly man from California, and we had bonded over a shared interest in linguistics. On a damp, drizzly afternoon, I accompanied him, though I decided to forgo the procedure myself.

We traveled to the town of Kalangba in the heart of Loko territory, on the other side of the river from Waridala. The person who was to administer the procedure was a friend of a friend's acquaintance and had been notified ahead of time. She was an ordinary-looking Sierra Leonean woman, stocky with round friendly features, wearing a bright orange lappa suit, the dresses made by local tailors from the bolts of cloth known as lappas. My friend took a seat on a bench and, without ceremony or hesitation, the woman took the paper off of a new razor blade and made three incisions on his bicep. Then she took the lid off a plastic container and rubbed a thick black paste into the cuts. Another woman who was passing by—the "daughter" of the woman making the incision we were told—stopped to provide some exceptionally vigorous rubbing to the wounds before she continued to wherever she had been going.

The woman in charge of the procedure made similar cuts on my friend's other bicep, top of the wrists, and the back of the calves. These locations seemed typical for the marks; other common areas were the shoulder blade and the back. Excess blood was wiped with a dirty rag; exclamations of pain were not forthcoming from my friend. Soon it was over. The procedure was surprisingly informal, as if she were preparing ingredients for a meal. She gave my friend a bit of extra medicine wrapped in paper to reapply into the wound the next day.

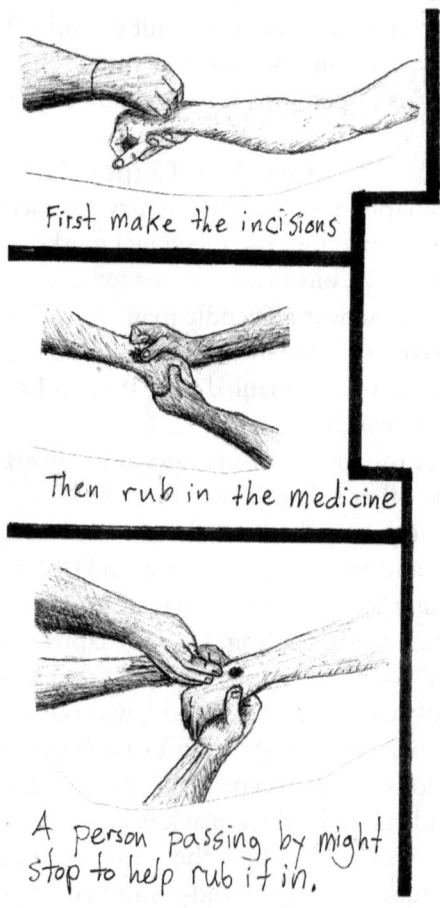

First make the incisions

Then rub in the medicine

A person passing by might stop to help rub it in.

    I inquired about the contents of the black paste, but, as to be expected, she told me it is a secret. She did show me her own scars when I asked if she had them—a line of scars on her back below her neck and another line of scars above her waistline. The scars looked quite different on her, compared to my white friend. Hers were the same color as her black skin, perhaps a little lighter due to the scar tissue. On white people, the scars stand out dramatically, black lines against pale white.

So now my friend was effectively inoculated against snake bites and witch guns. They say that with this medicine you can even step on a snake and it won't bite you. But does it really work? I don't know. Certainly, my friend went home with a badge that shows he had lived in far-off lands. But are marks like these just a cultural curiosity to be wondered at? Do they have some power that we don't understand? We cannot dismiss it as impossible, because even by science's own standards, we must watch and observe for a long time before we can make conclusions. Yet by its very nature, anything to do with witchcraft is secret, making confirmation by observation all but impossible.

Encounters with foreign belief systems, at best, help to show us the strangeness of our own. The diverse answers to big spiritual questions suggest that we don't have good answers, and instead we are carried forward by tradition and culture. These medicinal marks show us not only what is different among cultures, but also what is shared. People want strength and security in an unpredictable world, and they will do whatever they can to find it.

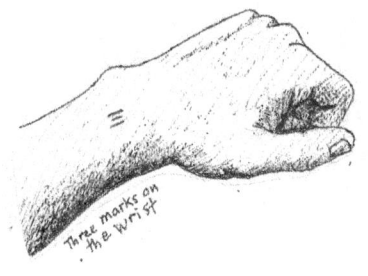

Three marks on the wrist

DONKI SALI

The biggest holiday all year is Eid al Adha, which the Maninka call Donki Sali. People go all out to celebrate, and relatives from across Sierra Leone gather in the place of their birth. The holiday commemorates the story of Abraham and Isaac—similar versions are found both in the Koran and the Bible—when Abraham obeys God's order to sacrifice his son Isaac. Abraham raises the knife, and only then does God substitute a sheep in Isaac's place. Donki Sali is a celebration of Abraham's obedience to God and everyone who can afford it sacrifices a sheep. This sacrifice is called *layon* in Maninka. Donki Sali/Eid al Adha happens during the Hajj season and the pilgrims on the Hajj in Saudi Arabia make the same sacrifice in Mecca.

In 2012 the holiday happened during November. The date follows the Islamic lunar calendar, so it changes each year. I decided to buy the *layon* for the old woman who lived in the same compound as me, Chernor N'dor Kuda. In the past, her children used to buy the *layon*, but that year none were able to. I was curious about the holiday so I thought buying the *layon* for Chernor N'dor Kuda would be a good way to learn more.

She kept telling me that Alhaji had a sheep for sale, referring to our mutual neighbor, but the man was traveling across the river where he was buying more sheep to sell and we were unable to meet up. I wanted to buy quickly, as I was told the price of a sheep climbs steeply as the holiday draws near. At last, Alhaji returned from across the river and I was able to make the purchase for a reasonable price of Le 160,000.

Chernor N'dor Kuda was delighted and blessed me over and over whenever she saw me for about two weeks. *Allah ni bariye*, she would say in Maninka, "May God bless you," and then she would lift up her hands. The appropriate response, I learned, was to say, *Amina*.

On the day of Donki Sali, the actual sacrifice occurred without much ceremony. After everyone returned from the pray field, they retrieved a knife and put some banana leaves on the ground to catch the blood. The deed was done by the old Arabic teacher, Pa Alpha. Chernor N'dor Kuda, other relatives, and I stood behind Pa Alpha as he solemnly slit the animal's throat, our hands on his back so we could share the blessings.

Besides the *layon*, a big part of the holiday was clothes. Everyone wanted to dress well. That year, a large group of people wore what they call *ashorbi* in Krio. You could translate this word as "uniform dress," though that does not quite capture it. The concept is this: Everyone buys cloth with the exact same pattern—some colorful Africana design—then each person takes the cloth to his or her own tailor and has an outfit made. On the day of Donki Sali, the group brought their *ashorbi* outfits along, and then at the dramatic moment, everyone put their outfit on at once and paraded around town. A good 40 people wore same *ashorbi* outfit, friends and relatives from Waridala and beyond. It was mostly women who participated, but a few men and children joined in as well.

Perhaps the most exciting thing about the occasion was the live band that came from Freetown and played Maninka music for two days in a row. The band had an electric guitar, an electric bass, a drum set, and at least three singers, all amplified by electricity from a generator. The sound of Maninka music is very distinctive but hard to describe. Despite familiar American-style instruments, the music has a wailing yet energetic sound.

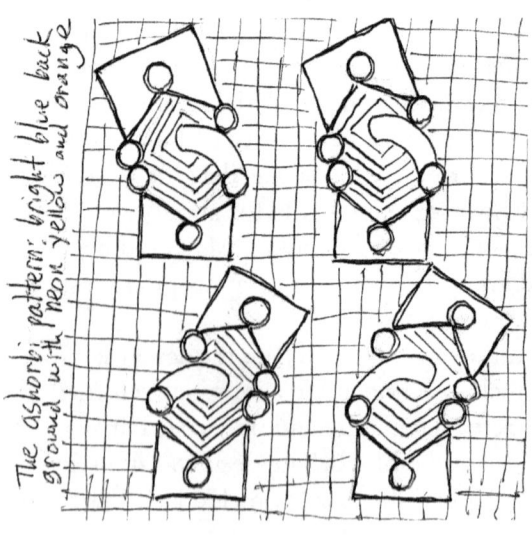

This music has a unique role to play at this event. These musicians are called *yelibas* in Maninka, which translates as "praise singer." Their job is to play music and let the people dance and enjoy themselves, but with a twist: The songs they play are about the people who are listening. It worked something like this: Everyone was seated on benches, watching, and people would take turns getting up to dance, either alone or in a small group. As the people danced, the singers would take turns improvising lyrics in praise of whoever was dancing. There is a two-step dance that everyone seemed to do, first to the right and then to the left, swaying back and forth. The person being honored is expected to give money to the musicians. When the money is handed over, everyone cheers. The lead singer (*yeliba*) was an outgoing woman and she singled me out and told me I needed to give her dollars when it was my turn to be praised. *E don! E don!* she said, "Dance! Dance!" I gave Le 10,000, a little more than what others were giving, and she seemed satisfied.

For a few days, the village swelled. The visiting relatives were more affluent than the villagers, hailing from bigger towns where economic opportunities extend beyond farming. These were the uncles and aunts and cousins who'd escaped the village, evident by their faces, unlined by long days in the fields. But they too were claimed by the same traditions of their less affluent cousins: Islam and sacrifices on Donki Sali and *yelibas*, showing how we can always leave home but never quite leave it behind.

RAMADAN

ONE MONTH IN THE ISLAMIC CALENDAR.
LASTS FROM NEW MOON TO NEW MOON

In WARIDALA

Ramadan involves an intensification of the practices the Waridala community is engaged in throughout the year: praying and reciting. It is called *sun kari* in Maninka and simply "fast month" in Krio. As was explained to me, fast month is not only about fasting from food and water—your whole person should fast: your hands, your feet, your eyes, your mouth. That is, besides alimentary fasting, people should refrain from immoral behavior, like stealing or gossiping. Some also describe Ramadan like this: God says for eleven months we eat rice and for one month we don't.

    The daily routine during Ramadan begins at 4 a.m., when the clock tower rings. The sound of the bell summons the women to begin preparing for the pre-dawn morning meal. Some might eat rice with chicken or fresh fish; during Ramadan, people often splurge and buy more expensive food. Others eat bread or drink tea. At 5 a.m., a man beats the drum at the mosque to tell people to prepare for the morning prayer. Sometimes a man walks through the village in the darkness, encouraging people to wake up, calling out, "*Na salat!* Na *salat!*"—a mixture of Maninka and Arabic meaning "Come to prayer!" By 6 a.m. people are leaving the mosque after prayer, the sky just beginning to brighten. After the first prayer, no more eating or drinking for the rest of the day.

This task is particularly challenging during those years when Ramadan falls during farm work seasons. In 2012 Ramadan fell during July and August, the heart of planting season. So by mid-morning, most of the village people had left for their fields. For the two o'clock and four o'clock prayers, the mosque was mostly empty because people were still working.

But by about 7 o' clock people would gather in the mosque for the sunset prayer, then go outside to break their fast together ("cut fast" in Krio). Every day different families volunteered to prepare the food to be shared. As the time for evening prayer drew near, children would appear, carrying pots and pans of hot food balanced on their head, on their way to the mosque. Particular foods were popular for breaking fast, especially the sweet mush made from rice called *pap*. They also sometimes made *sati*, which was made by scooping off the top watery layer out of a pot of rice as it is still cooking, then adding sugar and letting it sit, resulting in a sort of rice porridge. *Tow* was another popular dish, made from pounded cassava and is like fufu. Sometimes there was boiled cassava or a thick cassava stew called *yebe*.

Then they gathered after evening prayer, crouched in circles around the pots of food on the ground, men on one side of the mosque and women on the other.

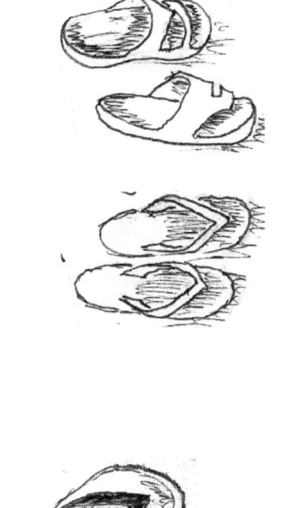

Sandals left at the door of the mosque by those praying inside

Like spokes around hubs, the people in each cluster reached their spoons into the shared pots for a scoop of food, together breaking fast.

The people followed a hierarchy. Old men were allowed to use a small bench to squat on when they ate; young men and boys squatted and sat on their heels. Sometimes, when I joined them, they tried to give me a stool to sit on because I am white and a foreigner; I usually tried to politely decline.

As the dusk deepened into darkness, we would finish eating and then retreat home to wait for the night prayer. At around eight o'clock, the bang of the drum would summon people again to the mosque. The night prayer during Ramadan lasted longer than usual because everyone observes *nafilah* together, a set of optional prayers that come after the required ones. *Nafila* involves doing 13 additional sets of prayers along with the four required for night prayer.

The last ten days of Ramadan were particularly special in Waridala. During this time people tried to stay up all night in the mosque reading the Koran. A night known as "the Night of Power" will happen during these last ten days (called *Aruba* in Maninka), but I was told that no one is able to predict on which night it will fall, so they try to study during all ten nights. It is said that the Night of Power is like a thousand nights of reading the Koran: The blessings a person receives will be magnified a thousandfold. In Waridala, they pick one night to observe the Night of Power as a community. Everyone gathered in the mosque, a generator providing light. The elders formed a circle at the center to read, and everyone else gathered around, listening or reading on their own. During this time the divider between the male and female areas of the mosque was lifted. By three in the morning the reading was over, and the old women sang songs in Maninka, their reedy voices mingling in traditional call-and-response songs. Then everyone left the mosque to go eat the large quantities of rice that the women had prepared, the night ending with proper Sierra Leone flavor.

I was the only foreigner in Waridala and the only non-Muslim. I knew that everyone else in town would be fasting and praying for Ramadan, so I decided to join them. The community was receptive. Two people gave me pamphlets about how to pray like a Muslim, which included English translations and transliterations of the Arabic prayers. People loved to talk to me about fasting: *Ee sun dor?* they would ask. Are you fasting? And then say, *Tele yeli?* How many days? The goal is all of them, of course (between 29 and 30, depending on the year), but not everyone is able and the people I talked to seemed to keep running tallies of the number of days they had fasted. I was able to do 19 out of 30.

In my experience, the fasting required careful planning so enough food and water was available in the morning and at night, as well as careful conservation of energy. However, if anything upset my routine—traveling, or sickness—I was not able to keep the fast.

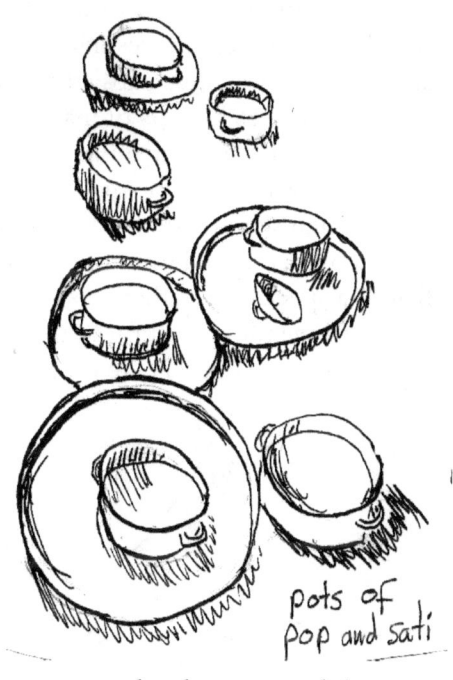

pots of pop and sati

One day of fasting was not too hard; one month is a challenge. An unexpected difficulty for me was the lack of sleep. Between waking at 4 a.m. and staying up for *nafilah* prayers, it didn't leave much time for sleeping. Once people started staying up all night the last ten days, I couldn't keep up and had to start going to bed early. Later, once Ramadan was over, I found it strange to see my food in the daylight, after so many nocturnal meals.

Finally, the end of Ramadan arrived, the day everyone was waiting for: Eid al Fitr. The celebration was preceded by a period of uncertainty because no one was sure which day the festival would occur, August 18th or 19th. The head imam in

Sierra Leone, I was told, waits for notification from Saudi Arabia before the date is announced on the radio.

Before Eid al Fitr arrives, everyone gives a *mudu* to the chief imam at the mosque. *Mudu* was explained to me as a gesture of thanksgiving and a form of payment to the imam for all the praying he has done for you during Ramadan. People paid one "pan" of groundnuts or one "pan" of husk rice, depending on which they were harvesting or able to spare. I had a different standard as I was not a subsistence farmer: The town chief said I needed to pay eight cups of machine-processed rice.

The date of Eid al Fitr was announced two days in advance; it was to be on August 19th. On the big day, everyone went to pray at a clearing outside of the village, alongside the road, a place referred to as the "pray field." Praying in the pray field is a special event that happens on pray day, but no one could tell me the reason for it; to my question "why?" they either said, "It is good" or "There is more blessing."

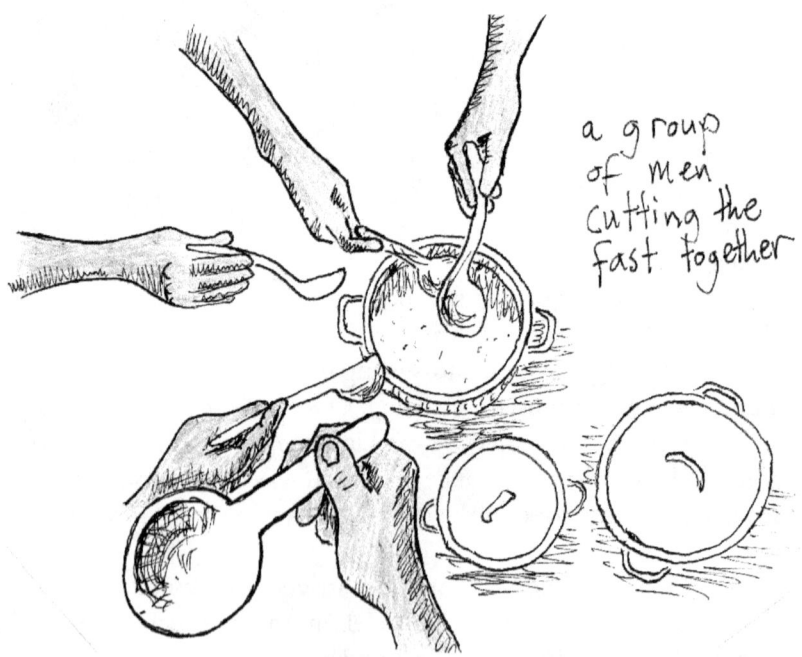

a group of men cutting the fast together

On the morning of Eid al Fitr, all the men in town went to "scrape" the pray field, that is, to remove the grass and weeds with shovels and machetes until only bare dirt was left. Bare-dirt yards are a sign of a well-kept home; a similar logic, it seemed, applied to the pray field. At about ten o' clock everyone gathered to go to the pray field, forming a procession as they walked together out of town. The chief imam was at the front, carrying a long staff, while the old women sang songs in Maninka. Everyone was wearing their best clothes, long, flowing robes for the men and layers of shawls for the women. At the pray field, people laid out prayer mats in long rows and a man handed out laminated sheets with special prayers to be recited in Arabic and English transliteration. The imam led everyone in two sets of prayers and then he gave a talk. At one point, the sun came out from behind the clouds and everyone started to sweat, so an elderly lady came around to serve everyone cups of water ladled from a bucket.

The imam dismissed those gathered and everyone returned to town where a good meal awaited; finally the fasting was over. The greeting for Eid al Fitr is *Eid Mubarak*—Merry Eid—and the children go around in their best, asking for money at all the houses saying, *Sal ma fo!* My house was popular because I gave them coins and not just groundnuts.

It was interesting how people didn't understand my "why" questions, such as about the pray field. They understood "why" to mean "for what purpose" (i.e., to get blessings). In a diverse and complex society, like in the U.S., discussion of explanations may be more common, but in the traditional world of Waridala, people have never had a reason to raise the question "why." The answer is simply, that is what we do.

Ramadan that year, for me, was a chance to see the threads that hold the community together: the daily prayers, the shuffling elders, the shared fasting, and the circle of spoons, dipping into a pot of pap at dusk.

THE HIPPOPOTAMI IN SIERRA LEONE

The huge head surfaces in the river. A massive snort, like a diesel engine. Grayish-purple skin, pink around the eye and nose, slick from the water. Black eyes glitter, and then the head disappears back under the water. This is a hippopotamus in the Little Scarcies River, in Outamba Kilimi National Park, to the far northwest of the country, near the Guinea border, miles from roads and towns. Certainly, it felt far from Waridala, although far downstream Waridala's Mabole River joins the Little Scarcies. This isolation, in part, is why hippos still thrive, far from the myriad troubles that humans tend to cause. Hippos – the same species *H. amphibius* that is found across Africa – are rare in Sierra Leone, around 100 total. In an aluminum canoe, a woman is watching the hippo. Her name is Lindsey Perry, a Peace Corps volunteer, and she is doing research.

For three weeks in 2013, beginning August 2nd, she camped out in Outamba Kilimi, observing this little-researched population of hippos. It was not an easy path. First, the roads were terrible. The road to Kamakwie, the nearest town, was a rutted, muddy mess. North of Kamakwie the road was even worse, passable only by motorcycle. Along the way it was necessary to cross the Mongo River. This involved a ride on an iron-and-wooden raft attached to a precarious series of pulleys that allowed a few men to pull the raft across the river by hand. After reaching the park, it was an hour hike by bush trail to the area where the hippos live.

The park administrators, however, proved to be an even bigger obstacle. A friend and I arrived at the park a few hours before Lindsey. The manager told us he was not expecting her at all. This was after months of meetings with the Ministry of Forestry. I traveled several miles and climbed a steep hill to reach the only place in the area with cell reception. I called Lindsey to tell her the motor car provided by the park authorities, which she was waiting for in Kamakwie, was not actually coming.

Lindsey had to hire local transportation, which carried her, her friend, and their gear to the park. The problem continued when she arrived. First, they told her she needed to have a cover letter before she could start. Then they told her she needed to have a guide accompany her at all times in the bush and she needed to provide food for him. All this was new information on the very morning that research was supposed to begin. Maybe the authorities wanted money somehow. The situation was extremely frustrating, although, unfortunately, not unusual at all. After a phone conversation on the cell phone hill in which both parties accused each other of being liars, after two days of waiting, and after the guide finally showed up, it was time to find the hippos.

We loaded up all the gear into the aluminum canoe and the guide took the boat down the Little Scarcies River while the rest of us followed the trail on the shore. After a good hike through the thick and dripping forest—and crossing a few streams filled with silty water—we heard the tell-tale snort of the hippos in the river. On shore were huge muddy trails through the brush, left by the hippos, pockmarked by the craters of their footprints. One set of footprints, the guided noted, was not from a hippo, but belonged to an elephant, a creature even more rarely seen.

After setting up camp, including erecting a tent whose poles had been forgotten, the research began the next day. Every day at 6:00 a.m., 12:00 p.m. and 6:00 p.m., Lindsey would go out in the boat with the guide to find the hippos. She would record their number, location, and behavior. Once a week she would do a transect on land, walking in a line through the bush, recording evidence of foraging from the hippos. Hippos can be difficult to study because they only come on shore at night to feed. However, Lindsey planned to record whatever she could find; this research was part of her master's thesis in biology.

One day, I went out on the research boat too. From the vantage point of the boat, only the hippos' heads were visible, as they gradually bobbed up and down in the middle of river, surfacing and sinking intermittently, always facing the current. Hippos do not really swim, I learned, and when in deep water they essentially bounce up and down to breathe. Whales and dolphins are their closest living relatives, with the similarity especially evident as surfaced with snorts of hot air like whales from the deep. Some of the hippos occasionally turned their heads to watch the boat, but most seemed unperturbed by the disturbance. Male hippos are territorial and stake out a claim on a section of the river. However, during August, in the rainy season, with the water level high, they gather together in loose groups. There were about seven hippos living near our encampment, each a 3,000 pound animal, as well as two little baby hippos, about a sixth the size of the adults, perhaps around 500 pounds.

The guide who came with Lindsey was a man named Sheka Gibril Bangura, a park ranger and very knowledgeable about the park. He told us about his job, which included patrolling for poachers along the Guinea border, not far from where we were, in collaboration with the police and the military. He told us he was paid very little for his work, but he was in the bush doggedly camping in the rain and looking for hippos, all while maintaining fast for Ramadan.

One evening, we went with the guide to a nearby village, Tandata, to look for some palm wine to drink. It was a long way to this tiny group of thatched roofs—we had to take the boat, then hike for what seemed like miles along a bush trail. At Tandata, Sheka greeted his friends, and I don't remember whether we even found *poyo* or not. We returned in the night, hiking through the darkening forest and then getting into the boat to finish the journey. The bugs were blizzard-like in our headlamps and I kept imagining angry hippopotami emerging from the watery gloom, intent on killing, but we eventually returned safely to camp.

Outamba Kilimi remains the best place in Sierra Leone to see hippos. If you are patient, you will hear their snorts in the water and see their shiny pink-purple heads, bobbing in the river that they call home.

Lake Sonfon

Traveling in Kuranko Territory in the Sula Mountains

Lake Sonfon, a green-blue lake set in the mountains. Or so I was told. People say the place is beautiful, they say it is magical. Some say it is impossible to cross the lake in a boat. Others say that you can see the prow of a ship protruding from the center of the lake. For a long time, I only knew the name and its shape, for it was marked on my map of Sierra Leone. Finally, I found a chance to go there, traveling by bicycle, alone.

From Waridala I rode my bicycle north on the Kabala highway. The road winds through hills and valleys, gradually climbing in elevation onto the Guinea Plateau. Near the town of Fadugu, I passed a rocky area, piles of stones along the road, sorted by size. A few women were working among the piles, carrying stones, or breaking larger stones into smaller pieces with sledge hammers. It seemed like brutal work. I was surprised again by this country, seeing how hard people had to work for so little. One of the women told me that people come from Kabala to buy the stones. Two thousand leones for one "pan"—about 50 cents for a container the size of a large salad bowl.

Some miles past Fadugu, a group of soldiers was hanging out outside of their barracks—12th infantry the sign said—and they were happy to give me directions towards Lake Sonfon. They told me to turn at the junction past the town of Makakura, but they didn't warn me how bad the road would be. It was utterly terrible, little more than a gash in the earth. The road was relatively broad and well defined, but rocky and steep, going directly up and directly down the hills. It was as if someone simply ran a large bulldozer through the landscape, without regard to changes in elevation, and no thought of planning for drainage or future maintenance of the road. A few other vehicles were on this road, old, worn-out-looking vehicles packed with supplies, a row of young men usually hanging from the bumper. I was both horrified and impressed that these drivers were able to coax their ramshackle cars through this terrain.

Perhaps the road was built for a few trucks to haul out a couple loads of some kind of mineral, and then abandoned, the local people then later taking advantage of it as best they could. The details of its construction are perhaps lost to time, but the road's condition fits a common pattern: foreign companies build rudimentary infrastructure to take advantage of Sierra Leone for its natural resources and then leave when they are done. Terrible roads like these made me appreciate the power of a functional government, especially for the building of infrastructure meant only to benefit the public good.

The sun was hot, and along the road the vegetation was dried and burned from heat and bushfires; this was mid-March, nearing the height of the dry season. Along the way I passed the occasional *warreh*, the camps where the Fulas, nomadic people who herd cattle, live. At each *warreh* I passed, I could see the circular fence made out of sticks and logs where the Fulas keep their cows, and the domed shape of the Fulas' distinctive houses, made of grass and sticks. It was entirely possible that the Fulas had been coming to this area with their cows for generations, before the road was even built, when the bush was empty and unbroken by roads.

 A few times I stopped for a snack of cow milk from Fula women I met walking along the roadway. They were selling milk in little plastic bags, which they carried in big buckets that they balanced on their heads. Every day the Fula women milk the cows and keep the milk in big plastic containers where it ferments into a thick sludge, similar to yogurt. The milk they sold me was mixed with sugar and some sort of grain. I bit the corner off the plastic bag and drained the contents. It was delicious on the hot day. The Peace Corps doctor had specifically told us not to drink the local milk, given the potential presence of harmful bacteria, but I was young and illness seemed like the least of my concerns.

 Just when I thought the hills and rocks would never end, I suddenly arrived in the town of Kondembaia, arranged around a large flat clearing with two huge cotton trees dominating the center of town. It was disorienting to arrive somewhere so orderly—and flat—after the chaos of the rough road I had been pedaling on. As I pedaled through town, crowds of people filled the streets in their colorful Friday robes, heading for the mosque.

 By now I was deep into Kuranko territory, the ethnic group that generally inhabits the remote and mountainous northeast corner of Sierra Leone. The Kuranko language is similar to the Maninka language of Waridala. It is said that the two groups split up a long time ago during a military invasion from the north. During the various skirmishes and troop movements, one group was told to wait under a plum tree. This group was separated from the rest and settled in the area where they found themselves, later calling themselves Kuranko, a variation of the phrase *kurdowa kordor*, or "under the plum."

I put to use some of my basic Maninka skills that I learned in Waridala while I rested briefly in Kondembaia and talked with passersby. Then I continued pedaling on through the blazing afternoon, stopping occasionally for water at small villages along the way. I soon learned that Kurankos consider themselves to be essentially Maninka, and the people I talked with were eager to converse with me in their native tongue. The language did sound similar to me, yet oddly distorted, syllables and phonemes rearranged. For example, in Maninka they ask, *E kende see da?* or "Did you sleep well?" In Kuranko, people say, *E kene kee ra?* I could see how these languages could be almost mutually intelligible, especially for a native speaker who had breathed the rhythms of these phrases for their whole life. In the U.S., with grammar books, compulsory education, and an all-pervasive mass media, language can begin to look orderly. Yet here, in this space between Kuranko and Maninka, I saw the wilderness of language, as it shifted and contradicted itself. For a moment, I saw that Sierra Leone does not have different languages, but a rich linguistic environment, where everything can be said in slightly different ways and each ethnic group stakes out a linguistic territory based on history and geography.

After passing the town of Benekoro, I encountered a brutally steep hill and it was necessary for me to push the bike most of the way. By the time I reached the top I was utterly exhausted, covered in sweat and trembling from the exertion. Here, at the top of the hill, as I wiped the sweat out of my eyes, I found a village they called Board House, because the handful of houses in this small community were all made from wood. I bought a snack of bread and mayonnaise from the one small store in town. The place had a transitory feel; trash was scattered on the rocky ground, board houses were half finished, and the occasional overloaded motorcycle roared by.

From here it was not far to Lake Sonfon. I bumped slowly down the bare rock road in the lengthening evening light. Finally, the lake came into view. I could see the flat expanse of water, almost green in color. The water glowed with a beautiful, almost iridescent hue I had never seen before. Then I realized what I was seeing was grass. Only a few large puddles remained at the center of the lake—the rest of the water had dried up. It was the middle of the dry season, after all.

I wasn't frustrated or disappointed to find the lake to be dry. All I felt was deep exhaustion that mingled with a vague sense that I was floating through a dream. I never expected to find a phantom ship prow protruding from the center of Lake Sonfon, but I also never expected to find no lake at all. But perhaps this too was the magic of the lake: Under the spell of false expectations and the tales of others, I had gone looking for something that didn't exist.

Farther down the hill, I found a small village I later learned they called Sengbeya. The village consisted entirely of low squat huts made out of sticks and mud. They were poorly constructed, tarpaulins over leaky thatch roofs, walls listing at dangerous angles. Refuse was scattered on the rocky ground. It was strange to come across a community in such an isolated place, after traveling so far on such bad roads.

House at Sengbeya

I stood straddling my bicycle, looking at this little village, and then at the green expanse in the distance that used to be a lake. I had no plan, no idea what I was going to do when the evening descended into night. But I felt no fear, only a vague sense that my body was still rocking, that I was pedaling, bouncing over rocks, even though I was now still.

One young man noticed me and invited me to sit next to him on a wooden bench that teetered on the uneven ground. He seemed slightly hesitant to extend this offer to this strange white person, but I gratefully accepted and soon I realized he was the friend I needed. This man, whose name was Foday Marah, became my host, and as he told me about Sengbeya, the place, although no less strange, began to make more sense.

People come to mine gold, he told me. He said the bare rocky areas like the one that surrounded Sengbeya and Lake Sonfon are good places to find gold. They call these rocky places *sola* in Krio. But one challenge: It is difficult to build decent houses on a *sola*. And latrines for that matter, as I learned when I was directed to an open area some distance away in order to shit. People come from different parts of Sierra Leone to this area and settle down temporarily in improvised communities.

Foday, I learned, was a Kuranko, born to the north in Kabala and he moved to Sengbeya several years ago to try to find a living. He showed me the little mud shack that he lives in, hardly big enough for an adult male to lie down in. He told me about the portable pump he owns for "washing" the dirt and gravel in order to separate out the gold. He and his helper, his *borbor*, walk two miles to the site where they were working. They would dig up dirt with hand tools and mix it with water from the pump to sort out the gold. When he finds some, Foday sells it in Sengbeya or brings it to the market in a town he called Badala that I had never heard of.

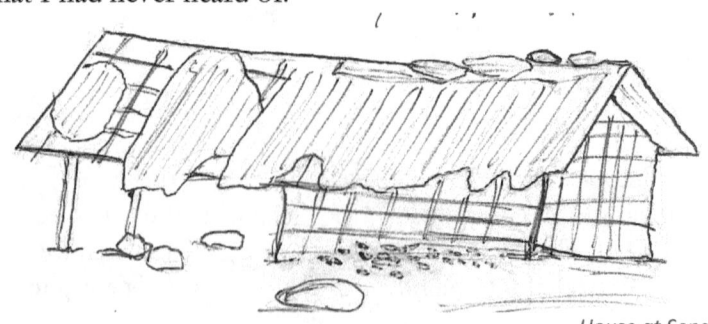

House at Sengbeya

Despite the rudimentary conditions, familiar Sierra Leonean customs were still evident: the hospitality towards strangers, the fondness for eating rice from a shared plate. Foday even brought me to greet the chief of Sengbeya, a semi-formal visit that served to notify the chief of my presence in town that night. The town chief lived in a shack that looked similar to all the others, although his had a very small and cramped veranda with plastic lawn chairs for receiving visitors. The chief even offered to give me a woman to marry.

That night I slept in one of the shacks, in a bed next to a young man to whom Foday had hastily introduced me in the night. I wasn't sure why the sleeping arrangements were made this way, but I was grateful to have a place to stay and humbled by this small community's generosity. It was one of the strangest nights of my life. I had to more or less crawl to get through the door of the shack and I slept fitfully in the cramped room next to a stranger. I expected to be robbed in the night, or worse. But perhaps that was the benefit of being introduced to the chief: Everyone knew I was there and therefore everyone would know if something happened to me.

Morning came as a relief. I said goodbye to Foday who left early to go to work. I sat for a long time that morning outside one of Sengbeya's shacks, watching people mining in the distance. Not too far away I could see a huge pit filled with dirty water. People with shovels and pickaxes dug away at the bank, moving the dirt down towards the water. Other people in the water put this loose dirt into pans and washed it, looking for particles of gold, it seemed. I was told that there are white people who mine there but I did not see them.

Finally, I convinced myself to stand up and continue riding, so I went back up the hill to Board House, and then took the junction that turned into another steep, rocky road leading to Dalakuru. As I arrived in this next town, I realized that Dalakuru is another mining community similar to Sengbeya except on a larger scale, although I still saw the familiar squat mud shacks and tarpaulin roofs. But here there seemed to be a different style of mining. People were digging shafts into the ground—they almost looked like wells—and a mound of reddish dirt was piled at the mouth of each hole. I didn't meet another friendly host like Foday Marah to explain to me what was going on, or what mineral was being mined, so I continued riding.

From Dalakuru, the road continued to go straight up and down a series of hills, as I had become used to by now. In the small village of Kunya, I stopped to talk to an old man sitting on his veranda, who hailed me as I passed. He was so friendly, and I was so tired, I couldn't refuse when he offered me a place to stay for the night. Ibrahim Sesay was his name—a proud Kuranko. By now I had left the *sola* behind, and the more familiar terrain of palm trees and brush returned, along with villages built around farming. Ibrahim's house was even made of concrete, painted a friendly blue color. We made small talk and listened to Maninka music until I went to bed early, still exhausted from the climb to Lake Sonfon the day before.

The next morning, I set out early for Bendugu and then from Bendugu to Bumbuna. Right before reaching Bumbuna, the road drops off a series of spectacularly steep hills. I saw some huge trucks on this road, going to and from the huge iron ore mine being worked by the mining company African Minerals, a British company. A huge crane and the detached bed of a gigantic dump truck passed by me, being towed behind these trucks, heading to what was clearly a very large-scale project. Seeing machines like this was a strange and striking contrast to the efforts of the miners at Lake Sonfon working only with hand tools and luck. I was reminded once again just how hard some people have to work for so little, as I had seen all along on the trip.

From there I left the mountains, where people kept offering to sell me gold, and returned to Waridala. When I had left only a few days before, I thought of Waridala as small and isolated, but now, upon my return, the little town seemed big and comforting and even luxurious—and the terrain flatter—compared to where I had been.

COWS vs. FARMERS

THE FULAS IN SIERRA LEONE

Mid-April 2012, Late Dry Season.

I went to have my machete sharpened by the blacksmith in Kamasara, a small Limba village about a half hour walk away by bush trail. A group of men and boys was there under the blacksmith's grass thatched hut; some were fussing with their hoes and machetes and some were just hanging out. The blacksmith was hammering near the fire, where the coals were glowing hot and orange as the boy spun the ramshackle bellows. The blacksmith periodically put the glowing orange piece of metal on a large rock under the *baffa*, using a hammer to bang it into shape.

All these men were farmers, except for one, besides me. He seemed to have come to the blacksmith's *baffa* just to chat. This was Amadu Barrie, the Fula who lived nearby at his *warreh*, and he invited me to visit his home. He was a thin man, perhaps in his forties, and seemed friendly and had a gentle smile, so I agreed. We followed a faint, faint trail through the bush. Amadu strolled among the vegetation casually, wearing jeans and a Western-style button-down shirt with a skull pattern on it. I was struck by his confidence and poise. Amadu's ethnic group is spread across West Africa and everywhere are well known for raising cattle and practicing Islam. In my experience around Waridala, the Fulas seemed to be respected, if reluctantly, for no other reason than they had a reputation for being wealthy. Fulas hold themselves apart from the other groups in the area, and even have a distinct look, tall and thin with narrow features and lighter skin.

Before we reached the *warreh*, we could hear it—the low of cattle in the distance. Then we could smell it, the rich scent of cow manure. Then the houses came into view, simple domes made from grass and sticks. The structures were clustered around the fenced area where the cows are kept. The fence was simple, made from pairs of logs driven into the ground and sticks laid at an angle between them. The edges of the gate were reinforced with stacked logs, the actual gate nothing more than sticks laid across the opening.

A Fula house at the warreh

Amadu showed me to his own house and gave me a place to sit outside, a bench made from sticks. He pointed out his family members to me, but it was hard to keep them straight and they're all related at the *warreh* anyway. Amadu gave me some rice and his children laughed at me as I tried to follow local tradition and eat with my hand. I was delighted to meet Amadu and I was fascinated to visit the *warreh*, just as the family of Fulas was fascinated with me.

Amadu genuinely seemed interested in making an American friend, and I periodically visited the *warreh* over the next year or so, including when the seasons changed and they moved their entire community to a hilltop. And I learned more about the Fulas, how the age-old conflict between farmers and herders still plays out and how Islam served as a foundation for everything they did.

entrance to a Fula home

My next visit with Amadu came about a week later. He had invited me to come watch them give salt to their herd. When I arrived, Amadu and some of his relatives were gathered around a sort of basket made out of sticks about four feet wide and two feet deep, located in an open field near the *warreh*. This basket held a thick, soupy mixture of mud and water, made with dirt from a termite mound, I learned later. Amadu took off his sandals and rolled up his pant legs, then stepped inside the basket. He was using his feet to mix everything up, I soon realized, as his brother added ingredients to the mud: orange bark, a dash of gasoline (for worms), some rubbing alcohol, and a dark liquid that they told me was from the washings from Koranic verses written on tablets (to protect against witches and devils).

Finally, they added some salt. Amadu's brother poured it from a 25-pound bag into a large calabash, mixed in a few leaves, and recited a prayer in Arabic. Then he walked around the basket and touched the calabash to the container four times, reciting more prayers. Then he emptied the calabash into the mud, along with the rest of the salt in the bag. All the male children were there, even little Alhaji, nearly naked and splattered with mud.

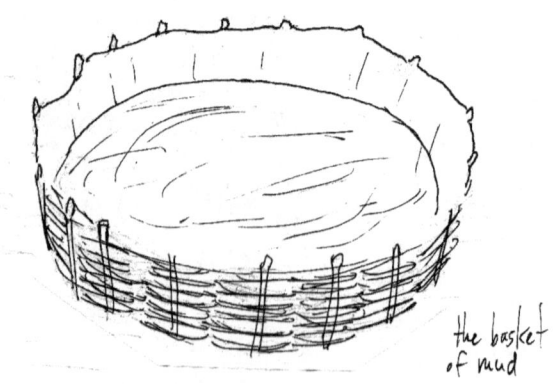

Now it was time to call the cows from the *warreh*, where they had been waiting. "Arh, arh, arh," Amadu called, while he simultaneously tapped on the lid of a pan. The cows came charging through the brush towards the salty mud, while the family just stood there, nonchalant, a short distance from the cows gathering around the basket, jostling for position. The cows were eager: They drank the mud like water, licking their lips, and some put their front legs into the mixture in their rush to drink. Some of them started to fight, locking horns and tussling. One teenage boy who was there explained to me that this was the cows' "pray day." When the cows drink the salty mud and the medicine added to it, they will be more likely to maintain their health and, Amadu explained to me, they will be less likely to go into farmers' fields.

Later we went to eat rice topped with cow milk. We had the meal sitting on the floor on the inside of one of the beautiful dome houses at the *warreh*. The cow milk was thick and fermented, almost like yogurt. Amadu gave me my own portion and a spoon to eat with; a woman came and poured what they called "butter" on mine, a thick oily liquid somehow derived from milk. The family all ate from the same big plate—Amadu and his brother and a sizable portion of their offspring. I counted ten hands in the rice. The youngest, Alhaji, was now completely naked and covered in dribbles of milk and bits of rice. When the meal was over, the chickens came in to clean up.

I marveled at the simplicity of the home. Nothing was in Amadu's house except a small bed and stacks of plastic containers for storing milk, with a few personal items wedged into the stick frame of the dome house. The interior of the house was quiet and cool, smelling of dry grass. The mud-plastered floor resembled smooth concrete, an effect, they told me, that is achieved by beating it, with what I wasn't sure.

Amadu told me about his family. A few of his children live in town and go to school, but many do not, helping on the *warreh* year-round. None of his daughters attended school; the Fulas believe that school might turn their girls from their traditional ways.

stacks of containers for storing milk

Amadu told me proudly that I will never see a Fula woman wearing pants. They always wear *lappas*, the loose wrap considered to be modest as it does not accentuate the hips and thighs like pants. Marrying a Fula woman is considered to be a great prize: They are universally praised for their beauty and obedience. Even though other groups in the region at times seemed resentful of the Fulas, perhaps this was actually envy.

sleepy calf

November 2012, Late Rainy Season

During the rainy season the Fulas migrate with their cows and their families and their homes. All I knew is they were no longer near Waridala, but had moved somewhere behind the town of Kamabai, which is along the Kabala highway. One day I happened to meet Amadu in Kamabai, as he was in town for an errand. He invited me to visit the *warreh* in their rainy-season location. "Why not come today?" he asked. And so I did.

We waited around for his father, who was charging his phone, but abruptly, we left without him. We followed a small footpath, leaving the houses of Kamabai behind. Soon we were surrounded only by the vegetation of bush, as the trail followed the flank of the steep hill that abuts Kamabai. The trail gradually became less traveled and shaggy with overgrown grass and branches. Suddenly the trail took a turn, heading straight up the hill. We climbed among eight-foot-tall konsho bean plants, a crop that grows in the Limbas' groundnut farms after they've harvested the groundnuts. Soon the land became too steep for planting, and yet the rocky trail continued straight up the slope.

Finally we reached the *warreh*. There was the fence made from sticks, the herd of cows, the cute Fula houses, the bare-dirt yards with the little stools that Fulas like to sit on. But we were only resting, I soon realized, as this was not Amadu's *warreh*. Someone gave me a cup of water and then we moved on.

We continued following the trail along the top of the hill, the trail brushy and rough. I could see that the land formation that we were traversing wasn't so much a hill as a rough plateau that stretch for miles. We climbed over steep saddles, among huge bare spires of rock that towered toward the sky. The land was lonely and isolated. We paused on one of the ridges to take in the view. From a vantage point like this, we could overlook the land for miles around, rolling hills far below us, palm trees and farms, all in miniature. It was like being in an airplane. Amadu pointed out some landmarks: the village of Sankoya, the road to Karina, the CSE road construction headquarters. Everything was small and distant and insignificant.

We met a Fula woman going in the same direction and we traveled with her, she and Amadu chatting nonstop in Fula. Finally, we reached an open ridge, in front of us we could see an impossible jumble of hills, steep and bare, seemingly untouched by humans. Then Amadu pointed out the *warreh*, on an adjacent ridge, overlooking these wild hills. The domed grass roofs of the Fula homes were visible poking up from amid the brush.

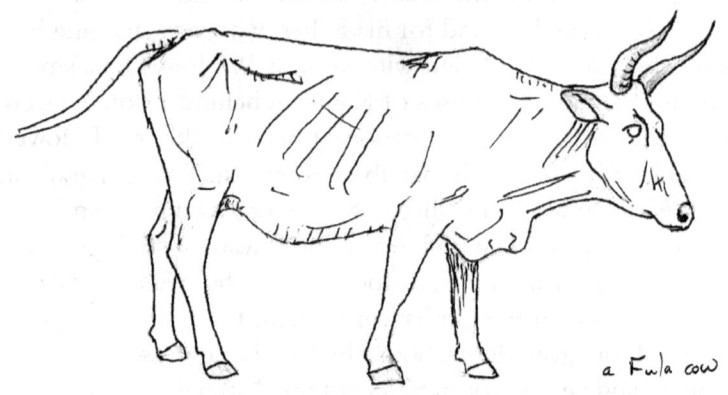

a Fula cow

Finally, after we passed another *warreh* along the trail, we reached Amadu's *warreh*. It had been a hike of two hours. I am not sure of the distance we covered in those two hours, but Amadu is a fast walker and it felt far away from Kamabai. The kids at the *warreh* all stared at me, but the *warreh* only consists of four houses—Amadu's and his brothers'—so there weren't too many eyes to stare at me. During the rainy season, the Fulas live on this hilltop, while everyone else makes their farms below. I wasn't sure how they brought the cows up here, although Amadu offered a vague explanation about a different route that was longer with a more gradual incline. In the dry season, Amadu and his family will migrate again and go back down. Amadu told me they usually move once the water on top of the hill dries up, usually near the end of December. By that time, the only crop still in the fields is cassava.

The mark Amadu brands on his cows

When we arrived, we went into one of the houses and rested. It looked just like the house I had been in when I visited Amadu at the previous location near Waridala. There was a bed, stacks of containers to store milk, the sweet scent of dry grass, and not much else. I promptly took a nap. When I awoke, all the girls were pounding rice in the *mato odo*, preparing to cook a meal using the fresh fish that Amadu had brought from Kamabai. Amadu told me that he had recently married a second wife. One of these girls who was pounding rice was his new wife, he told me. Amadu is 42, he told me, and the girl he pointed out certainly had not reached twenty yet.

I went with two adolescent boys to check on the cows and then we bathed in a clear stream that ran across a bare rock face—the spring, it seemed, that sustained this small community until it dries in the dry season. Life suddenly seemed peaceful and simple out here in the bush with nothing except the clothes on our back and a piece of soap to wash with. One of the boys asked me questions about America.

Then we returned to the *warreh*. I realized that I was very hungry, but the rice was not done cooking. Everyone sat together and chatted, and now it was Amadu's turn to ask me questions about America. He translated my answers into Fula for his relatives, who were packed on a bench nearby. Amadu tried to teach me a little Fula, the greetings, the names of basic objects. Fula is a beautiful language; it has a melodic sound and even when a Fula speaks Krio, this song-like accent sometimes shows. For example, *Ambelkejan* is "good morning" in Fula. When they say it, the phrase seems like a song. Some of

Amadu's family at the *warreh* could speak Krio, but they were uncomfortable with it, especially the women.

At last, it was time to eat. We ate outside on a bench made of sticks and I shared a plate with Amadu. We ate two plates of rice, actually, because there were two women cooking. It was one of the best meals I have ever had, made all the better by the spectacular surroundings. Amadu made it clear that he was the elder one of us, by giving me the subordinate role of finishing the last rice on the plate, while he scooped a bit into another bowl and finished it that way.

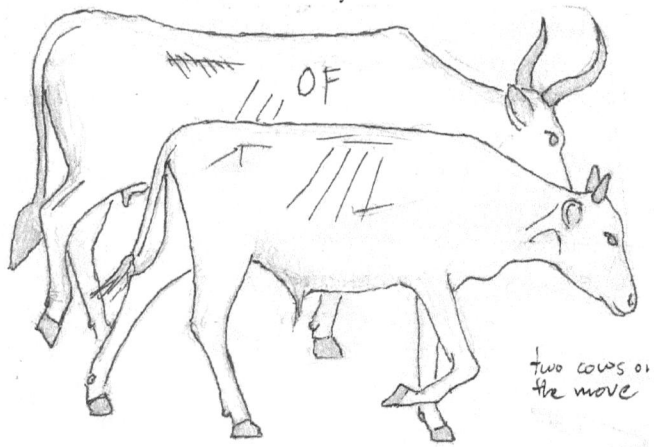

two cows on the move

In the gathering darkness, Amadu and a few others performed the evening prayer. They spread their prayer mats on a big flat rock and prostrated themselves toward Mecca, in the same direction as those wild hills in the distance. I lay back on the stick bench and watched the stars come out, one by one, and felt the peace of the night settle over me. In the distance, the lights of a nearby town were just barely visible; later, they told me it was Bumbuna. Before we retired for the night, I gave Amadu a Le 10,000 note as a gesture of appreciation. They had me sleep in the same house as the women and children. They spread out a mat on the mud floor and gave me a blanket. Someone closed the woven palm leaf door. The sounds of activity in the *warreh* slowly faded as people settled down. I quickly fell asleep and slept deeply.

In the morning, I woke to the sounds of the *warreh*, people talking, the sound of the *mato odo*, cows lowing in the distance. I was given some cold rice with milk on top. One of the women with whom I had shared a house the previous night mixed the milk for me with a sort of beater made out of a stick; she held it between her palms and twirled. And then I headed back down the hill. Amadu only visits Kamabai once a week, so he did not return with me, but he sent me in the company of his young wife and some of her friends. They were going down to Kamabai to sell milk. Each woman had a plastic container of milk balanced on her head; they had to duck carefully to pass under low-hanging branches. As they walked, they conversed rapidly in Fula. At the other *warreh*, the one that we passed on the way up, one woman teased me in Krio: "You done get some fine women today! You de go with am?" She was wondering if I was going to marry them and take them to the U.S. with me. At the stream at the bottom of the hill, the girls stopped to bathe and put on their town clothes and makeup, as I waited some distance up the trail. Then suddenly we were back in Kamabai, the houses, the people, the noise.

May 2013, Late Dry Season

By this time, Amadu and his family and their cows had long since returned to their location near Waridala. The rains were going to return, and the farmers were beginning to plant, so it was time for the Fulas to move once again. One day when I visited, Amadu told me that his brother-in-law was moving his herd across the river and Amadu intended to go with him. He asked that I wait at the *warreh* for his return, but I insisted that I go too. But I did not quite realize what I was getting into.

They let the cows out of the fence and they took off at a run through the brush and trees. Amadu and a handful of men and boys followed behind. A boy gave me a stick to use as a switch and told me, "Let's go!" The cows moved like liquid through the trees and brush, speeding up to go downhill, swirling around in the narrow areas. The cows stayed together but occasionally one would break off from the herd and someone would have to chase after it and direct it back to the main group. "Arh, arh arh," they cried when they wanted to coax a cow to come closer. *"Mai, mai, mai,"* they said to urge the cows along, "Let's go," in Fula.

We passed new groundnut fields, the farmers at work, watching the passing herd warily. Cows from other Fula herds were scattered around in the bush as we went, and these cows tried to join. It was necessary to drive the other cows away to keep them from getting mixed together. We were on a cattle drive, heading through the bush towards their rainy season territory; they called it "following" the cows in Krio. We passed Manjaka and Manjobi until we reached the river. The cows milled around, a mooing traffic jam, until they plunged into the river and they were across.

My neighbor in Waridala, Usu, was a farmer. He said to me, "Fulas don't give money to anyone, even when their cows spoil a farm. They only share their money with their wives." And Amadu's father told me: "People like cow milk, people like cow meat, but they don't like the cow owners. White people make fences and bring food for their cows, but we don't know how to do that." And so, the traditional tension continues, the Fulas living in an uneasy harmony with their farming neighbors. Fulas may visit the blacksmith, but usually not to have a hoe fixed, because come rainy season, the Fulas won't be planting, but they and their cows will be moving somewhere new.

MOUNT

BINTUMANI

April 17 - 24 2013

Mount Bintumani, located in the heart of the mountains of northeast Sierra Leone, is the highest point in West Africa at 1,948m (6,391ft). Summiting it only requires a few days of hiking, but the hard part, it turned out, was just getting to the trailhead.

Our trip began in Panlap, outside of the northern regional capital of Makeni. I traveled with two other Peace Corps volunteers and the plan was to ride to the base of Mount Bintumani, leave the bicycles in a nearby village, and hike to the top. The only other transportation options would be renting a motor vehicle for an outlandish sum or riding on the back of motorcycle taxis for hours down terrible roads. Bicycling seemed like the least unpleasant option. From Panlap we rode down the dusty orange road to Bumbuna, a town right at the edge of the mountainous plateau that covers northeastern Sierra Leone.

After Bumbuna, we soon found out, the road consists of one giant hill, the gravel surface eroded into a "washboard" pattern from the frequent traffic and the steeply sloped roadway. We basically had to push our bikes, loaded down with gear as they were. After the initial climb, the road followed a series of undulating valleys until the town of Bendugu, a surprisingly lively town for being so isolated. After Bendugu, the road became markedly rougher, smaller, and less traveled. Traffic mostly consisted of the occasional motorcycle taxi, as evident from the single track worn into the road. We camped near the road that night and continued early the next morning.

In Alkalia, another surprisingly well populated town, we paused for a breakfast of fried dough, which we bought from a roadside seller, who fried it in a large, wide pan. While we were stopped, a man offered to fry up some grubs for us to eat. Despite some apprehension, we accepted. The man showed us the delicacy before cooking them: white, two inches long, and still squirming. They live in the rotting trunks of dead palm trees, we were told. To prepare them, the man used a small twig to pierce each one, innards spilling out, white and chunky like ricotta cheese. Then he picked out a few dark specks—the bitter parts, he commented—and put the grubs in the pot to sauté in their own juices, no added oil needed. As the grubs sputtered in the pan, gradually they stopped squirming.

Then the big moment came. It was too late to back out. Our impromptu chef even provided us with a spoon. I cautiously scooped up one of the grubs, put it in my mouth, and chewed it. It was quite good, actually; it tasted like a buttery artichoke, the creatures' diet of wood giving them a distinctive vegetable taste.

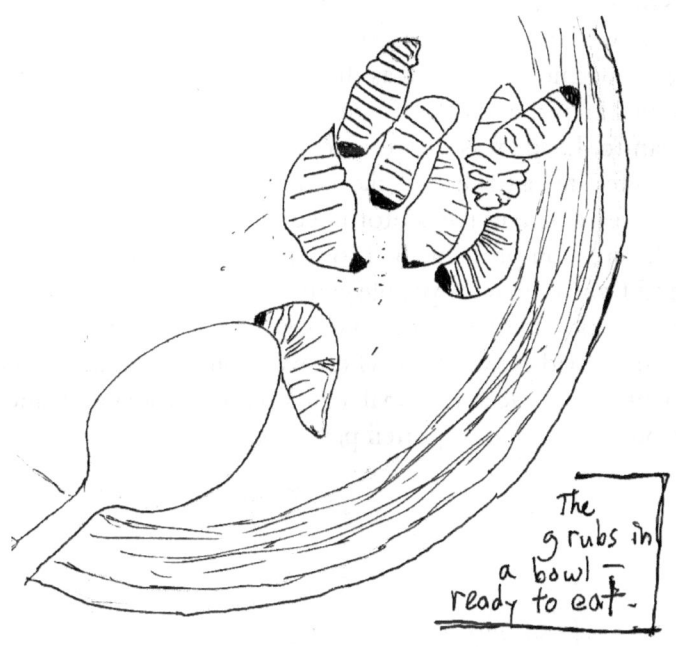

The grubs in a bowl – ready to eat.

After Alkalia, the road became more rutted and rockier until we reached the town of Yifin. The name of this town means "black water," in Kuranko, the language of the locals. The Kuranko people traditionally live in the mountains of Sierra Leone and consider Mount Bintumani to be part of their home territory; they call it Loma in their own language which simply means "mountain." In Yifin we were a big sensation with the children, just like in all the other towns we passed, and a crowd of them gathered to watch the white men eat, talk, and repack their bags. The adults were no less curious, peppering us with questions: Where are you going? Where are you coming from? What is your mission?

We talked to the chief of the town and he politely asked us for a *kola*, an indirect way of asking for money. We continued to encounter this more traditional understanding of money—a sign of respect and goodwill rather than a fee or price—as we got closer to the mountain.

From Yifin we continued on towards the village of Konombaiya, where we were told we could find guides. The road was still very bad—rocky and steep; tree trunks cut in half with a chain saw served as the bridges over numerous creeks. Outside of the village of Kuruto, there was a small palm-thatch lean-to. Inside was a sort of statue made from dried mud, about two feet tall and shaped like a torso with no arms and no neck. A few feathers and twigs protruded at either side of the "head." The creation probably had something to do with secret societies, and I could imagine people gathering there in the night, at that potent boundary between the bush and the village, participating in unnamed ceremonies. There was a sinister air about the mud figure, so crude and primal, invoking something dark and secret from humanity's forgotten past.

The strange shrine near Kuruto

After a few more tortuous miles we reached Konombaiya, the alleged starting point for our climb. After two days on bicycles, pedaling on atrocious roads, my two companions and I had finally arrived. This was the right place to begin a hike up Mount Bintumani. At least so we thought. First, we had to wait for the town chief. He was at his farm in the bush. By evening time, the chief had returned to town. We sat down with him on a bench in front of his grass-and-mud house.

He wore a worn prayer robe and a floppy brimmed hat with the Coors beer logo emblazoned on the front. He was a friendly man but didn't speak English or much Krio for that matter. Some bystanders translated into Kuranko and we told him we wanted to climb the mountain and we wanted a guide to show us the way. The chief agreed.

Great big ties of grass ready to re-roof a house in Konombaiya.

That night, the last member of our group finally arrived: He had taken a different route, on motorcycle taxi, and spent the last part of the trip traveling in the dark. He seemed to be a little stunned and told us the trip had been utterly treacherous. His motorcycle taxi driver drove recklessly on these terrible rocky roads and it was all he could do to hold on for his life. Eventually, he was able to relate that he had passed through the village of Sinekoro, which he had been told was the right place to go up the mountain.

The two villages, Konombaiya and Sinekoro, were competing, it seemed, both claiming to be the "right place." They were competing for the prestige of leading a group of white foreigners like us up the mountain, and most of all, competing for a share of the large amount of money which they believed white people to possess. At this point, it became clear that going up Bintumani was not just a matter of putting on a pack and hiking, but required a lot of communication skills as well. We were at the intersection of cultures, these small villages trying to negotiate the terms of their relationship with the visiting white people and with the encroaching modern world.

After some discussion, we eventually decided to continue on to Sinekoro. We were hoping the road out from Sinekoro would be better than the one we came in on through Yifin.

The next morning, after leaving some "*kolas*" for some of the people who had helped us in town, we set out for Sinekoro. We followed the small bush trail, which required more pushing of the bikes over some steep hills. When we reached the village of Ken-ya, we were told the path becomes completely impassable for bicycles: foot traffic only. We had to hire a few men to carry our bikes while we carried our gear. The last seven miles to Sinekoro we followed the trail through thick forest, jumping from boulder to boulder, navigating steep inclines.

Houses in Sinekoro

Finally we reached Sinekoro, a small and poor village like all the others in the area. Most of the houses were mud with grass for roofing, or a sort of palm-leaf shingle was also used. There wasn't a well in town, we learned later; all the water came from a nearby stream. The chief of the town, Musa Mara, talked with us, and we told him we wanted to start hiking that very day, and we wanted a guide (or a "director" as they called it in Krio). However, the chief told us that we would have to wait until the next day because everyone had already gone to their farms.

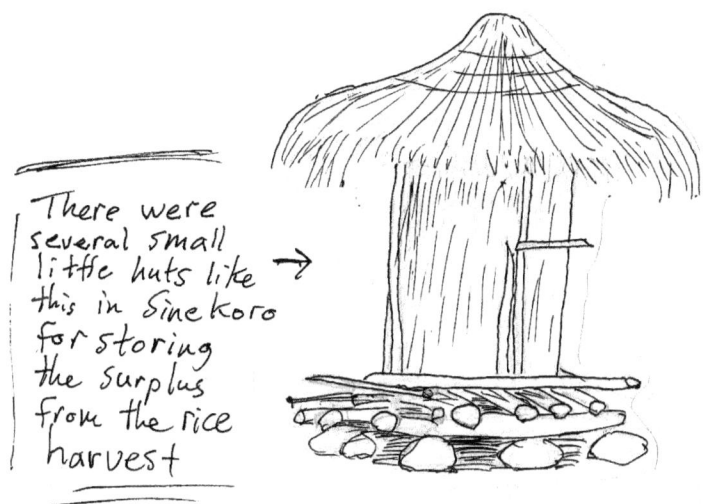

There were several small little huts like this in Sinekoro for storing the surplus from the rice harvest

Late that afternoon we had a meeting with the chief and one of his advisors. We needed to pay a *kola* of 30,000 each for the big men in town, including the chief. Then we realized they meant 30,000 pounds. And when they say 30,000 pounds, they meant 60,000 leones. In some of the local languages, like Kuranko, people still talk about money in terms of pounds. When Sierra Leone first became independent and started printing its own money, the leone was originally linked to the pound and was worth two pounds. Some people, especially older people, still talk about money in pounds, essentially halving the amount of leones printed on the bill, i.e., if they say 5,000 they mean 10,000.

The upshot was that we thought 60,000 was a steep price. We tried bargaining and persuading in Krio and I even gave my best try in Maninka, a language related to Kuranko. Finally we got the *kola* down to 7,500 pounds (15,000 leones) per person.

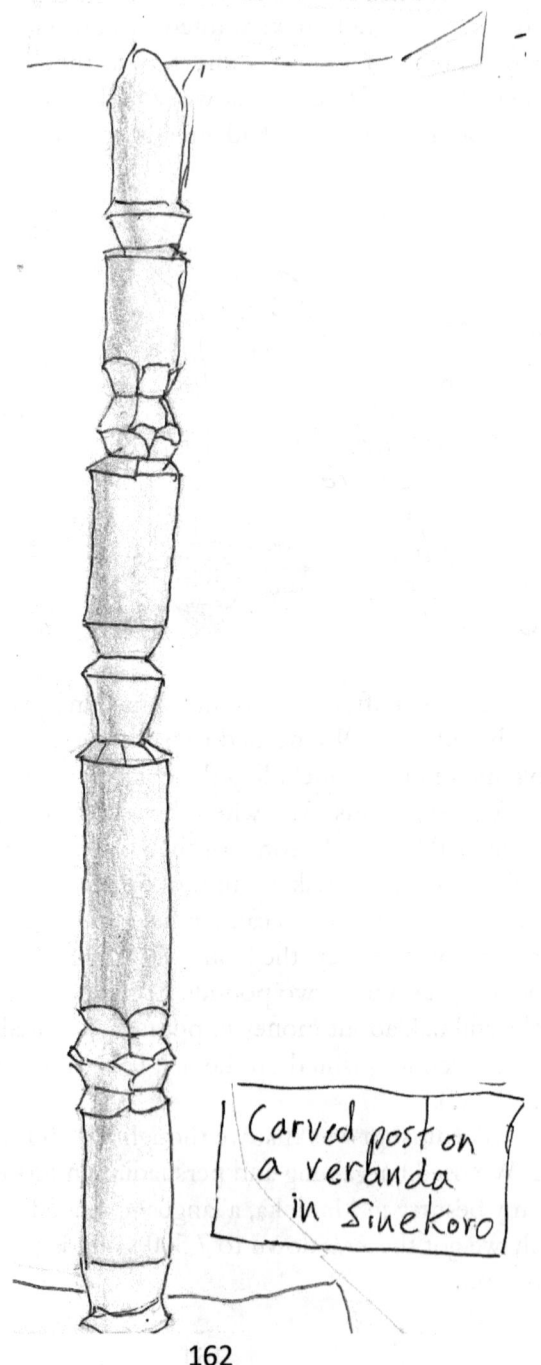

But we still had to wait to get our director to guide us up the mountain. Finally, after darkness had fallen, the chief said he was calling a meeting and the town crier started summoning people. Everyone gathered around in a loose circle, and in classic West African style, the men spoke in order of seniority, each giving a speech, beginning with the chief. Everything was in Kuranko and we had no idea what was going on.

As the discussion continued, finally some kind soul at the meeting took pity on us and started translating bits and pieces of what was being said. We finally realized that the meeting had nothing to do with us or our trip. Instead, the meeting had been called because an NGO was in the village digging a well and the men who were supposed to be learning about the operation of the well were going to the bush instead of staying to learn about the well. It sounded like a disaster of a project, though I wasn't quite sure why the chief had insisted we participate, other than perhaps that he hoped with a few white people in the meeting he might gain some publicity for the plight of his village.

Finally, the meeting concluded around ten o'clock and the chief hastily introduced us to the appointed director. He was a young man, not much more than 18, named Hassan. Of course, we had to bargain with him also and we huddled in a group behind the chief's house and "talked price" as they say in Krio. The discussion was made more complicated because Hassan actually works for someone else. He told us that the town is broken up into sections and certain people in each section are eligible to work as a director. The opportunity to be a director rotates each time a new visitor comes to climb Bintumani. The person whose turn it was had delegated the task of directing to Hassan, although we would still be paying this other person. From a starting point of Le 300,000, we got them down to Le 20,000 each for the four of us. That night we camped in the middle of the village, the children running around and singing songs until after midnight. At last, the village was quiet except for the sound of insects.

The next morning, we set out with our director and another young man named Samuel, a friend of Hassan's whom we recruited informally. After hiking along the stream valley—a flat area with farms—we entered into the brush, then into the forest, huge thick trees, with wide buttressed roots. Here was the reverent silence that usually accompanies high ceilings. Then the trail started going up, straight up, among the trees and brush. We were slipping and sliding in leaves and duff, scrambling and scampering up, then we broke out into relatively open flat ground, the soil orange and rocky. Then we were back into the trees again—big trees, undergrowth, leafy ground, the occasional stream. Then the land became steeper and steeper again and still we went up, always up, over fallen logs, pulling ourselves up by roots and vines.

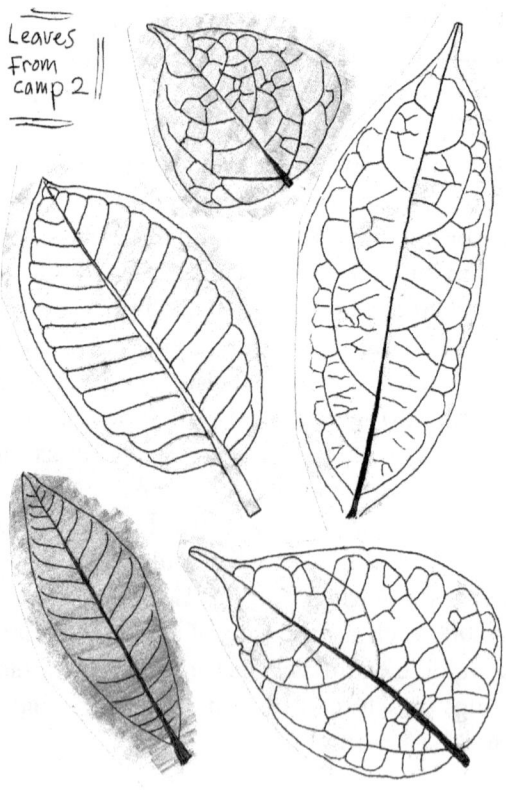

Leaves from camp 2

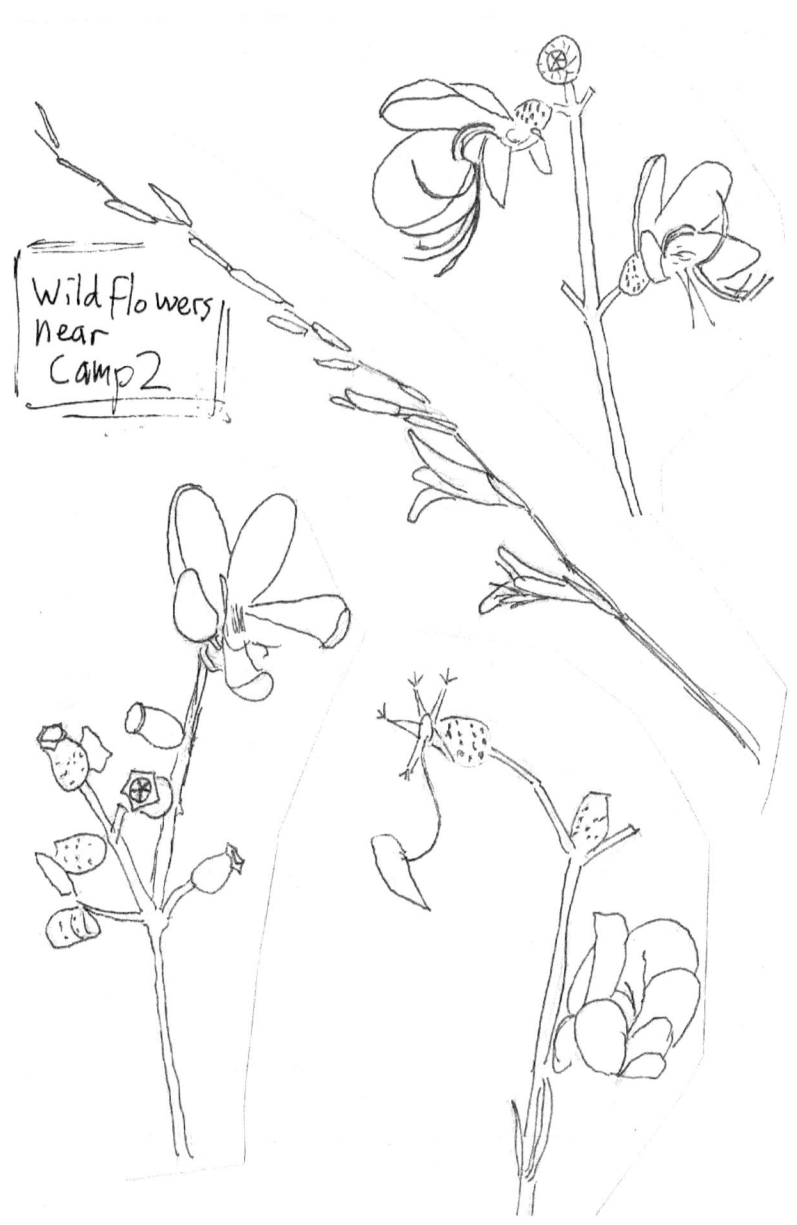

I experienced a mystical moment as we were climbing up. I was aware of the mountain as a giant rock beneath us, beneath the trees and leaves and dirt, solid and unmoving, yet somehow breathing and alive, stretching to the sky, wreathed with a coat of dirt that sprouts huge trees, trees that were irrelevant to the stone. And at that moment the mountain's unmoving movement seemed like true love somehow.

At last we came to Camp 2, as it was called, a sudden flat and open spot, hillocks of green grass and flowers, rounded weathered stones and boulders. We went across to the campsite located under a grove of trees and set up our tents. Hassan and Samuel made a bed out of leaves. That night we looked out over the dark hills below us and we could see the orange ribbon of flames from dry-season bushfires far below, appearing as if they were floating in the blackness.

We talked with Hassan and Samuel that night. They told us how they went to primary school in the village then completed high school in Kabala, the closest city to Sinekoro. Yet the community does not give the respect, they said, because they do not do "community work," i.e., farming. The elders, according to Samuel and Hassan, think that school is just vanity. Gradually the conversation moved on to other things and Hassan showed us the scars on his upper arm and chest—old wounds from a "witch gun," he said, referring to the traditional weapon controlled by occult powers. He said that the bullets from the witch gun were still in his body, and only Limba traditional doctors have the medicine to remove the bullets. The conversation illustrated how Hassan and Samuel are at a crossroad between the traditional and the modern, graduating high school but bearing the marks of traditional witchcraft.

The next morning we woke early to go to the top of the mountain. We went with Hassan, while Samuel stayed behind to cook us lunch. On this last part of the hike, we walked over green hills and patches of exposed bedrock, the soil too poor for trees, it seemed. The top of Mount Bintumani was now visible, looming bigger and bigger.

The atmosphere was hazy, perhaps due to the bushfires of the late dry season, and visibility was poor. Still, one got an intense impression of vast distance and space on this last part of the hike. We saw what Hassan called bush goats—small, dark creatures running furtively through the grass and rocks. We followed the bush goats' trails, intermittent flat paths among the hillocks of grass that we were stumbling over.

The summit of Bintumani

There was a steep climb up a grassy hill, then we started up the spine of a steep ridge leading to the top of the mountain. Below us we could see smaller hills surrounded in a misty haze. The top of the mountain is crowned by a block of sheer rock. We circled around to a point where there was a natural break in the sheer face. Here, grassy hillocks formed a series of hand and footholds and we pulled ourselves up the near-vertical incline. I was scared. Everything that I could see besides what I was holding onto looked very far away; it was disorienting.

Finally, the top. It was flat and grassy with patches of exposed rock. We added a rock to the cairn we found there, took some photos, and then headed back down. For a moment, though, we were on the top of the world, or at least the top of West Africa.

The rocky crown at the top of the mountain

    I was scared to go back down, backwards down the steep incline we had just scaled, but it wasn't as bad as I thought and soon we had made it onto slightly less steep terrain. When we returned to Camp 2, we ate and rested for a while. One of the other volunteers took out his harmonica and started playing and Hassan seemed nervous. He explained to the volunteer that if he played that instrument in town, people would beat him. It seemed that the sound was similar to an instrument or song used in their secret societies. I was struck by the differences between our respective cultures: Americans find power and creativity in the individual, while Kurankos find that same power in the group, in traditions, in rituals. Individuals unconstrained by the group were threatening, dangerous even.

    Then we headed back down the hill toward Sinekoro. On the way, Hassan picked up a reddish-pink fruit which resembled a small oblong pomegranate, and he sliced off the top with his machete. Water sloshed out. Inside were two rows of soft bright-yellow seeds. Sucking on them produced an intense sweet flavor, almost like candy. Hassan pointed to more of the fruit hanging above us in the tree branches, and he said that they are a favorite food of the chimps in the area.

the view from the top

On the way down, we met another guide who had taken people to the mountain only a few days before. The man told us that the community had taken away the money he had earned. The elders had taken it from him in order to buy tools to work on the road. The man expressed frustration with the current system. There should just be a flat rate, he said. Yet the community has its own hierarchy, and it is not open to change. Hassan said he intended to give his share of the money we paid to his mother for safekeeping and then go into hiding.

a small cairn on the top of the mountain

This traditional system of Sinekoro may be losing ground, as the government of Sierra Leone is trying to turn the area into a national park. We met two men in Konombaiya who said they were from the government and demanded to see our permits (we had no idea what they were talking about and they eventually left us alone). Someday in the future, perhaps the government may try to take a more active role in administering the area. And someday, too, youth like Hassan and Samuel will be the old men in the village and they will run things their own way. But for now, traditions prevail in Sinekoro, and visitors to Bintumani have to follow them as best they can.

N° 2 RIVER

[Fisherman's Boat]

PICTURE THIS: white sand beaches, green palm trees and the blue Atlantic stretching to the horizon. But picture this too: except for a handful of people, the beach is empty. But such is the reality of Sierra Leone: post card-perfect beaches ready for tourism. Yet without the postcards and without the tourism. What happened? Bad infrastructure? Bad publicity? Isolation? A ten year civil war? Malaria? Probably a combination of many factors. In more developed countries, it seems as though representations are often more real than the thing itself: the media storm of photographs, TV programs, and ad campaigns is so intense, at times we feel most at home in this digitalized, computerized, pixlized world. So when I visited one of Sierra Leone's more famous beaches (relatively speaking) a beach known only as River No 2, I found the place to have a sort of innocence, as if it were curiously unaware of what it really is. River No 2 (apparently called No 2 River by the locals) is located on the Sierra Leone Peninsula in the Western Area. To get there, it is necessary to pass through the giant traffic fiasco known as Freetown and charter a taxi to follow the unpaved Peninsula Road. The road is currently undergoing

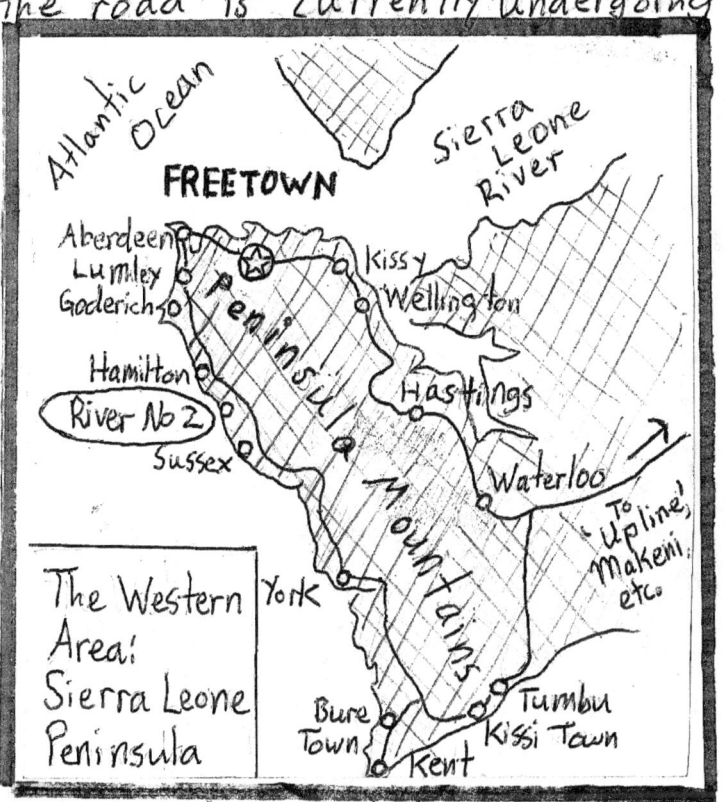

The Western Area: Sierra Leone Peninsula

improvements and, during the rainy season, becomes a maze of giant mud puddles. River No 2 is a combination of small fishing village and resort, though the term 'resort' seems too opulent and

Beach Huts

ostentatious to describe the collection of small bunker-like accomodations and thatch-roofed huts. There was surprisingly little commercialization: more people try to sell you things when you ride on a bus in Sierra Leone than at this beach. There were a lot of foreigners there, which by Sierra Leone standards, wasn't much more than ten. A generator ran during the night, but no light in our room due to a short.

In the midst of this attempt to accomodate tourists, the daily rhythms of village life also played out, as people engaged themselves in more traditional livelihoods, which centered around fishing. A handful of wooden boats were beached on the shore, many of them painted with bright

Out Fishing

colors, and at certain times of the day, a crowd of women would gather near the boats before they would disperse, carrying plastic tubs on their heads filled with fish. It was easy to spot the barracudas that were caught that day, as the pointy tail and pointy head of the fish would be poking out of opposite sides of the tub. Other boats were usually visible bobbing in the swells off shore.

River No 2 has an organization that seems to bring these two halves of the community together, called the N°2 River Development Association. This is a local cooperative run by the people of the village, in which profits from the beach are divided among the community members.

Offshore Islands

The water was a fine temperature for swimming, the sort of temperature where you don't notice at first that it is raining on you. The actual river of

A Boat Waiting to Go out Fishing

River No 2 is small and seasonal but during the rainy season it has a brisk current that can carry a thrill-seeking swimmer right to the surf. Crowds of birds gather on some parts of the beach, including Arctic terns enroute to one of the poles.

If a person is inspired to do a little nocturnal skinny dipping, it is possible to see the eerie glow of phosphorecence in your wake, as points of light appear like stars as your limbs churn the water

Even though River No 2 is a place ostensibly for holiday, it still has the same Sierra Leone feel of the rest of the country: a local might chide you for not greeting properly; there is a woman selling hot rice and sauce in a shack by the road for dirt cheap prices; the slow current of village life eddies by; and life doesn't seem at all tied to strict measurements of a clock, but is instead defined by the rhythms of the seasons, the drip of the rain, the heat of the sun, and the pull of the tide.

Home made key chain at the resort

And the foreigner wonders how it might ever be possible to leave. But soon enough the carefree young man driving the beat up taxi will return, and it is time to squeeze in

Empty Beach Chairs

Someday maybe River No 2 will have its own postcard and a more glamorous name (still haven't figured out where River No 1 is). In the meantime there are just the dilapadated buildings, the hiss of the ocean and the white sand beach without footprints.   26-7-2012

The School

The Sign in Front of CJSS

In a House

The secondary school in Waridala is called Community Junior Secondary School, CJSS for short. Junior secondary school is the same as middle school in the U.S., at least in definition, though the similarities don't last much beyond that. The school was located across from where I lived, in a big house in the style of the others in Waridala: crumbling concrete steps, big veranda lined by ornate concrete railing. At some point in the past, it had been painted yellow with blue trim, now faded and peeling.

On the first day of school, I came to the building early, ready and eager to tackle the challenges of education in Sierra Leone. But there were no students. Eight a.m. sharp and no students. I sat on a bench on the school's veranda and stood up again. No one. I wasn't sure what to do. Finally, a student passed by, without any uniform, and informed me in Krio: "Better school no de," literally "Better school's not there," which means something like, "Real school hasn't started yet." I had previously been told that on the first week of school, many students do not show up, and some of the teachers don't either. But I didn't expect that absolutely no one at all would be there.

It takes a few weeks for school to get going and for everyone to come regularly. School seemed like a season. It doesn't happen all at once. Gradually the students begin to come. And eventually they do come. They walk to school, coming from more than twenty tiny villages spread out in the bush. They trickle down the dirt road from Manjaka, follow the forest trail from Kamakinkali, cross the river in a dugout canoe from Makahe, and some from farther villages. Their uniforms are shocks of white and blue against the green forest and the drab houses of the village, making them easy to spot as they linger on verandas and gather under the mango trees.

I.

First was morning assembly, when the students lined up according to their form: Form One, Form Two, and Form Three, roughly equivalent to sixth, seventh, and eighth grade. To announce the beginning of morning assembly, a teacher gave a large brass bell a shake. Usually this happened at eight in the morning, though the time varied somewhat; nothing is too consistent in Waridala. The late students jogged down the dirt road and ducked furtively between houses, hoping to escape attention. For each form there were separate lines for girls and boys. It was not a big school; when I taught there the total population was only a little over one hundred if all the students came, which was rare, so usually the lines at assembly were not long. The students lined up outside, facing the veranda of the school, where one or more of the teachers stood and barked orders in English, sometimes in Krio, and occasionally gave a long speech about studying hard and doing well in school. This was the time of day when the students were most orderly. They stood quietly and listened, for the most part, which wasn't usually the case during the rest of the day.

All the students wore white dress shirts with blue piping on the sleeves; the boys wore dark blue pants, and the girls wore dark blue skirts. During Form One and Two the boys wore short pants, but in Form Three they wore long pants. They were supposed to wear a short blue necktie, but on any given day, there were many bare necks, and only a fraction would wear the school badge sewn onto their front pocket, as required.

It was difficult to estimate their ages; the only thing clear was that they were of a variety of ages. Generally speaking, students in Sierra Leone are older than their corresponding peer group in schools in the U.S. Due to the constraints of village life, including the lack of money, or the help the family needs on the farm, it takes students longer to complete their education. By the time students reach Form Three the equivalent of 8th grade, some are 17 or 18 years old. One student in my Form Two class told me he was 25. Some of them, however, if asked their age, do not know. Age is a vague concept in Sierra Leone, partly a result of cultural differences, and partly, perhaps, because many of the students were born near the end or right after the disruption caused by the recent civil war.

Families are less likely to send female students to school. Some still think that it is not their place to go to school. In 2012, according to national policy set by the government, it was necessary to pay in order to go to junior secondary school, 25,000 leones for one term of JSS; 75,000 leones for the year. That was about $17 for a year of schooling, a significant amount of money. People are poor and families are big. If they have limited funds and can only send some of their children to school, they might choose to send boys. Girls going to secondary school also face the threat of sexual violence or exploitation. It was common for teachers to sleep with female students in exchange for grades or favorable treatment. It was officially against the law, and contrary to the Teacher Code of Conduct, but this did not discourage the practice.

The Sierra Leone government recognized the challenges female students faced and subsidized the school fees for female students. The government reimbursed any family with a female student a whole year of school fees for JSSI; the government paid for two terms of JSSII; and for JSSIII, the government paid for one term. Yet this subsidy was controversial for some. I heard male teachers rail against it, arguing that the government is only able to pay the teachers a paltry amount, yet seems to find the money to pay school fees for girls.

Morning assembly was when sometimes the teachers inspected the uniforms. Shirts were supposed to be tucked in, which is usually still happening during assembly. The girls were expected to have their hair braided, in tight rows against the scalp. They were diligent about their hair, and teachers rarely criticized them, unlike the boys. The boys were supposed to have their hair cut short; at assembly, the boy line should be a line of shaved heads. As a test, a teacher sometimes pinched the hair on all the boys' heads. If the teacher could grab hair, the student got a smack on the head.

Occasionally one teacher got especially creative in this regard. After assembly, he would take a razor and shave a circle on the side of the heads of the boys whose hair he deemed to be too long, making a bare patch which the boy then tried to cover with a book or a hat, out of embarrassment. Needless to say, this caused quite a stir and everyone laughed. Invariably, these offenders came to school the next day with a newly shaved head.

The students were not supposed to wear flip-flops to school, or "slippers" as they call them in Krio. The problem was shoes are expensive, and flip-flops are the footwear of choice for rural people. For a while at the beginning of the term most students complied with this rule, but gradually, more and more slippers appeared among the ranks at morning assembly. On some mornings, the teachers would do a roundup and go down the lines and take the flip-flops and put them in a bag. The offending students went barefoot for the rest of the day.

Next, the teacher leading assembly usually would make them raise their hands above their heads and clap a few times in unison to get everyone's attention. Then they would sing songs. The teacher leading the assembly often said something like, "Form One, who can give us a nice song?" The students were reluctant to volunteer to lead a song, so usually finger pointing and giggling ensued, until someone started singing. The songs all had the same sort of call-and-response structure in which the leader sings the first verse alone, then everyone comes in and sings that verse, and so on. They sang a variety of songs, some Christian spirituals, some in the local languages, and of course, the school song. It goes like this:

> Come, come, come
> Come to CJSS
> The school of Waridala
> Come to CJSS
> Do not waste your time
> Your time is very precious
> Come, come, come
> Come to CJSS

This song was rather ironic because the students were quite adept at wasting time, but they sang it at least a couple times a week. However, the students were earnest about their singing and it was always entertaining to listen to them sing, especially on days when attendance was particularly robust.

Next, they prayed. CJSS is nominally a Muslim school and meets from Sunday until Thursday, honoring the Muslim holy day on Friday, but during morning assembly, the students say both the Christian "Our Father" prayer and the Muslim "Al Fatiha." This daily practice reflects Sierra Leoneans' view of religion. In short, Sierra Leoneans don't seem to see significant difference between Islam and Christianity. It is the same God, people say. Families are split between Muslim and Christian religions, without conflict. When a person moves to an area dominated by the other religion, they often convert. In this regard the country is remarkably pluralistic and tolerant: The conflicts that divide Muslims against Christians in other parts of the world seem almost unimaginable here. The idea of prayer in school, which periodically inspires outrage in the U.S., is a comforting tradition in Sierra Leone. It is not just in schools: At village gatherings or government meetings in the capital, people begin with prayers, both Christian and Muslim. And the Christians and Muslims know both prayers.

To finish assembly, all the students sang the national pledge and the national anthem. Sometimes they sang them in Arabic, and sometimes they sang them in English. Everyone stood at attention when the students reached this part of the assembly, even the farmers passing by on the way to the fields and the women on the nearby verandas. For a country recently torn apart by a terrible civil war, the words of the national anthem seemed to be particularly poignant:

> High we exalt thee, realm of the free
> Great is the love that we have for thee
> Firmly united ever we stand
> Singing thy praise, o native land
> We raise up our hearts and our voices on high
> The hills and the valleys re-echo our cry
> Blessing and peace be ever thine own
> Land that we love our Sierra Leone

And then assembly was over. If none of the teachers or the principal had any lecture to give or announcements to deliver, line by line the students filed into their respective classrooms. This practice of the daily assembly was an important part of the school day, happening each school day at schools across Sierra Leone. From what I heard from other volunteers, and from what I saw from visiting, other schools in the country had very similar morning routines.

From my perspective, morning assembly was a strange spectacle, particularly the teachers' role, in which they engaged in a sort of authority theater. It almost seemed exaggerated, over-the-top. I was certainly not capable of behaving in the ways that the other teachers did, like taking their slippers, pulling their hair. It all seemed ridiculous to me, a violation of personal boundaries, not to mention illegal, at least to my American sensibility. But it was my job to teach students in Sierra Leone. And that really is the basic contradiction. What did it mean to teach students who came from a culture that I didn't belong to? Certainly, multicultural education is an important part of any classroom. But the kind of differences at stake seemed deeper than I could imagine. It wasn't about cultural identity, or religion, but what it means to go to school. And everyone else knew what it meant except me. At first, I thought morning assembly was a tangential part of education; but I eventually came to understand that morning assembly was a core part of the meaning of school, for students and teachers. The drama of morning assembly *was* school, in a way. I am sure that many decades later, every last student will remember the routine of morning assembly and how they were supposed to behave.

Between the end of assembly and the beginning of class, it might be possible to observe an important tradition in Sierra Leonean schools: corporal punishment. Locally they call it flogging, and a thin cane is the tool of choice for this task, which doubles both as a means of discipline and a pointing device for the blackboard. Being late was the most common reason for flogging. Students at CJSS were not prompt, and throughout assembly they were usually still arriving. Once assembly was over, the latecomers were unequivocally late. The flogging was not consistent, but once in a while the teachers would take a cane and give the latecomers a few blows in the posterior region. The students would make a scene, dancing around and yelling before they ran up the stairs to class. While no doubt unpleasant, it was always a little unclear to me if there was an element of performance on the students' part.

Not paying school fees was another reason the students were beaten. The Le 25,000 the students were supposed to pay per term trickled in slowly. When lack of payment had dragged on long enough, the vice principal chastised the students during assembly for not paying, then waded into the classrooms and flogged them, rousing a flurry of upset cries from the students. Other occasions for flogging included wrong answers and the failure to pay "extra fees" to a teacher that requests them.

All the teachers at CJSS were ardently committed to it – and it was common practice at other schools. "These are African children," is the common refrain. "Some of them just don't listen." Flogging was officially against the rules of the Ministry of Education, but this did not stop teachers. Many were convinced it is a basic part of education in Sierra Leone and would not be persuaded otherwise. I heard parents say this at meetings as well.

I found the practice reprehensible. In my view, people needed to learn to solve problems and communicate with words, not with violence, yet the fact that teachers flogged did not inculcate this lesson but in fact encouraged its opposite. And besides, it was disruptive, and the other kids got excited and wanted to watch and it became difficult to teach. That first year I was there, an accident happened, in which a teacher somehow poked a boy in Form III in the eye. Apparently, the teacher intended to strike a student, and during his windup he accidentally struck the other student in the eye.

The principal, Mr. Sesay, was one of the few who were anti-flogging. He decided to ban flogging the year I came to CJSS. He said that female students should only be flogged by female teachers and since there were no female teachers at CJSS, the whole practice should be eliminated. The problem, however, was finding some system of discipline to replace it. We tried American-style detention after school, but that did not last too long because it was a battle to get the students to stay after school and the teachers were not committed to it. We also tried kneeling down in front of the class, an alternative punishment sometimes used in Sierra Leone, though the students mainly found this entertaining.

Finally, the principal left school for a couple months for another job, and flogging came back, along with that common refrain: "These are African students. They need to be flogged. They don't listen." It was a self-fulfilling prophecy, a circular argument forever proving itself. When flogging is taken away, there are no new ideas or motivation to organize a new system, so there is general disorder until teachers begin to point out again, "Well, look! They need to be flogged." Attitudes are not easy to change. Change has to happen at the level of the community, even the whole country. The failure of the flogging-reform campaign was a frustrating and discouraging experience.

II.

After morning assembly, the students would go into their classrooms, talking, bantering and shoving each other. The school was housed in what was originally a private residence for a big family. In 2005, when the school was started, this was the only structure available in town, and the school was housed in that building in my first year of teaching there, in 2011, and through all of 2012. The government was constructing a new and bigger building during the time that I taught there.

The house had crumbling steps leading up to a large front veranda. On the inside was a main hall with smaller rooms off to the side, a typical floor plan, able to accommodate a large extended family. However, the structure wasn't a good fit for a school. Form One, the biggest class, and Form Two shared the main hall. A piece of particle board about waist high served as a partition, so all the noise from one class easily carried over to the other class. Form Three got its own classroom, one of the smaller rooms. However, although Form Three was only about thirty students in size at the time, they couldn't all fit into the room, and they spilled out onto the veranda.

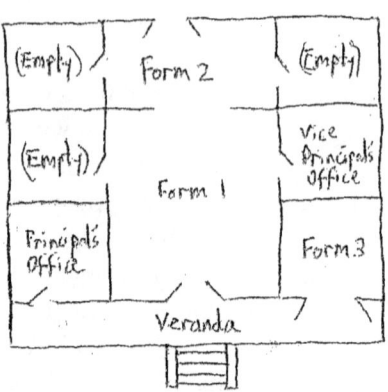

Floor plan of the "school in a house."

    The students sat at desks of rough-hewn lumber; one board served as a place to write and attached to it was another board that served as a place to sit. They squeezed into the desks, sometimes three students to a desk, arranged in rows, facing the dusty chalkboard. The walls were yellow and stained and the floors seemed perpetually gritty, even though the students, as part of their morning chores, would sweep out the classrooms.

    During class, students hunched over tattered exercise books, carefully copying the notes written on the board. These exercise books were central to the students' education. Copying down what is on the board and then memorizing it was the routine drilled into the students from when they first go to school. This approach, in part, stemmed from Sierra Leone's history as a British colony and the long-ago adoption of what at the time was the British style-curriculum. Their exercise books were made from thin sheaves of notebook paper, stapled together, with a reprinted photo of some soccer star on the thin cover. This flimsy book was the most important tool the students used in their education. And, for the most part, the only tool. No computers, no internet, not even any books, at least not very many. CJSS was fortunate enough to have government-supplied textbooks for core subjects, though I found the Language Arts textbook disorganized, at an inappropriate reading level, and mostly useless.

I owned a small stack of graded readers intended for primary school students and when I would bring them in, the students used to go wild, forming a big mob and fighting over them when I tried to hand them out. The JSS students seemed to feel no shame whatsoever about reading books written for little kids. They fought with special enthusiasm over a little book called *The Lorry in the River*. In a school without books, a book vacuum exists, and the students seized whatever they could find.

The students had a system for how they would write in their exercise books: everything written in blue ink, with red ink for the headings, and pencil for diagrams or pictures. It was a system they adhered to carefully. But mistakes happen: They spelled things wrong, left out words; and wrote with messy handwriting. For some of them, I wasn't sure how they were able to use their notes later.

Reading and writing was a great chore for them; the best students had at most a basic proficiency. The lowest students could not read or write. When I asked them to write something for an exam, these students produced a random series of words and letters. It was clear they spent years struggling to copy words from the chalkboard, but never figured out how to put them together to make meaning. Others engaged in lengthy labor to make the most rudimentary sentences with atrocious spelling.

When I saw the students faltering like this, I felt terrible. It was a failure on behalf of the education system. For students to go to school year after year yet to still be bereft of basic literacy skills meant something was wrong. Such failure seemed like a violation of human rights: Reading and writing is a fundamental skill, essential for developing various human capacities. Without it, people are denied something akin to clean drinking water and adequate nutrition. The hardest part was the students I was teaching were at a point in their schooling where they should have learned to read and write already. By JSS they should have been learning to improve on their literacy skills. So for the lowest students, it was too late, because for the rest of their peers, it was time to move on. For these students, I was not sure what I could do, besides delivering yet another death sentence to their confidence when I returned an exam with a grade of 4%. Though it was not my fault, I felt complicit.

III.

For the rest of the day the routine usually went like this. In secondary school, each class stayed in the same classroom all day long; the teachers rotated to the different classrooms according to subject. The core subjects were Language Arts, Maths, Science, and Social Studies; electives included Agricultural Science, Creative Practical Arts, Business Studies, Home Economics, Technology, and Arabic. This last subject got particular emphasis in Waridala: Out of a staff of seven, there were two Arabic teachers. The principal convinced me to teach Creative Practical Arts, in addition to Language Arts, but I only lasted one term, the absurdity of teaching definitions about art and design being too much for me. I do remember doing a lesson about leaf rubbings with crayons, which I think may have violated community beliefs about leaves from the bush, but at the time I didn't know any better.

The typical class period was forty minutes long, but some of the core subjects were allotted a double period. At the end of each period, the bell would get two shakes to mark the time. At 11:00 a.m. there was a twenty-minute lunch. During lunch, a handful of women came and sat on verandas near the school, selling such West African specialties as fried dough or fufu. Often the students did not have money to buy lunch.

When a teacher entered the classroom, the students were supposed to stand up and greet. The prefect said, "All stand!" and all the kids stood up and said in unison, "We are standing up!" Then the prefect said, "Greeting!" and all the kids said in unison, "Good morning, Sir!" I was supposed to respond to them, "Good morning, how are you doing!" and they said, still in unison, "We are fine, thank you! How are you, too?" The kids in Form One used to greet me in this way about half of the time when I entered the class. In Form II they only did it occasionally, and the kids in Form III didn't do it at all. The routine was drilled into them during primary school, it seemed, and it took a couple years before it wore off.

The official language of instruction in Sierra Leonean schools was English, which seems like it would make it an easy transition for a teacher like myself who speaks English. However, I have a heavy America accent and I said things differently than Sierra Leonean teachers. Often my explanations were met with blank stares of incomprehension, because I spoke too quickly and used too many words. But even when I repeated myself, spoke more slowly, and simplified my vocabulary, the problem still remained. For all the students, English was a second language. The students at CJSS spoke Krio and came from a variety of ethnic groups: Maninka, Loko, Limba, and Fula made up the majority, while there were one or two Themnes and Mendes. Each student at CJSS spoke at least one of these languages at home. No one spoke English at home.

Learning English is essential at school because it is the language of instruction, but teachers do not spend time actually teaching the students to use English. It seemed kids were supposed to pick it up as they go along. For language lessons, students often received instruction about grammar and parts of speech, useful lessons to improve one's proficiency but confusing at best for a student who is still learning. As a result, students in Sierra Leone begin learning about all sorts of subjects in English often before they have a grasp of the language.

Yet when I tried to provide more interactive lessons, it was confusing, even for the best students. Working with a partner was strange to them and I was unable to explain it effectively. Having kids come up to the chalkboard to do practice exercises was very novel. What they really expected was to write things down in their exercise book and memorize it. A big portion of the class time always involved the students writing down the notes from the board into their exercise books. Sometimes it seemed as though students began to confuse learning with having written down something in their books. For exams, which happened twice a term, the students were expected to go home, memorize what they had written down in their books and rewrite it for the test.

This was maddening to me and at the time seemed inexplicable. But I think the expectations students had were due to Sierra Leone's culture of hierarchy, at least in part. An important man is a "big man," as they say in Krio—a man who has wealth and contributes to his community in a big way. While teachers were poorly compensated, they had their own higher status as keepers of knowledge at school. Children are at the bottom of this hierarchy; they do work, run errands. They rarely get any of the meat in the pot at home.

In some ways, the hierarchy makes the teacher's job easier. There wasn't the sort of talking back and surly attitudes that are present in American middle schools. The Sierra Leonean students were certainly loud and wild sometimes, but they usually did their best to be respectful to teachers. Another effect of the hierarchy was that the students did a lot of work: They carried water to the school for drinking, swept the classrooms in the morning, picked up trash in the school compound. Some days were "work days," when all of the students brought hoes and machetes; usually the girls brought the hoes and the boys bring the machetes (cutlasses in Krio). On these days the afternoon classes were canceled and the whole school would go out "cleaning." The boys cut brush with the machetes and the girls dug up the grass and the weeds, creating the bare-dirt yards that the village people were so fond of. Often the school had a cleaning day in preparation for a holiday or important event and the students went around and cleaned throughout the village.

But at the same time, this hierarchical worldview was one reason my interactive lessons never worked. The people who know things (teachers) were supposed to pass on information to people who don't (students). Disrupting the model of repeating and memorizing went against the social order.

IV.

At 2:00 p.m. the day was over. Midday is the usual time in Sierra Leone for the big meal of rice, often the only meal of the day, so the hungry students wanted to hurry home to eat. A loud clanging of the bell could be heard, signaling the end of the school day. The students surged out of the classrooms, restless and hungry young bodies filling the veranda of the school and spilling into the bare dirt yard. Just like in the morning, they lingered under the mango trees and talked on neighbors' verandas—and then gradually they disappeared, some to their homes in Waridala, others walking again down the red dirt roads and bush trails to the small villages where they lived.

After school, I would stand on the veranda of the school, leaning against the railing and watching the students go. Exhausted, with a hoarse voice. And I would think to myself: What just happened? To begin with, any given student in my classes probably understood only about half of what I said, due to my accent and their generally poor English. If there was an exam, there was probably a lot of cheating, or "spying" as they call it in Sierra Leone. I probably had to tell them a half a dozen times to be quiet. I said over and over: "Get out a piece of paper!" "Stop talking!" "Start writing!" "Why don't you have a pen?" Their English was limited and the language is hard. They just wanted to copy off the blackboard. They came late all the time and only two kids in the whole class did their homework. Attendance was sporadic for many students, especially those coming from distant villages. Sometimes one of the villages had a "jam" in the middle of the week and half the students danced until dawn and slept through class the next day.

But one underlying factor made everything harder for the students: People in Sierra Leone are very poor. They suffer from easily prevented diseases. Many grew up malnourished, their bellies swelling. Decent health care is hard to get, doctors hard to find. Most of the handful of motor vehicles in the country barely run, and people ride bicycles that would be scrap in the U.S. There are few jobs besides working as a subsistence farmer or as a petty trader providing the few items that a subsistence farmer needs to buy. For those who are educated, the job market is slim; they can work as a teacher or maybe for an NGO.

Even being a teacher is hard. The government pays them little, around Le 500,000 a month, which is around $100. It was a small group of teachers and they did their best: Mr. Kamara, the vice principal; the other Mr. Kamara, who taught math; Mr. Gibate, who taught agricultural science; the two Arabic teachers, Mr. Conte and Mr. Turay. The fact was CJSS only had three classrooms, so only three teachers could teach at a time. My second school year, there was an effort to hire a woman as a teacher. She moved to Waridala with her family and lasted only a few months. Village gossip drove her away.

Getting certified to be a teacher is similar to a two-year technical degree in the U.S., but, because it is time consuming and expensive, some people try to work as teachers without certification. These teachers are known as "community teachers" because the government does not pay them. Principals in need of extra teaching staff will hire them and pay them using the proceeds from the students' school fees. It is a prime situation for corruption. The key to the whole system is what they call the "voucher," the official document that contains a list of all the teachers on the payroll at the school. A teacher who is not qualified will masquerade under a different name, a name that conveniently happens to appear on the voucher. Sometimes the name of a teacher who is retired or dead remains on the voucher, and other people collect the money instead. At the beginning of my first year, the teachers were all talking about what they called The Package, a monetary bonus that was funded by a collection of international aid organization like the IMF or UNICEF or some other groups. The Sierra Leonean government, however, refused to release the money. The teachers accused the government of corruption and they even threatened to strike. The government refused to pay for months, and when they finally did, it turned out to be a paltry sum.

Poverty exists as a system, and while it is not an effective system, it works. The schools do not have books, so the students take notes off the blackboard and copy them into their exercise books. People are too poor to buy concrete and wood and metal roofing to make a house for themselves, so they go into the bush and find the materials there. Teachers do not get paid regularly, so they enlist extra help on their farms from the students. And while it is true that strategies like these are grim signs, they also suggest creativity and even grace. Even in the face of difficult circumstances, people find ways to survive and even to thrive.

One of the more interesting local strategies, I thought, was the practice known as an *osusu*. Rooted, it seems, in agricultural traditions like the rotating *katee* work teams, even the teachers had *osusu*. For a fixed period, everyone in the *osusu* contributes a sum of money to a shared pot; each person in the *osusu* gets one turn to collect all the money in the pot for use as they see fit. I participated with the CJSS teachers for one round. Every month we were expected to contribute a portion of our paychecks and the payout, as I recall it was around 700,000 leones, the equivalent to over 100 dollars at the time.

It was tempting at times to question what I could really do to help. The poverty in Sierra Leone was present long before I came and will be there long after I left. I accomplished nothing at all, at least according to the sort of geopolitical terms by which modern governments operate. Reform efforts don't always seem to help because they do not fit into the system in place. What if a school gets a donation of computers and doesn't have electricity to power them or technical knowledge to work them or fix them? One school near Waridala received a generous donation of books from Europe and they were written entirely in Gaelic.

But being a Peace Corps teacher often seemed defined most of all by the little moments. Hearing stories about the students' lives. Joining the teacher *osusu*. Or teaching a class of middle schoolers something they never knew, like what the word "favorite" means. Or that the earth orbits the sun. Or whether there are Muslims in America. People everywhere have the capacity to express themselves-through a system of signs and sounds—and to learn to hear the secret music of these symbols. It is a teacher's task to help others cultivate this capacity, and on the good days at least, I knew that there is no job more important.

We haven't had a riot in eight years, the announcer says over the loudspeaker. Don't do it now!

Sports—an important part of school—always take place during the dry season, traditionally a time of leisure and plenty for the farming communities. The dry season falls during the second term of the school calendar. Planning for the annual Waridala sports event in 2012 began months in advance, in January, a task shared between the primary school and the secondary school. Periodic planning meetings were held, with a chairman, secretary, treasurer, etc., events that often dissolved into arguing. The first thing to do was to raise money for a sound system, food, printing, and other costs.

We started by getting sponsors for each "house" or team. Mayeteh Construction sponsored Red House, Child Fund for Yellow House, Sierra Leone Association of Journalists for Green House, and Pa Alimamy Bangura of Kenema for Blue House. We delivered letters saying that a house had been named after their organization and asked for a financial contribution.

This, of course, seemed a bit like the opposite of how sponsorships work, but no doubt the incentives for sponsoring a village sports event are meager. The sponsor for Blue House, Pa Alimamy Bangura, was the section chief for the neighboring region and he lived in a town across the Mabole River. As he was perhaps one of the potential sponsors most likely to provide support, I was recruited by another teacher to take a motorcycle ride to personally deliver the letter to him. We had to carry the motorcycle across the river and ride down farm trails and rutted roads, but Pa Alimamy received us with hospitality. No one ever told me if he donated, or how much.

One weekend, all the teachers and many of the students went on what they called a "rag parade." All the males dressed up as females and the females dressed up as males and we crossed the river, where many of the students live, going from village to village asking for money. People in Waridala thought it was funny to see me in a skirt, head tie, and pink tank top. A few of the teachers led the students various call-and-response songs in Krio, such as:

Auntie, give me money, duya
Auntie, give me money, duya
If na rice, we want am
If na konsho, we want am
If na pepper, we want am

Since these were poor farming villages, we received lots of crops as donations instead of money. Although, as the song implied, we gladly accepted these sorts of donations as well.

Eventually the teachers themselves contributed money for the event, Le 70,000 each, and Le 100,000 from those with positions of responsibility, like chairman. We were supposed to earn that same money back and even profit from the proceeds from ticket sales to the event. At least so I was told.

The students had to prepare was well. One afternoon we organized "balloting," an event for assigning new students to a house. They take turns choosing from among scraps of paper which will determine what house they will belong to for the rest of their time attending the school. Another afternoon was "arbitration," when the students took turns standing next to some chalk marks on the wall, and a teacher measured their height. Based on their height, the students were divided into classes: the tallest being Seniors, followed by Intermediate, Junior, Feather, and Infant. These classes determined whom they would compete against on the day of the event.

Finally, a few weeks before the event, it was time for the students to clean the field. They came to school with hoes and machetes, to trim the grass and the bushes at the field. They usually worked for an hour or so and then they would dissipate. This is also around the time when classes at school simply stopped happening. Students would come for assembly, clean the field for an hour or so, then go home. At some schools, no teaching takes place at all for a month or more during sports time. At Waridala, the teachers decided to have the sports event close to the end of the term, to preserve as much teaching time as possible. Not going to class is very much in the spirit of the dry season. There is less farm work during this time of year, so people visit friends and hang out. This attitude easily permeates the school culture as well.

After cleaning the field, the students built a fence around it, so admission could be charged. Then they made a *baffa* hut for each house, where the students will stay during the event, and a sort of pavilion for the "high table" where all the guests of honor will sit. The students made all these structures with materials from the bush. First, they fixed sticks into the ground, then built a frame onto these sticks, using more sticks and vines. Then they made panels by weaving palm leaves between the sticks. A few of the older students climbed up the nearby palm trees to cut down the leaves.

The weeks before the event is also when practice happens. The students come to the field and run and practice handing off the baton and doing the high jump. Each house has a house master—a teacher who is in charge and is supposed to help their house practice.

At last, the day arrives; sleepy Waridala swells with visitors. The generator starts up to power the sound system and the beat of Sierra Leone popular music spreads through the village. There is a "march pass" to start off the day, when all the students line up with their respective houses and parade through town. It is a riot of color. For the event, all the students acquire the brightest t-shirt and shorts they can find in their respective house colors, often embellishing with matching socks or ribbons on their head. Some girls braid yarn into their hair that match their house color.

After the march pass, the running and jumping began. The announcer called out each event on the loudspeaker, summoning the participants to the field. When an important guest arrived, the announcer announced his or her arrival and said whether they brought an envelope—a gift of money for the organizers of the event. As the day went on, the score for each house was recorded on a blackboard in the middle of the field. Each event earns a certain number of points. Besides the spectators, many people came to sell food and drinks. Other people brought food and drinks to "serve" their friends, that is, to give to them as gifts. During the event, I was pressured into racing in the "House Master" 100-meter race, for Blue House, which I lost. People kept playfully reminding me about that for several weeks after the event.

On the afternoon of the second day there was a rainstorm that interrupted the competitions. By the time everyone reassembled at the field, it was time for the all-house relay, always the last event, when boys and girls from Senior, Intermediate, and Junior all race in one long relay. This is the race that is worth the most points, too, so the crowd gets excited. During the race, Green House did something that brought the ire of the others houses. I wasn't quite sure what happened in the middle of the commotion, but it looked like there was going to be a fight.

But suddenly the announcer began reading off the results. First, he just read the numerical scores, to try to quell the tension. Then he read the results: Red House won, followed by Green House, then Yellow, with Blue in last place. The members of Red House began cheering wildly. This was also the point at which the announcer warned the crowd that there hadn't been a riot in eight years and urged them not to do it now.

It is not the sort of thing that you tell crowds that are about to riot, I'm sure—at least not if you want to stop the riot.

But, probably in spite of the announcer's warning, the crowd did begin to disband peacefully. No riot, at least not that year.

Eventually I did get some of the money back that I had contributed during the planning stages, although I was told that the event didn't break even. At least that was what I was told. The event was not very transparent, to say the least, and I'm not sure what happened to all the money.

Sports disrupt school for weeks and are a source of squandered instruction hours and general disorganization. But the best part is seeing your students succeed. In class, they struggle through words written in a challenging foreign language and endure corruption and corporal punishment. Yet on sports day, they run as fast as they can and go all-out because it is their chance, for once, to win.

A WULA KA JAN

The mosque at Madina Loko

THE DISTANCE IS FAR:
A Trip to the sports in Madina Loko

The students are running, yet as they run, we can see that they are children no longer, but young adults. Their bodies move with the power and grace of a fully developed human being. They have on brightly colored t-shirts and shorts: some with red, some blue, some yellow. Their black skin glows from the sweat and sun and each step they take kicks up a small fountain of dust. They have no shoes, some wear socks, some are barefoot. A huge sound system hooked up to a generator plays Sierra Leonean dance music and when the runners cross the finish line, the crowd cheers. This is sports in Sierra Leone, a one- or two-day event of track and field competitions and dancing, and on March 7th and 8th, 2013, the students and staff from CJSS Waridala traveled to Madina Loko to witness the sports their school was putting on.

There is no easy way to go from Waridala to Madina Loko. It is necessary to follow a series of bush trails. The few who had bicycles used them. The rest of the students and staff walked. The people of Waridala were surprised when I said I was walking and they told me: "*A wula ka jan!*" in Maninka, i.e., "the distance is far!" However, in the village, even short trips are big journeys, so I did not take the warning too seriously. I guessed it was probably ten miles.

The day before the trip and the morning of, my veranda was filled with students looking for help to fix their worn-out bikes so they could ride to Madina Loko. By the time I got everything cleaned up, I was one of the last to leave Waridala. I walked under the hot, dry-season sun, all vegetation dried and scorched. It was a hot and sweaty hike, but these were the moments that I loved the most in Sierra Leone: the small villages with long rhythmic names, the chance to meet all sorts of people, and the sense of peace and freedom. Out here in these bush villages, many accessible only by trail, they follow an ancient, timeless rhythm and the modern world seems like a faint dream.

The village of Kakola

I passed Karina, Mayongbo, Masasa, Kakola, Maboroba, Sherifula. In Masasa there was a funeral, the town filled with visitors sitting under the mango trees paying their respects to the relatives. In Kakola I drank palm wine twice. In Sherifula, I talked to a man named Salu Sheriff about education and how small villages must build schools for themselves because the government doesn't help. The sun was brutal and the people in Waridala were right—the distance was far. But at last, I came to the final obstacle of the journey: to cross the Mabole River. I climbed into the dugout boat and a naked little boy paddled me across using a stick. His naked playmates wrestled with each other in the brown water nearby, splashing and shouting, cascades of water sparkling in the sun.

Madina Loko is a Maninka town like Waridala. The "Loko" is affixed because the town is located inside of Loko territory. It is a moderately sized town, the main street lined with old concrete houses, like Waridala. A brand-new, beautiful mosque rises in the middle of town. A generator lights up the building for night prayers. I was told that construction originally began before the civil war and, after considerable delay, it had been recently completed; a local woman who moved to the U.S. funded the construction.

Upon my arrival, I learned that someone in the community had passed away, and according to Muslim tradition, the deceased must be buried as soon as possible, so the whole community came to a halt. As a result, the beginning of the sporting event was delayed until evening time when, finally, the event would begin. At last, in the lengthening evening light, the first races began, and the students started running in the dusty sports field right at the outskirts of town, competing until darkness fell.

At that point, all the people from Waridala gathered at the house that had been designated for us to stay the night. Now, it was time to eat. According to local custom, hosts are expected to feed their guests. Getting "served" is an important part of any trip for a Sierra Leonean. However, the cooking was delayed, due to the burial, and some grumbling could be heard among the students. Finally, the food came, rice and sauce piled on huge plastic plates two or three feet in diameter. The students crowded around, crouched on the ground, eating with their right hands. Boy and girls eat separately, and a big plate was designated for the teachers to share among themselves. Everyone ate quickly and quietly, the silence of satisfaction hanging in the air.

The next day, the running and jumping continued. The whole sports field had been enclosed by a fence made of palm leaves, and everyone paid Le 2,000 to enter. Many people came from the community and beyond to watch. Others came to sell snacks to all the spectators. During this time of year, the farmers have finished their harvests, so everyone had free time and maybe even a little money. The atmosphere was festive and I felt caught up in it too. The students from Waridala didn't compete—I wasn't sure why—they only watched and showed off in their best clothes. By the end of the day, Blue House had won, besting Yellow House and Red House.

That night there was a dance, this time the palm-leaf fence enclosing a much smaller area, and people could again pay a small fee to enter. I always found these rural village-style dance parties thrilling: The thumping beat of Sierra Leone dance music gushing from six-foot-tall speakers, pressed up against strangers, the heat of the day dissipating as the thick cool air of the bush at night settles, while the stars spill out overhead.

The next morning, we woke up early to return to Waridala. A big crowd of people accumulated at the river as everyone tried to cross at once: The Waridala people with their bicycles, some boys on motorcycles from Kamabai, and a few locals from Madina. General chaos took over as everyone clamored to get a spot in the boat. People, bicycles, bundles of unidentified items, even a motorcycle were crammed in. The boat was pushed away from the bank, voices quieted for a moment, and immediately the vessel dipped low from the weight and water began to spill over the sides. Everyone started yelling again and a few people got out and another attempt was made. This time the boat slowly glided across the river, the waterline inches from the top edge of the boat. After reaching the other side, the boy guiding the boat across immediately turned around and went back for another precarious load.

The trip to Madina Loko to see the sports summed up Sierra Leone well: rough, disorganized, and hot, but always exuberant and fun.

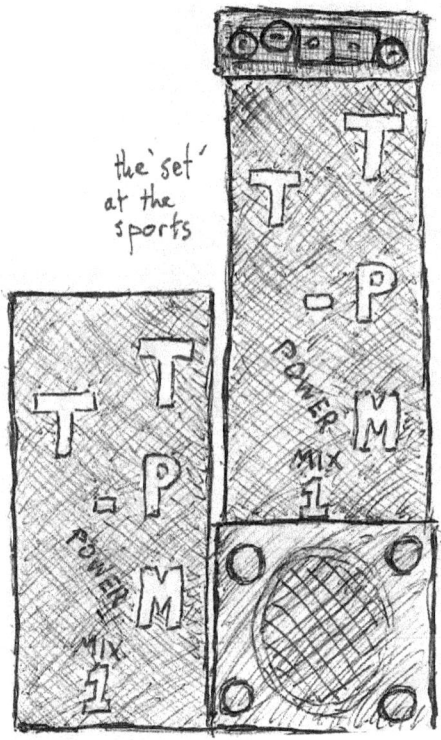

I speak fluent English because I was born and raised in the U.S., but my students at CJSS struggled to read and write the simplest sentences in English. It was not their native tongue, after all. Yet they had to learn it since English is the language of instruction in schools. But during their lunch break, they spoke in the dancing rhythms of Krio, the hard consonants of Limba, the percussive syllables of Loko, the rapid lilt of Maninka. These were the students' native languages, wild and unconstrained by grammar books, formal education, or governmental mandates. These languages were the places where they live. They laughed and flirted and gossiped in Krio, Loko, Limba, and Maninka until the lunch break was over, then returned to the classroom to those hollow, empty words written in English on the blackboard.

    I came halfway around the world to this impoverished village—a place that sings with languages and cultures far different from my own—in order to teach these students my own language. It was an improbable situation, yet for these students, the entire future of their education depended on their ability to grasp this foreign tongue.

    My job in Waridala was the result of an agreement between the Sierra Leonean government and the American government, sending me along with 49 other Americans to Sierra Leone to teach. For those of us who were to teach English, we were told that teaching English is about teaching grammar. Learning English begins with the definition of a noun: "A noun can easily be defied as the name of a person, place or thing," and moves on from there: "The type of nouns include abstract, concrete and proper nouns." After teaching nouns, the teacher is supposed to move on to verbs or adjectives or maybe pronouns. I knew this method well because it is how I learned Ancient Greek in college. In first-year Ancient Greek, we opened our big, thick textbooks and began with how the noun works in Ancient Greek and then advanced to more complicated topics. In higher level courses, we sat at a table and translated from Ancient Greek texts and discussed the more complex grammar structures and points of style. Learning in this way was appealing to me because I love grammar. I love its logic, its rules, and order that it puts on the sprawling chaos of language.

At one point during our introductory training, we had the opportunity to practice teaching on some local students. When I saw the low academic skills of the students, the grammar-based approach we were learning seemed inadequate. The students hardly knew English at all. They needed to solidify their reading and writing skills; they still needed to learn to make meaning from the written word. The ability to name the parts of speech and define a noun did not seem to contribute to that goal. Knowing English grammar and knowing English, it seemed to me, are very different things.

The problem with this grammar-based method in an African context is that there is no common language in which the students are already literate. They are not using the grammar rules to understand a second language in terms of their first language; they are simply learning grammar rules of a language they don't really know. This isn't teaching the students how to read and write and speak in English but teaching them about English. And grammar is difficult. Native English speakers in the U.S. learn to read and write before they learn parts of speech. My doubts about this method were heightened during the practice teaching session, when I asked students to identify nouns and verbs in a sentence. Most could not. Their understanding of a noun did not go beyond the definition.

At Waridala, I began my classes with discussions of nouns and verbs. I tried to make them child centered and link the grammar lessons with things that I thought the students would be familiar with. However, it seemed there must be a better way. In a book about teaching English as a second language, I read about the communicative approach to language learning, a perspective that maintains that we use language to do things, to greet, to buy, to say sorry. This means that learning a different language means learning to do things with the new language. With the communicative approach, students learn to greet, give advice, complain, or give instructions in the new language. Lessons are tied to a specific context.

I found the basic idea to be fascinating and tried to incorporate it into my teaching. I began with basic listening comprehension lessons. I gave the students a template for describing an object:

It is used for _____ (activity)
It is made of _____ (substance)
It costs_____ (price)
It is _____ (color)
It is _____ (shape)
We can find it _____ (location)
What is it?

For example, I would use this template to describe something; the students would have to listen to the description and then name the object I was describing. Then I would ask them to try to pick an object and describe it for themselves. I also tried lessons like this: I would draw a series of different designs on the board, each one slightly different. Then I would describe each one in a random order and the students would have to listen in order to identify the order in which I described the pictures. The important element in these lessons was that they were about communicating. In these examples, if a student understood the lesson, it meant communication was happening.

However, I soon realized this communicative approach wasn't going to work. At the simple level of basic comprehension, such as in the activities mentioned above, some of the students could follow the lessons, but to go further to more complicated tasks was not working. The problem was that the communicative approach requires a lot of independence on the part of the learner. Students are expected to do things on their own in a new language. This didn't work in my classroom. A big problem is that the students in each class were at mixed levels. Some had strong skills, some were emerging readers, and some couldn't read or write at all.

But more than this, my approach was contrary to what my students expected at school. In Sierra Leone, the knowledge that students acquire at school consists of facts. Define livestock. What are the three theories of man's origins? Define first aid. Define a noun. What are the three kinds of human migration? What are business studies? It is the teacher's role to disseminate these facts. The teacher writes them on the board, reads them to the students, explains what they mean, and leads the students in repeated choral recitations of what is written. Most schools in Sierra Leone do not have books. It is the students' task to write down these facts in their exercise books and commit them to memory in time for the exam.

In Language Arts class, like all the other classes, students are accustomed to receiving facts. They want to copy and memorize, not produce language, and they need a teacher in front of the class telling them what to do. Yet I could not let go of the idea that I needed to teach them to understand how to communicate in English.

By the end of the term, I was disheartened. I needed to try something new. After some reading I tried incorporating the audio-lingual method into my lessons. This method was developed by the U.S. government during World War II to teach soldiers new languages like German, French, Japanese, and Tagalog as quickly as possible. The Department of Defense hired behavioral psychologists and linguists to create a system in order to accomplish this goal and the Audio-Lingual Method is what they came up with. The procedure is simple. The new language is learned through the study of written dialogues. The sequence of instruction is grammar based, but grammar is never explicitly taught. Rather, the students memorize the content of dialogues through repetitive readings. Here is an example of a dialogue I used in class to teach students about introducing themselves and asking questions in the present tense.

      Dialogue 1: Greetings and introductions.
      Sorie: Hello, how are you?
      Isata: I'm fine. What is your name?
      Sorie: My name is Sorie. What about you?
      Isata: My name is Isata. It is nice to meet you.

Sorie: It is nice to meet you too. Where do you live?
Isata: I live in Sierra Leone, in Bo.
Sorie: Do you go to school?
Isata: Yes, I go to Sierra Leone JSS.

    I could create various dialogues of this sort on all sorts of topics and incorporate various aspects of language I wanted to teach. I would lead the class in a group reading of the dialogue, then repeat the reading with variations, like by row, or boys and then girls. Later I would have them do fill-in-the-blank activities or write a letter introducing themselves. Teaching in this way was a relief to me because it was so simple and straightforward, and it fit more closely with the way in which the students are accustomed to being taught. The students were used to reading aloud from the board in choral fashion and memorizing and they loved having examples they could imitate.

    However, the audio-lingual method, too, had its drawbacks. It cannot be used to teach certain writing skills like mechanics, or topics such as literary devices, areas in which I was expected to provide instruction. Moreover, I had difficulty finding an effective way to test the skills I was teaching them. An activity like fill-in-the-blank is a simple solution but many of the students had difficulty making the imaginative leap. For example, if I used a question sentence for a fill-in-the-blank task, many of the students would answer the question rather than fill the missing word into the blank.

    By the start of my second year, I was frustrated and tired. Finally, I decided to come back to the beginning and teach my students grammar. In the end, it seemed like innovative techniques I tried were lost on my students, who simply had different expectations for school than me. Learning about grammar was simplest because it was easier for them to understand what I was asking of them. The trick, it seemed, was to make sure the grammar lessons were selected and taught in a way that allowed students to practice and improve their reading and writing skills, rather than simply learning the grammar. (For this reason, I still didn't teach parts of speech.)

I spent the whole first term of my second year teaching my Form Two students about the past tense. The past tense was challenging to my students and when we started learning about it, they hardly knew any past tense forms at all. Every week I would give them a list of past tense forms that they had to memorize, and we practiced writing on topics that required use of the past tense. I made flash cards on card stock which I used with the whole class to help them study. The past tense forms of verbs were simple to teach, they are easy to test and the students understood what was expected of them.

I came to understand more about what it means to teach English because I came to understand that teaching English is not a monolithic concept, not a unified practice; it means different things in different contexts. In Sierra Leone, to learn English is to be sophisticated; it is to tap into the power of the colonialists. Indeed, this is how Western education originally came to Sierra Leone. The British built schools to teach the local elite—originally the Krio—how to serve Her Majesty's empire. Today, Sierra Leone educators and students continue to try to emulate the British, from the structure of the education system to the curriculum, to the language of instruction. The English teacher in Sierra Leone is supposed to approach the subject of Language Arts as if the students are citizens of Britain, already fluent in English. The best students learn to play this confusing game comprised of signs and symbols borrowed from a distant culture. The rest of the students are left behind.

To learn another language is to learn another culture, an often-repeated maxim. This basic insight was implicitly acknowledged by Sierra Leoneans, most of whom seemed to see English-based education itself as something foreign. People speak positively about the value of education, yet they believe that education comes from somewhere else; it does not really belong to them. The Maninka contrast *wala karan* with *tubabu karan*. *Wala karan* is the traditional study of the Koran; the phrase refers to the wooden *wala* tablets that Mandinka children use to learn Arabic. *Tubabu karan*, on the other hand, means literally "white person learning."

What is it that motivated these students to come to school? They walked through the bush in flip-flops. They crossed rivers. They endured beatings at school. They struggled through a foreign language. Some didn't even know how to read. They faced challenging national and international exams. A dismal job market awaited them when they leave school. Their parents sacrificed scarce money to pay the school fees.

Perhaps people believe that God will bless those who learn to read and write in English, just as God will bless those who learn the holy language of Arabic. Perhaps people believe that English education is a form of white man medicine that will somehow grant their children the kind of wealth that exists in English-speaking countries. Perhaps the prestige of the English language is so strong that people will go to great lengths to simply be close to it.

But maybe the best way to think about schools in Sierra Leone is that children are learning to be Sierra Leonean. That is why school, and teaching English, seemed so strange to me. The content of lessons and units that students learn at school is only part of the education they receive; how they learn is equally important. Just because I didn't get it didn't mean it was meaningless. The hierarchy between teacher and student taught important lessons. Even little details are important. For example, reciting both Arabic and Christian prayers during morning assembly is a key part of Sierra Leone culture, and for the rest of their lives the students will be expected to say both types of prayers at all sorts of meetings and gatherings, regardless of their personal religious affiliation.

One unique thing about West Africa, including Sierra Leone, is its diversity of languages, a densely packed concentration of tongues found nowhere else in the world. As a result, multilingualism is a fact of life; almost everyone knows a second language, if not a third or fourth. This multilingual environment calls into question the distinction between first and second languages. The students who were in my classes spoke Loko or Limba or Maninka or Fula at home with their families. Some of the students had parents from two different ethnic groups, so they learned both languages. They all knew Krio and spoke it with their friends at school or at the market. These students didn' necessarily have a first language. There was a spectrum of languages through which they moved and they used them in different contexts. No one ever formally taught them these languages; they learned them as the situation demanded. In this context, English is not necessarily a second language, but another language to be used in its own particular context—in this case, school.

  West Africa needs a unique approach to education and to teaching language, one that celebrates linguistic diversity. The emphasis on a single language, English, in school and the degradation of the other local languages as "vernaculars" is an anachronism from an earlier colonial period. Some changes have been made. In the early 90's, when Sierra Leone was spiraling into civil war, one of the temporary governments was the NPRC, National Provisional Ruling Council. The NPRC introduced several changes to the education system, including adding local languages as courses of study in the national curriculum for junior and senior secondary schools: Krio, Ka Themne, Hu Limba, and Mende, the four most widely spoken local languages in Sierra Leone. Many schools, especially in bigger towns, offer classes where students can study the local languages. Of course, there are at least 17 local languages spoken in Sierra Leone; many other languages are still left out. And some places have no clear linguistic majority, making it difficult to offer classes in a local language. At times people seem to view the local languages as symbols of ignorance. Incorporating them into the school system helps to turn them into a subject worthy of study in their own right. I would love to see more local language literacy, the end of English-only rules in schools, and English taught like the foreign language it is. I think academic Krio would be a powerful tool. Krio is not broken English. It is its own language. It has an alphabet and a body of literature. Why not start writing textbooks in Krio? Why not start conducting classes in Krio? An academic Krio could be developed, used to express the ideas found in a school setting.

From the Village to the City:
Paying the Way for School

It started when the BECE results came out —Basic Education Certificate Examination—the exam everyone takes after junior secondary school. A passing score on the BECE is required to advance to senior secondary school. For reasons known only to the African bureaucracy gods, the results from the BECE are not released until October or November, well after school has already begun.

In 2012, the results from the BECE reached Waridala in early November. It was a dramatic day, as last year's students gathered around the school office to pick up their results. These results would determine who would go to Senior Secondary School, SS for short, and who would stay in Waridala to retake the test, or start working full time on the family farm. A girl ran through the school grounds screaming with joy at her good results. Others walked quietly away, likely due to less than preferred marks.

One student came to the school that day who hadn't sat the BECE with the others; he'd taken it two years before. He'd passed, but he hadn't been able to find the money to go to SS. Waridala and the immediate area nearby does not have an SS; getting the money and connections together to go to a different school in a different town can be a significant obstacle to some. This student came to see the results of the exam, just to watch. His name was Foday S. Mansaray. I'd seen him around the village; he seemed like a nice kid, so I told him I would pay for SS this year if he wanted to go. He said yes. The next day he wrote me a letter thanking me.

I wanted to help, I told myself. By late 2012, I had become enmeshed in the workings of the local community. The poverty was grinding, relentless. My work at the school, at times, felt useless. Yet the community welcomed me with such generosity. I felt obligated to help where it seemed I might be able to. Paying for school fees seemed like a small gesture. I set a boundary for myself: I would only pay for education-related expenses. In retrospect, helping Foday was a mistake. Sometimes no help is better than a little help, a nudge of assistance that changes expectations and perceptions far out of proportion to the actual material extent of the assistance. Even after being immersed in village life for 18 months, I didn't quite realize the extent of the poverty, the corruption. And my prudent-seeming personal boundary of only paying for education proved to be an utter fiction, meaningful only to myself.

Foday like most students in the English-based schools, didn't know English particularly well, but spoke Krio and especially liked to converse in Maninka. He was short and muscular, his polio-weakened leg a contrast to his strong arms. His mother died when he was young, allegedly at the hands of witches who turned into bees and stung her to death. He has no photograph of his mother, but people say that he looks just like her and he told me that sometimes he looks in the mirror to imagine what she looked like. His father was still alive but very poor and did not support Foday. From what the other teachers at CJSS told me, he was an excellent student when he attended. From my perspective, he seemed like a good student to support.

The first task was to find a place for him to stay. It is common for students to live with relatives who will give them a place to sleep while they are going to school, and some rice to eat from the family pot. Foday's uncle, a farmer in Waridala, began using his connections to find Foday a place to stay in the nearby city of Makeni so he could start going to school. November passed, then December, and then it was January. School had begun again. Still no place to stay. I should have taken this as an ominous sign. I should have ended it then, when he couldn't secure a place to stay. But I told Foday we needed to make a trip to Makeni ourselves to look for a place. Makeni is big enough that living on one side of town and going to school on the other side would be impossible. The issue of distance was particularly crucial for Foday. He had polio as a child and the disease weakened one of his legs, so he walks with a limp. In retrospect, this mark of disability—minor or inconsequential in my eyes—made all the difference in the local community, steeped in traditional beliefs. Friends and relatives—crucial to the livelihood of any Sierra Leonean—didn't step up to help him, even though they could have. It was unclear if they felt that given his disability, he would never be able to reciprocate any assistance—or if it was something more insidious.

Oblivious to what I was getting into, on the agreed upon day, I gave Foday some money to go to Makeni. I rode my bike and met him there. In Makeni, Foday and I met with a teacher name Mr. Tarawalie, a man who used to teach in Waridala and had married a lady from the village. He served as a kind of liaison while we looked for housing. We went around to several compounds where people from Waridala were living. Mr. T inquired whether there would be a place for Foday to stay. By the end of the day, we had heard only one answer: no. One person we asked blamed the housing shortage on African Minerals, a foreign mining company—many people had come to Makeni looking for employment and they were taking up a lot of the extra beds. We headed back to Waridala that evening, disappointed.

A few days later one of Foday's friends called him and said, "Why didn't you tell me you were looking for a place to stay?" This was a young man about Foday's age named Alhaji, who was from a nearby village and had attended CJSS in Waridala. He was now attending school in Makeni and he said that he knew where Foday could stay, so we went back to Makeni to set everything up.

The nearest school to the room that Alhaji had found was MCA, Makeni Comprehensive Academy, the same one that Alhaji himself was attending. Foday, Mr. T, and I went to meet the vice principal for the admission interview. At first, I didn't understand quite why we were going to the vice principal's personal residence—although as I was soon to see, everything in Sierra Leone is personal. The vice principal, a stout, middle-aged man named Mr. Gbanti, was sitting on his veranda, shirtless. It was immediately apparent that Mr. Gbanti was blind. We had to announce our presence loudly and introduce ourselves to him. It turned out that Mr. Gbanti had been Mr. T's teacher when Mr. T had been in primary school. Mr. T was excited to see him, but Mr. Gbanti didn't quite seem to remember his old student. Mr. Gbanti explained that he went to the doctor for cataract surgery a few years ago, something went wrong during the surgery, and he's been blind ever since. Mr. T explained the purpose of the visit, and Mr. Gbanti dutifully listed off from memory the various fees required for entering the senior secondary school at MCA.

    School Fees: Le 90,000
    School Colors: Le 80,000
    Stationary Fee: Le 25, 000
    Development Fee: Le 25, 000
    Uniform: Le 40,000
    ID Card: Le 6,000
    Total: 266,000

The total amount, 266,000 leones, was about $60—a significant amount for many, and a frequent reason why students stop going to school after JSS. Yet it was a manageable amount for me, even on my meager Peace Corps stipend. Then Mr. Gbanti looked at Foday's BECE results. He had to have one of his older sons, who was nearby, read it off for him. Foday had passed six subjects out eight, with an aggregate of 27, aggregate score being a sort of comprehensive score derived from the scores in each subject. Mr. Gbanti approved of what he heard and recalculated the aggregate score in his head just to be sure. I took out the 266,000 leones, counted it, and gave it to Mr. Gbanti.

All this time, Mr. Gbanti's wife, or some female relative of his, had been cooking a big pot of rice on the veranda. Now she was taking the pot of rice off the coal pot and scooping hot rice into a variety of bowls, plates, and containers. Mr. Gbanti was served a big plate of rice and sauce, and his guests received plates as well. When we were finished, Mr. Gbanti put on a collared shirt with a bright pattern, a pair of sunglasses, and picked up his cane. He was ready to go back to school. It seemed that he had come home for his lunch break. Foday's friend, Alhaji, guided the man down the street.

We were not through yet. We still had to have a meeting with the principal. We walked over to MCA and through the campus, which consisted mostly of a series of dirty white one-story buildings and a big dirt field. MCA is big; there is a primary school, a junior second school, and a senior secondary school. The students were gathering in the courtyard, all white-collar shirts and royal-blue pants and skirts. Then we went into the principal's office, a cramped space with books and loose papers strewn about on the shelves and on top of the big desk that took up most of the room. The principal was a big strong-looking man with a hug handshake and a huge smile. He sat behind the desk, dressed in a blue Africana outfit with a matching hat. We made introductions, explained the reason for our visit, and showed the principal Foday's BECE scores. Then Mr. Gbanti gave the money to the principal. He counted it and said it was not enough. The principal explained that there was a transfer fee because Foday had not selected MCA as his school of choice when he took the BECE. Mr. T tried to bargain with the principal (even the price of going to school is negotiable it seems), and finally the principal accepted. The principal signed some papers and gave Foday a receipt and an admission number. Foday was now a student at MCA.

Then we went to the market and bought school supplies, notebooks, pens, a pair of shoes, a bag, and other things. By now I could see that I was face-to-face with deep and dire poverty: There was nothing keeping Foday from a bench on the veranda of a house in Waridala except me. I even had to buy him toothpaste.

By this time, it was already two weeks into the second term. This wasn't a problem though. Every student entering Senior Secondary One for the first time is late. The BECE results are released late; students have to find the money, a place to stay—although they still have to pay fees for that first school term that they missed.

Foday had a difficult time. First, this wasn't the end of the fees. Besides the official fees, there were many unofficial ones: fees for evening classes, weekend classes, even fees for collecting homework. At Foday's school, he told me later, the teachers mandated that all the students buy photocopied pamphlets of the teachers' notes for each subject. The students were then expected to study the pamphlets and later the teachers would draw questions from the pamphlets for the exams. Getting food to eat was also a challenge. For a while Foday's neighbor was giving him some rice every day, simply out of generosity. Then that situation changed, for reasons that were unclear, and the neighbor had to stop giving the rice. Then he wasn't getting anything at all. He called me to tell me the problem, but he said that he would be able to endure some hunger because, as he said, "Thanks to God, I am not a greedy person." He made it through the rest of the year getting by on the generosity of friends and meals of dried cassava powder, *gari*, when he could afford it. His housing situation was never quite secure. The room he started living in had originally been rented by an *okada* driver. The driver had suddenly vacated the space, leaving it open for Foday. It turned out that the driver had been involved in a traffic accident and someone had died, so the *okada* driver had gone into hiding in order to avoid prosecution. He had not yet returned but was said to be likely returning soon; at least Foday was able to utilize the room while he was at MCA.

The extra fees that he had to pay at school proved to be exorbitant. Those who pay can pass their classes, and those who can't, don't. Foday's friend, Alhaji, who had showed him the room originally, started driving *okadas* rather than going to school, but he was able to pass because he could use some of the money he made from driving to pay the fees the teachers ask for.

But the biggest problem was that Foday was not promoted to the next form. Students are supposed to receive a 50 percent or higher cumulative score in all the classes that they take in order to advance. Foday had a cumulative grade of 49.8 percent. Usually, this number would have been rounded up to

50, and Foday would have been promoted, but for some reason the person who prepared the grades did not round up the number. Most likely it was an effort to get more money from Foday and, in turn, from me. But I didn't take up the indirect demand for a bribe. In a system where no one plays by the rules—or the rules are made up as they go along by those in power—I chose to do the right thing. But was it really the right thing? Perhaps Foday's entire cumulative grade was fictional. But I had come up to the boundary I had set for myself—that I would do what it took to pay for his education. They said he didn't pass, so I told Foday that that was all I could do. Him staying in Makeni for another year to retake first-year SS hardly seemed like a sustainable option anyway. He asked me for other things—a camera, anything. He grew increasingly desperate.

    He wept when my two years as a Peace Corps volunteer were up and I left Waridala. Yet, not knowing what else to do, I stuck to my original boundary. I had given him a chance, and it didn't work. The true weight of the poverty in Sierra Leone was on the other side of this line. Only later did I see it from Foday's perspective, that there was no difference between educational attainment and all the other parts of his life, that I briefly lifted him from his difficult life in Waridala, and then dropped him right back where he came from, except worse off, because now he no doubt faced the scorn of his friends and relatives. I let him down, and I didn't realize it until later. It was a difficult situation I was in, immersed in poverty yet at the same time removed from it by virtue of my race and nationality. I realized I made a rash decision, sending Foday to Makeni without understanding what I was committing to. But at the same time, I can't say that I did the wrong thing; faced with such systematic corruption as that which Foday faced, I am not sure there are any good answers.

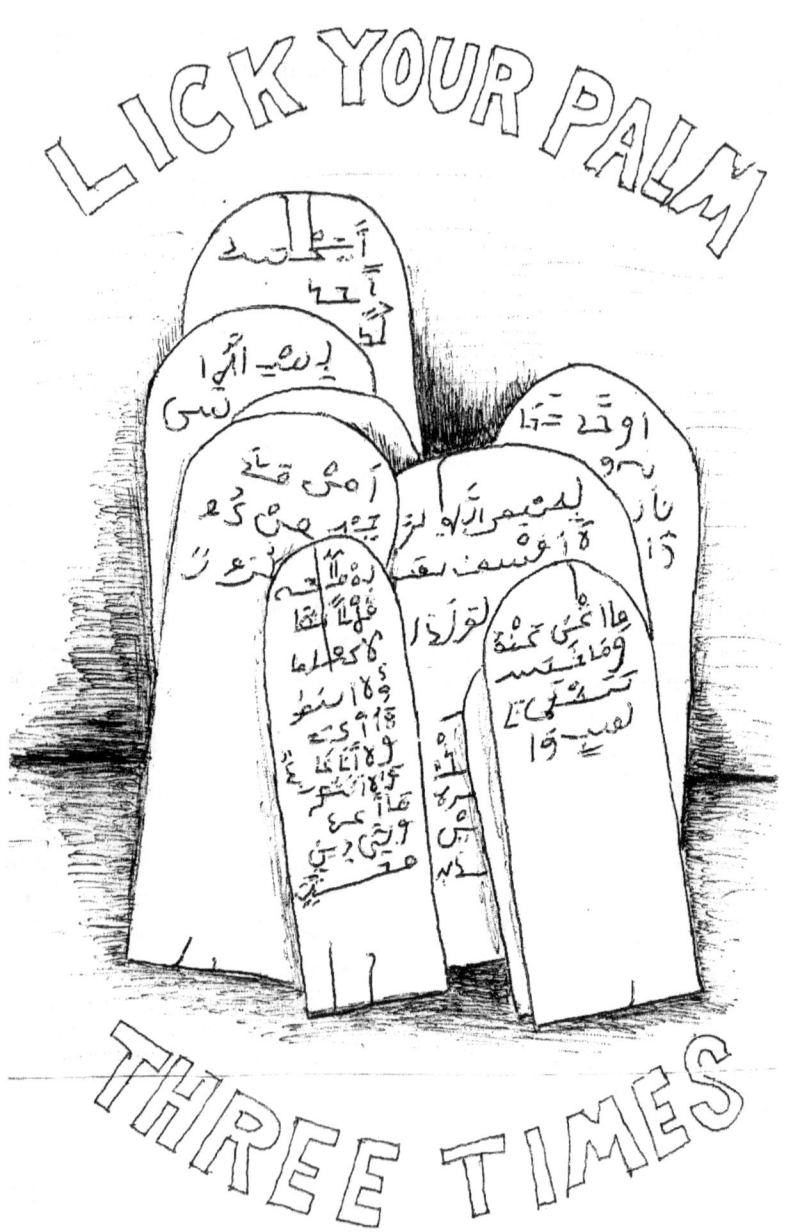

When a Maninka child in Waridala becomes old enough, around five or six years old, their parents bring him or her to the *karamorko*, the Arabic teacher. The teacher takes the child's hand and writes in ink on the palm: "*Bismillahir Rahmanir Raheem*," an Arabic phrase meaning "in the name of God, Most Gracious, Most Merciful." Then he sprinkles on a little salt and tells the child: lick your palm. The child obeys, tasting the mingling of salt, sweat, and ink. Now rub it on your forehead, the teacher commands, and the child rubs their hand on their head. The child performs this ritual three times. Once the ritual is complete, the child has entered the traditional Koranic school as a *karanden* – a student - and is ready to begin to learn Arabic.

The *wala*, a smooth-sanded board the shape of a tall, narrow gravestone, is central to learning Arabic. This board is where the verses from the Koran are writ as a ten, using the traditional ink and pen. Pa Saio, one of the village elders, described to me how it works. I found him one afternoon in front of his grass house in the shade, sitting on a bench wearing a close-fitting cap and a *wala* board on his lap. The pen is called a *kala*, Pa Saio told me. It is made from a species of grass of the same name. Elephant grass is the English name, a tall, vigorous grass that grows more than 10 feet tall in the rainy season, until it dries up and burns in the sun and wildfires of the dry season. During this season, before the land burns, the Maninka man finds a well-dried clump of this grass. He cuts a short length and slices off one end diagonally, so it comes to a sharp point. Then he makes a small split in the tip so it will hold ink. The ink is called *duba*, made from the bark of a species of mango tree they call *walsa*. It is boiled with water and another kind of leaf for a long time until it turns into a thick black liquid ink. I watched Pa Saio closely as he wrote. He dips the grass pen into the container of ink taps off the excess and carefully writes a few letters in Arabic. The pen squeaks occasionally against the wood and the ink stands for a moment in intricate liquid welts on the surface of the *wala* board before it dries and soaks in.

The kala squeaks occasionally against the wala and the dufa vibrates for a moment in intricate duets on the surface of the wala and wala melts on the surface it dries and before it soaks in.

Some kalas, made from elephant grass dried by bush fire

When the children are young, the teacher writes for them, but older students write for themselves. Once the student has learned the Koranic sura written on their *wala* board, the board is erased and a new sura is written. To erase, water is applied and the student scrapes it with a rough leaf called a *mweka*. Some people consider the water used to wash away the verses to be special, for it is infused with the sacred syllables of the Koran. They add this water to the water they use to bathe, believing that doing so will help prevent illness and bring good fortune. Some write a sura from the Koran pertaining to devils, wash it off, then mix the washings with milk and honey. It is said this drink will give special protection against devils. Some powerful teachers are said to have access to their own personal devils, and the washings from words written by these teachers have been imbued with the power of their devils.

The students come five days a week to the Arabic teacher's veranda, early in the morning, sleep still in their eyes. A few girls can be counted among the students, but they are largely boys. Their chanting can be heard from my house, a few houses away—they don't read silently when they practice—and gradually their volume swells as more students arrive. As latecomers arrive, the others make room on the long benches on the veranda of the teacher, a local man named Komanda Conte. They remove their flip-flops before coming onto the veranda, then look around for their own *wala* board. Then they begin practicing, reciting out loud and tracing a finger right to left as they read.

Occasionally, they pause to look around, the pauses gradually becoming more frequent until Mr. Conte yells at them in a mixture of Maninka, Krio and Arabic to keep studying and brandishes his cane. Periodically, a student comes to kneel before Mr. Conte's seat and asks how to pronounce a phrase which has been forgotten. He reads the indicated passage, the student repeats the example, and then sits down. Discipline is strict: On this day Mr. Conte gives one kid lashes for being so late.

When a student thinks he or she has memorized the sura on the *wala* board, it is time for a test, the *"wala for,"* literally "speaking the *wala.*" The teacher holds the *wala* board and the student recites, receiving one lash for each mistake. If successful, the student moves on to a new sura. It is not clear how much the students comprehend: The focus is on memorizing the sounds. After all, the purpose of this studying is not to facilitate communication between people, but to worship. The important thing is the passing of the sacred words across the lips. Traditionally, the student would memorize the whole Koran and only then go back and learn the *tafsir*, the meaning.

Mr. Conte is not paid for his work. The Maninka believe Arabic teachers will be paid in the afterlife. The teacher's work is not without benefit, though, as any time he needs help on the farm, he can ask his students to work for him.

Traditionally, in the dry season, during the harmattan when the cool winds blow and the nights become chilly, students study around a bonfire to keep warm. The students all bring a *yonson*, a small bundle of firewood collected from the bush, which is their contribution for fueling the fire. This tradition of studying around the fire is where Maninka Koranic learning, *karanta*, gets its name. "*Karan*" means "read" and "*ta*" means "fire" so *karanta* literally mean "fire reading" or "fire study." On the cool harmattan mornings and evening, the commotion of the children's studies are moved from the teacher's veranda to a circle around the fire. The harmattan season is supposed to be a time for the students to intensify their study: The rice harvest has been brought in and there is little work to be done until the rains come again. The fire is a symbol of this intensified period of

Karamor with warm hat in harmattan

study, as the children get up early and stay up late to study.

The first year I was in Waridala, I saw this tradition taking place, the orange glow of the fire lighting up the faces of the young people gathered to study, long after the town became still and dark. But the next year, the students did not make a fire to warm themselves while they studied. The students said the teacher was too busy and the teacher said the students didn't want to carry wood.

The truth is life is changing in Waridala and old traditions no longer carry the weight that they once did. Arabic learning has many rivals for the attention of the youth: music, money, the lure of larger towns with more going on. Perhaps the biggest rival is the English-based school, two of which opened in Waridala in the last 20 years, a primary school and CJSS, the junior secondary school. More people seem to be deciding that English-based school has more benefit.

However, as a teacher in the local English-based school, I observed how the model of Arabic learning continues to live on in the English-based school system. The students memorize, and understanding of the words is not prioritized. Just like with Arabic learning, the meaning somehow seems secondary to learning the sounds of the words and phrases. The teacher at the English-based school is expected to be very similar to the Arabic teacher. The teacher provides an example to emulate; discipline is administered with a cane; and when necessary, his students provide labor on the farm for free. My students did seem to act like Arabic students. They wanted me to read first and they repeat after me. When they read alone and found a word they don't know, they asked me to pronounce it. Rarely was the issue of meaning broached. My classes were filled with students who could copy from the blackboard but couldn't take meaning from written text. They memorized the definition of "livestock" and the names of laboratory equipment as if they were lines from a sacred text. After all, in Maninka, the word for "read" and "recite" is the same: *karan*.

SCHOOLS FOR AFRICA

THE STORY OF THE CONSTRUCTION OF ONE SCHOOL IN SIERRA LEONE

In 2012, the government of Sierra Leone, with the assistance of the Islamic Development Bank and the World Bank, constructed a new school in the village of Waridala. To understand what happened, we could begin with what was unseen: that the construction of this new school in rural Sierra Leone was allegedly political favor; that the principal of the school, the contractor of the construction, and the town chief all allegedly obtained personal benefit from the project;

that the villagers secretly complained about the school, because the classroom takes away their children from their traditional jobs of the farm, like driving the birds away from the rice crop.

But perhaps the real beginning was when the ground was first being cleared, the first physical signs manifested. That's how I knew the project was actually going to happen. The new site was located in a clearing right outside of Waridala. On that day, the students were working – for this one of many tasks that they were expected to complete as part of the new building projects – the male student swung machetes as they cut the long grass a brush; the female students scraped the ground with hoes. They were still wearing their school uniforms, white shirts with dark blue trousers or shorts for the boys and dark blue skirts for the girls. It was a work day, as they call it: School had been dismissed so students could work at the new school site, clearing brush.

a student cutting brush with a machete

For seven years this community had a junior secondary school, the equivalent of middle school, called Community

Junior Secondary School, or CJSS for short. This school is recognized by the government, meaning teachers receive regular salary. Government approval is rare in the rural Sierra Leone and most village schools are not officially recognized. These unapproved schools are called "community schools" and the teachers are paid from the school fees that the students pay rather than government coffers. Government approval means teacher salaries are more regular and more ample; as a result, a government school should be a more stable institution.

So the name CJSS is somewhat confusing. While it is in fact a government recognized school, at its inception it was not, and the "community" was retained in its name, perhaps for no other reason than convenience and continuity.

However, this school in Waridala did not have its own building; classes took place in a house. The house had crumbling steps leading up to a large front veranda. Inside the concrete structure, a main hall dominated the floor plan, with small rooms off to the side, a typical arrangement designed to accommodate a large extended family.

But at last, the Sierra Leone government, under the auspices of NaCSA, National Commission for Social Action, designated the funding from international donors to build a new school building. The process began in 2011, the same year I moved to Waridala, and I had the chance to witness, up close, the process. With little fanfare, apart from the rhythm of the students' machetes cutting the brush, the project began.

I

In mid-2011, the rainy season, within the first couple months of my move to Waridala, representatives from NaCSA came to explain the project to the residents, a "sensitization" as they called it. They arrived in a muddy Land Rover and held a meeting on the chief's veranda. At the time, my grasp of Krio was still rather weak, but "community-driven project" was the key phrase the NaCSA people wanted to convey on that day. This meant that the community had to elect a CMC, a

Community Management Committee, which in NaCSA lingo means the group of people in charge of handling the money. The other part of "community driven" involved the people of the community providing their labor for the project, such as cutting brush and digging the foundation.

Soon, some of the men from the community began working with the construction company in Makeni to "knock blocks" as they call it. They had a big pile of sand, a bag of concrete, and some water. One man used a shovel to mix the concrete and sand while another added water. Then the man shoveled this mixture into a small rectangular form, turned the form over and out popped a new concrete block, ready to dry in the sun: one block "knocked." During this time the contractor's vehicle, a battered white pickup, raced through town at regular intervals, going to the river to collect sand to bring back to the site of the new school.

At one point in this process, a whole stack of newly knocked concrete blocks had to be condemned. The foreman had decided to reduce the amount of concrete added to each block, pocketing the difference. These extra-sandy blocks were weak; fortunately, someone noticed the difference. These blocks were too soft to be used for the foundation and had to be saved to make the walls.

Concrete proved to be a contentious part of the construction process. At the time, one bag of concrete cost 44,000 leones, about $10, which was a significant amount of money. For this school project, hundreds of bags of concrete were coming into the village, and everyone wanted some, to patch up a cracked wall in their house, to put a new concrete railing on their veranda, to plaster a cracked floor. All these much-coveted bags of cement were stored in the basement of the mosque, a location that would serve as a neutral site and perhaps a deterrent to theft.

One day, I watched as the contractor's truck piled high with bags of cement arrived from Makeni. The boys who worked for the contractor piled out and began carrying the bags of cement in the basement on their heads. The small brown bats who live in the basement woke up and fluttered around as the boys stacked the bags in the basement, and the powder leaking out of the bags gradually stained the boys' clothes and cheeks gray. Once the bags were unloaded, the storage room was to always be locked. However, despite the precautions, a few home renovations involving concrete started up in the village during this time.

Soon after, there was another NaCSA meeting, which took place at the new school site. The final layout of the buildings was to be decided. Many people attended this meeting: the contractor, the NaCSA representatives, the architect, the principal, the elders from the village. Eventually the meeting turned into a heated debate about the orientation of the school. Were the structures to face the road or be oriented perpendicular to the road? At the time, such details seemed to me not to warrant such an impassioned conversation. Only later did someone explain to me what the debate was really about. Some of the stakeholders in the project, including the contractor, the principal, and the town chief, wanted to reduce the size of the final structure; they would keep the extra money for themselves. It seemed the orientation of the building would impact its dimensions and hence how much money certain people were able to put in their pockets.

Finally, after the debate about the layout of the school, the NaCSA officials marked out the layout of the buildings with string and sticks: a block of classrooms, an administrative block, and the principal's living quarters. The digging of the foundation began soon after; as a community-driven project, the task of digging belonged to the men in the village. They dug with shovels, shirtless and sweating under the tropical sun.

Soon the foundation was completed, and school administration called the students again for another work day, this time to carry the hundreds of blocks that had been already "knocked" to be used for the walls. Mr. Sesay, the principal, commented that the students needed to provide labor because they would be benefiting from the project, an accurate summary of many people's views in Sierra Leone. All the students came to the site of the new school and, balancing the blocks on their heads with practiced ease, they made short work of the task.

II

From here, the project proceeded in fits and starts and deadlines were broken. Indeed, the principal had originally told me the school would be finished after the first term of the school year – by the end of 2011 -- though by now the third term was nearly finished – well into 2012 -- and the building was not complete. The money for the project was to be released in three stages. The foundation was one stage, the walls were the next stage, and the roof and finishing were the final stage. It was a well-funded project—someone told me the total budget was Le 514,000,000, over $100,000, although I was not sure if that as accurate or not.

During this time, I occasionally would visit the site of the work. However, the men working on the project at that point, skilled masons and carpenters from the nearby city of Makeni, started yelling, "*Opoto yemanie–what?*" at me. This was the phrase that Themne children yell at white people, meaning "White person, I am hungry." Apparently, children began adding "what?" to the end of their slogan in anticipation of the typical white person's befuddled response. So, when the grown men at work on the new school started telling me, "*Opoto yemanie–what?*" I decided to make a point of avoiding the work site.

This major building project in a small village made a big impact. The construction crew was housed in Waridala and there were the usual dramas and allegations of affairs. Perhaps the most striking change the construction brought was the daily presence of an automobile in town. No one in Waridala owned a car. There is a road to Waridala, but it is not a very good road, usually traversed by people on foot, bicycle, or occasionally a motorcycle. Now every morning the contractor's white worn-out pickup truck was roaring through town, piled high with bags of concrete and tools, workmen hanging off the sides. The vehicle had a problem with the battery, and on many mornings it was unable to turn over the engine. A group of men would gather to push the truck down the short hill leading out of Waridala, right by my house. Usually, the engine would then cough to life but sometimes it would fail to catch. Then the men, grunting and sweating, would have to push the truck back up the hill to try again.

It was a big event any time the truck had to go to Makeni to pick up supplies. Everyone would try to get a ride. On these days a crowd of people would gather around the truck, usually arguing and yelling. They would pack in the cab and the rear bed until they were nearly overflowing. Then the truck would take off, leaving the rest of the crowd behind in mid-argument, the cab and the bed full of people dressed in their best to go to town.

III

Finally, the walls and roof of the school were completed, though delays had been considerable. For some time, a rumor went around that the whole project had been held up because the minister, who had to provide his signature, was away in Ghana. At one point the elders from the village went to the site of the school to perform a sacrifice, of a goat, to help ensure a successful outcome to the building project. Eventually, school closed for what would be called "summer holiday" in the U.S. from August to September -- with the new school still not complete. By now it was well into the rainy season and the prime time for building, the dry season, had slipped away. NaCSA was putting pressure on the contractor to finish up. During this time the people of Waridala were busy planting their crops and engaged in the fasting required during Ramadan.

One evening during Ramadan, the principal came to the village. The principal lived in another town, only coming to the village when school was in session and would leave during the holidays. He met the village people breaking fast for the day; they were outside the mosque crouched in circles around pots of food on the ground. "*Sala la Mohamed*," the principal said, meaning, "I begin the name of Mohamed."

"*Salalaw taslim,*" the people said in response. The principal's invocation of the Prophet's name told them he had a message to tell them, so now they waited to hear what he had to say. It was about the school. Time was running out, the principal told them, and there was still a lot of work to be done. "I need help from the men," he said in Krio. "It is necessary to dig a drainage ditch along the back of the school. It is not a lot of work, but it needs to happen tomorrow." Immediately the group broke out into a flurry of shouting as people stood up, discussing, and finishing eating at the same time. Some waved spoons in the air to emphasize their points. Finally, one man among them was able to quiet the group and speak for them all.

"We all trust you, Mr. Principal," he said. "And you know that if you ask us to do something, we will do it for you. The problem is with the contractor. When we work for him, he does not give us anything. He delays and he delays and we never see anything." The group broke out into shouting again. At last, the principal announced that he intended to contribute 100,000 leones to the men doing the work, in addition to whatever the contractor promised to pay. This seemed to satisfy the group and they gradually disbanded to their homes.

Soon after this the men completed the drainage ditch and within a few weeks the school was finally complete. It stood immaculate and out of place in the humble forested surroundings. It was made up of three buildings. One building contained the classrooms: one classroom each for Form One, Form Two, and Form Three. The other building was the administrative block, containing a staff room, an office, the principal's office, the vice principal's office, a library room, and a home economics room. The administrative block was in fact bigger than the actual school, a strange incongruity. In the rear of the school was the principal's quarters. There was also a brand-new set of latrines and a well. The new school site was located a bit outside of the village, so when you were at the school, you couldn't see the village at all, or any signs of habitation. All you could see were palm trees and the unbroken brush of the surrounding forest. Occasionally you could see small, dark monkeys moving through the trees. Sometimes big birds called great blue turakos came to roost nearby, with bright-blue feathers and yellow crests on their heads.

the new school

IV

One morning during the long holiday, some commotion started in the village and someone told me that white women were coming to see the school. People put on their best clothes and went to the new school to await the arrival of the white women. The village women all wore Africana *lappa* suits of bright colors and the men wore colorful Africana shirts and trousers. When the three white Land Rovers finally arrived, all the village women sang a song in Maninka and clapped to keep rhythm. I wasn't exactly sure who these white women were or what they were doing. All the people in the village told me was that *fadabge musu nu yi na la*, that is, the white women are coming. It turned out that the women were representatives from the World Bank, one of the organizations that had helped to fund the project. The women, I eventually figured out, were coming to Waridala to interview the community members.

For the meeting, everyone gathered into one of the rooms in the new school building and all the important people were introduced, in order of status, as is necessary in West African culture. The people from Waridala were eager to have me translate for the visitors. During the meeting, I paraphrased what was said in Krio into English for the two visitors and did my best for what was said in Maninka, although my skills in that language are rudimentary at best. In some sense, however, the accuracy of my translations was not the important thing: It was a source of pride for them to have a foreigner living among them who was able to understand their language on even in a basic way.

One of the questions the two World Bank women brought to the community members was, what kind of impact will the school have on the community? The women tried to elicit answers from the males, females, and some students, though it took some encouraging to get members from the latter two groups to talk. The World Bank people also asked them what skills people have in the community and what challenges they face. The men of the village said they know how to cut brush using machetes and plow land with oxen. They said that the school helps them get training to be carpenters in town. The women said they hoped the school would bring more people to town who would buy soap, onions, and homemade cakes.

The two women listened carefully to the responses, though when it was over they didn't even stay to eat rice. The representatives got back in their Land Rovers and departed. In Sierra Leone if guests come, it is expected that they will eat rice; if the guests aren't served properly, the hosts will be embarrassed and the guests annoyed. Especially in rural areas, there is no difference between work life and personal life—all guests are personal guests, even if they come for work purposes. The rapid departure of the visitors showed there were two different sets of customs being followed.

In a sense, there were really two meetings that happened at the same time. The World Bank people were in one meeting and the Sierra Leoneans were in another. The two meetings just happened to take place in the same location. In the World Bank meeting, the two white women were seeking grassroots feedback from a sampling of local men, women, and children about the effectiveness of the projects that the World Bank was funding. In the Sierra Leone meeting, the people followed the traditional protocol. The more important males speak first, never say anything negative to guests—and they believed fervently that these two women were going to bring them money. Both meetings seemed successful to the people involved. The World Bank people recorded the comments, and the Sierra Leoneans believed they made a persuasive case to the World Bank representatives to send them money.

But there were many things that the two visitors could have learned that remained unsaid. The village people assured them that the school brings significant benefit to the community. The reality was more complicated than that. A realistic assessment of the situation shows the school had no immediate benefit to the community at all. The only occupation in Waridala, after all, is subsistence farming and this does not require any schooling. The vast majority of students who attend this school fail the national exams at the end of Junior Secondary School, their families having sacrificed scarce savings to send their children to school. The students who are successful in their exams move away from the village for schools and jobs in distant cities; their departure leaves the village bereft of the most promising young people. And during the school year, all the children in town have to go to class and leaving no one to drive the birds away from the rice crop. These problems are not just present in Waridala but can be found in any rural village across Sierra Leone. The benefits of a more educated populace are numerous, but those benefits are difficult to see from the vantage point of Waridala.

V

Soon after this meeting the school year began, yet classes at Community Junior Secondary School were still taking place in the old house in town; the new school building was locked and empty. It was said that NaCSA was holding onto the keys; it was said that they were organizing a grand opening for the school; some even said the president would be coming. No one really knew for sure, but it was an election year in Sierra Leone and campaigning was beginning. The opening of a new school seemed like a good place to have a rally.

It was around this time that the political dimension of the project began to become clear, and stories, such as the following, began circulating. In Sierra Leone there are two main political parties, APC, the All People's Congress, and SLPP, the Sierra Leone People's Party. The two parties are mostly indistinguishable, but people often align themselves with a political party based on ethnicity. For example, the two biggest ethnic groups in the country, the Themne and Mende, traditionally belong to the APC and SLPP respectively. The Maninka people's political allegiance traditionally lies with the SLPP. However, for the presidential election in 2012, the APC, the party of the incumbent, attempted to sway the Maninka people to join, at least those living in the Waridala area. A deal had been made, I was told. The APC government appointed a Maninka originally from Waridala to a high-profile government job—ambassador to Iran. There was one condition: He had to get his hometown to switch parties. In the course of this endeavor, the man used his contacts in the government to arrange for the construction of a new school building in Waridala.

Now the election was a month away and the date was finally set for the official opening of the school. Traditional drummers were invited to perform at the occasion. One group was to represent each of the three ethnic groups that form a majority in the school's population: Loko drummers, Maninka drummers, and Limba drummers. In anticipation of the occasion, people bought ingredients to cook large quantities of rice and sauce. Rumors about whether the president would be there were still circulating until the very evening of the event.

On that evening, a van full of APC supporters showed up. They were dressed in red outfits, the color of the APC party. This was not unusual; visits from the APC had become frequent and some people in the town were beginning to change parties. The APC held a meeting under the mango tree in the center of town, which soon devolved into shouting and arguing. I learned later that in the meeting, the APC people announced that the president would not be coming to Waridala after all, but would be making a short visit instead to the nearby village of Karina, another Maninka village, where he would lead a rally. For this reason, the APC representatives encouraged the people in Waridala to cancel the opening of the school. It seemed that the Sierra Leoneans saw the new school in some sense as belonging to the president and that it would be disrespectful to inaugurate it without his presence.

The people in Waridala, however, were quite offended at the cancellation of the opening and threatened not to attend the president's rally the next day. In retaliation, the APC people contacted a higher-up in NaCSA and ensured that the school would be effectively locked until further notice. I was shocked by this development. The opening of the school would be further delayed and all the supplies the village people had purchased would spoil, being miles away from effective refrigeration.

Fortunately, on the very next day, the opening of the school proceeded as planned. I don't know how it happened but somehow the keys to the school were obtained. The Limba drummers had left, but the Maninka and Loko drummers were still around town. The ensembles took turns circling around the town, their organic polyrhythms echoing on the verandas. Small crowds of people followed the drummers around, dancing and clapping. Periodically, the drummers would pause in front of someone's house and the revelers would form a circle.

the young Loko dancer

One of the revelers would enter the middle of the circle and dance a sort of solo while the others would watch and cheer. Upon exiting the circle, the dancer was expected to give money to the drummers, a gesture which is always met by hearty cheers from the onlookers. The Loko group brought a young boy to the event who seemed to be a star dancer of sorts; he had on a headdress and held a whistle in his mouth and danced with wild abandon, doing handstands and cartwheels. There was something timeless about the rhythms and dancing of this celebration, emerging spontaneously from these moving bodies like sweat on a brow.

That day there was a big community meeting at the new school, no president or ministers in attendance, only farmers from the nearby villages who send their children to this school. It was said the official opening would happen later. According to the protocol at meetings, everyone had to be introduced and everyone had to give a short speech. Representatives from the different villages were invited to speak. I was surprised that many of them chose not to speak in Krio, but instead they requested that a person serve as an interpreter, to translate their native tongue of Loko or Maninka into Krio. These individuals claimed not to be able to speak Krio very well, and then launched into long speeches. In this isolated rural area, not only do people not know English, but they also don't know Krio very well, the ubiquitous language of markets and radio stations across Sierra Leone.

This language barrier highlighted the gap between the local communities and the English-based education of the schools. Few people in this part of rural Sierra Leone have ever been to school. Moreover, their discomfort with the Krio language shows they haven't even traveled much in Sierra Leone. Most of their lives were spent in the village and on the farm. These people send their children to school but know little about what happens there. The language of instruction at school is a foreign language to these families, as are the activities that take place there. Notably, among the people who work at the school, no one was born in the area; they all come from other places. The school is run by Themnes from Makeni; the principal and most of the teachers are Themnes who hail from other places. There is not necessarily any animosity between any of the ethnic groups but Themnes who run the school belong to different social circles and their families live in other towns; thus the divide between school and the local communities only becomes wider.

At last the new school building for Community Junior Secondary School in Waridala was open: new chairs, new benches, fresh paint, a shiny new tin roof. The familiar routine developed; the students came to learn, take notes from the board, and then go home at the end of the day. There were periods and lunch breaks and exams. Certainly it was a huge improvement from the old building, where there were no walls separating the different classrooms and the students didn't quite fit in the available space.

This building project highlights a persistent tension within education. Schools require buildings and books and blackboards—concrete, tangible objects. Yet these things are not education, which is unseen, invisible. Building a new school was a long and complicated process. Yet this work was simple compared to the work of bringing education to rural Sierra Leone, the end product of which exists only in the mind. The students and teachers and government officials who work at the schools in these rural areas navigate a tangled network of different languages, cultures and traditions, and the job has only just begun.

Epilogue

Six months after the construction, a few minor problems with the building were apparent, probably because of the embezzlement of funds. The latches on a couple of the doors broke. The blackboards were of poor quality and were difficult to erase. There was supposed to be solar power for the school, which never happened. The old principal, Mr. Sesay, left for a new job, but still had not resigned his position at the school. So the post was essentially empty, and remained so for quite a while as the slow machinery of the Sierra Leone governmental bureaucracy ground its gears. In the meantime, the vice principal was acting in his place.

The election came and went peacefully on November 17th, 2012, the first one solely administered by Sierra Leone since the war. The incumbent, Ernest Bai Koroma of the APC, was victorious. A vocal minority of the Maninka in Waridala switched to the APC for the election, but the rest stayed with the SLPP. The school, whether or not it was really a political favor, did not seem to sway people.

Obviously, significant corruption was involved with the construction of this new school. Yet the sort of informal favors often called corruption are an integral part of the culture in a small rural town like Waridala. Quite simply, Waridala does not operate by an economy of money. Everyone works as subsistence farmers; what they grow, they eat. At certain times of the years, they have no money at all. What they can't get from their own labor, they get from informal favors. They borrow. They beg. They make deals. "*N'kordor, n'kordor,*" the Maninka address their elder brother or sister, "Do you have any assistance for me today?" Rather than an economy of money, Waridala operates according to an economy of favors.

These informal favors follow certain rules. More important people have more privilege, yet at the same time they have greater obligations to their dependents. This means traditionally speaking, Alhaji Baba Fofana, the town chief in Waridala, should expect a cut from the new school project, simply by virtue of his seniority. At the same time, an important man like Alhaji Baba is expected to support his relatives who are less fortunate. Money and the concept of a zero-sum exchange was exported to Sierra Leone by the British, yet more traditional, informal ideas about exchange persist. In impoverished rural Sierra Leone, these informal favors are how people survive. However, what about people who are part of the modern economy in Sierra Leone and receive paychecks? They play the traditional game of favors but at the same time still benefit from a modern-style economy.

To join the modern world, Sierra Leone will have to leave behind some of its traditions; in the meantime, even relatively small projects like the Waridala school quickly become mired in corruption as everyone tries to get their share. The cost of the project was tremendous, especially considering that some of the work was done for free by the men in the village. But that is the cost of doing business in Sierra Leone.

Study the Koran with the Maninka

Long ago the Maninka people came to Sierra Leone as traders from the distant interior, places today known as Guinea and Mali. They brought their Islamic religion with them. Ever since then they have regarded themselves as among the bearers of Islam in Sierra Leone. Waridala used to be known as a center for Islamic education. Students came from around the country, sent by their families to live and work and study with the Maninka: Mendes from Bo, Themnes from Makeni, Yalunkas from Kabala.

One day I asked the town chief, Alhaji Baba Fofana, to tell me more about those days. I found him sitting under the awning made of palm fronds that stands in the center of town, where he often spends the afternoons, sitting in a plastic chair, fan in hand, dressed in white prayer robe and cap. Upon seeing me, he immediately offered me a chair and listened carefully to the questions I posed to him in Krio. He began his answer with complaints about the children these days, just like old people the world over like to do.

"In the past the children in town were not allowed to run around or play ball all day long," he said. "Only at night, after their work and studying were finished were they left to their own devices and allowed to play their games."

He told me in more detail about how Koranic learning in Waridala used to work. The Koran students used to live in Waridala for seven to fifteen years, studying every day. The students reached certain milestones in their study of the Koran, the *yasi*, the *ka*, and the final one, the *baraka*, when the student is finished studying. When a group of student reaches one of these benchmarks, the community used to hold a celebration, a *wala la bor*, where the village cooks large amounts of rice and everyone feasts.

Although the Koranic teachers not paid for their work, their students served as a formidable workforce on the farm. And the teachers did occasionally receive contributions from families. For example, every year during the Muslim holiday of Eid al Ada, students went home on a 10-day holiday to visit their families. When they came back, they were expected to bring the teacher a *banda bila*, a gift such as rice, chickens or goats. These were not only gifts to the teacher, but offerings to God, and the families hoped to receive blessings in proportion to what they gave.

When the students finished their studies after seven to fifteen years,, the fathers come to take their children, who were now young men. Often, the students, who were now adults, would leave Waridala with a Maninka wife, the daughter of one of the many families in town. When the fathers come to collect their children, they are expected to come with a *karan sara* to give to the teacher, one last offering to their child's teacher. The best and most fitting offering is a cow, though not every family can afford that. Upon their return home to their families, they would bring with them a deep knowledge of the Koran, eventually becoming Koranic teachers in their own communities.

"The teacher used to carry a whip when he taught the children," Alhaji Baba told me. "One mistake, the students felt it." The chief made a gesture with his hand to demonstrate the consequence of a mistake. He told me the whip was the *karanbinye*, the "study bullet." I was opposed to whipping children for their mistakes while studying, but the chief told me this anecdote with such a look of pride that I did not dare share my opinion.

"Back then, there was not a single person who did not go to the mosque," he continued. "Every Friday, everyone would go to the mosque. Back then, there was less sickness. In morning, we had a bitter medicine that we used to take." He touched his fist to his lips to indicate sipping from a cup. "A certain leaf was collected from the bush; boil it; add honey and lime to the pot; and then cover it for seven days. When we took this medicine, we never had a problem. No one dared to bring rum through town; this town was too holy. If a container of alcohol even entered the perimeter of the town, a case would be brought to the chief and the offender would be punished. In those days, the people in this village didn't sell all their crops in order to get money. People kept their harvest in reserve, so they had enough food to eat all year long.

"The back then, the elders didn't trust English education." Now the chief looked at me, right in the eye, implicitly acknowledging that I teach English classes at the local school. It was not a menacing look, but it was not friendly, either. His look simply acknowledged that my presence in the village and the existence of the school where I teach would not have been allowed in Waridala not too long ago.

"No one spoke in Krio in this village, or English," he continued. "Only Maninka and Arabic. The elders thought that if their children went to learn at the white man's school, they would not know their fathers. They would begin to drink. They would begin to smoke. They would stop working for their families. The elders thought these schools the white men were bringing would turn their children to *kafir*, Arabic for "unbeliever."

"Change came gradually. A few of the families decided to send one or two of their children to the white man's school, so they could learn the white man's language and so they could translate for their fathers when the white people came to the village. The elders didn't want the white people to rule us. More and more people began to send their children to school. They saw educated people go abroad, to England, America. They saw educated people become ministers. They saw people get money. Now, today, almost everyone sends their children to school. People believe if your children don't go to school, it is a problem.

"Today, everyone is rushing for money. They sell their harvest to get money and then later in the year they are hungry and they suffer because they do not have enough food to eat. There is more sickness, there is more malaria. People don't believe in the old medicine. If you get sick, you have to go to the clinic and pay 200,000 leones. Now the headmaster at the primary school is selling rum. Selling rum! In Waridala!

"Today, all the students of Arabic have gone. The population of Waridala has shrunk. We still have the traditional Arabic learning, but it is very small. Only families in the village send their children to learn. But not all the children in the village learn the Koran. It is not like it once was. The families in the village marry each other now because people don't come from outside. Two schools have been built in Waridala. They teach Arabic, but not much time is devoted to it, an hour here or there. All the rest of the learning is in English. How can the students learn Arabic like that?

"But the school brings much benefit," the chief assured me, as he drew his narrative to a close. This final assurance was a diplomatic gesture to me, I knew. But it was also a reluctant acknowledgement that his town had to join the modern push for English-based education or be left behind. Alhaji Baba clearly felt uncomfortable with the changes that had taken place in Waridala, but he also seemed to know that it would be useless to try to fight them.

I thanked the chief for his time and returned to my house. My head was spinning from the conversation. I was struck by Alhaji Baba's pride in his town's history, and his sadness and frustration with how things have changed. Certainly, his was not an objective account of the past and Alhaji Baba's recollections were colored by the warm glow of nostalgia. I had heard from other people about how hard the Koranic students used to work on their teachers' farms, about how poorly they were treated and about how little food they were given. But his story made sense to me. It explained why Waridala has these grand old concrete houses, gradually crumbling away with each season, while every other village nearby is made up exclusively of grass and mud houses; why Waridala has such a large mosque; and why someone decided to build a clocktower in town, such a strange and out of place landmark. In the past Waridala was a much more important place. People invested in the town, people in the town had money; Waridala used to matter. Gradually, everything changed. The construction of the Kabala highway—the main north-south artery of the area—bypassing Waridala about three miles to the east probably contributed to the town's decline. Sierra Leone's economic and political difficulties hit hard everywhere, even in Waridala. Now only the oldest in town—like Alhaji Baba—remember how things used to be.

ELECTION

2012
SIERRA LEONE

On the radio, a woman's voice, scratchy but audible, is reading the national tallies for the votes cast in the presidential election in Sierra Leone's 2012 election. Most of the candidates were minor and only received a few thousand total votes nationally. Then the woman, continuing to read slowly and methodically, reads off the tally for one candidate, a total that was clearly far bigger than the other candidates. A sound begins, not on the radio, I realize, but outdoors. It is the sound of cheering, as the people in town simultaneously hear the numbers announced on the radio and reach the same conclusion. Ernest Bai Koroma of the APC party, the incumbent president, has officially won the election. As the cheering swells and rises up over the rooftops of the town into the twilight sky, as children run through the field outside the window in excitement, the voice on the radio announces what the people have already realized just moments before.

Here in this town, Kamabai, the population is majority Limba, so support for the APC runs high. It is said not a single Limba in Sierra Leone belongs to another political party. On the main street, a short distance away, I can hear the thump of the bass as Sierra Leonean dance music begins, people starting up generators and turning on huge speakers to celebrate. Ernest Bai Koroma received 1,314,881 votes, 58.7 percent of the total and enough to avoid a runoff against the nearest challenger. One week after polling day, November 24th, the results of the 2012 election in Sierra Leone had finally been announced.

In the chaos that surrounded the announcement, people temporarily forgot that three weeks before the election, a murder took place in Kamabai. The victim was a middle-aged woman, married, with adult children, in good standing in her community. She lived on the main road down the hill by the second speed bump. One afternoon, she went missing. No one knew where she went, no one knew what happened to her. Some said her mutilated body was found behind the school. Some said a policeman was among those who found it. Yet no one wanted to say anything publicly. Because those who speak out are those who might be investigated as potential suspects. Instead, there were only rumors. For, if the rumors were at all true, this was a ritual murder, committed by a traditional doctor. The woman's body was dismembered. The body parts and the blood were utilized in ceremonies. Cannibalism is the word they whisper. That election year, someone decided to resort to dark arts, to assure a victory for their candidate and their party.

The government began organizing for the election in early 2012. In January of that year, the principal at CJSS, Mr. Sesay, temporarily left his job in order to work as a Ward Coordinator for the National Electoral Commission, or NEC. Teachers and principals formed a major part of election personnel and, as the election drew closer, more and more of the staff at my school were absent to fill positions at the NEC. The reason, it seemed, is that teachers have a basic education and can read and write and speak a little English; qualifications like these are not easy to find.

A month or two after the principal left, voter registration began, administered by the NEC. They called this process "exhibition." Temporary exhibition centers were opened throughout rural Sierra Leone, often a mud-and-grass house or a local school, marked by a few posters plastered on the wall and some white and orange marking ribbon. The official voting age is 18, an ostensibly precise number that in practice is quite vague. In rural areas there are no hospitals, no doctors, no birth certificates, and little documentation of any kind. Families are big and keeping track of time is imprecise. As a result, the age of any individual is a guess at best. No doubt filling out the parts of the registration paperwork concerning age and date of birth required some creative arithmetic. After the residents made the trip to their local exhibition center to give their names and addresses, they had to make a second trip back to confirm their names and addresses and pick up their plastic laminated ID card. For many people, this is the only form of ID that they have. Unfortunately some kind of mix-up occurred when the ID cards were distributed to the different exhibition centers and many of the cards went to the wrong pick-up locations. NEC then had to organize a "re-exhibition" to try a second time to unite all the ID cards with the correct people.

A month before the election, in October, the Sierra Leone Parliament closed its doors and the campaigning officially began. All campaigning was banned until this time. The two major political parties are the APC, All People's Congress, and the SLPP, the Sierra Leone's People's Party. The APC's color is red and its symbol the rising sun; the SLPP's color is green and its symbol is the palm tree. The two largest ethnic groups in the country, the Mendes and Themnes, dominate politics. The SLPP is the party of the Mendes in the south; the APC is the party of the Themnes in the north. The rest of the seventeen ethnic groups, for the most part, ally themselves with one of these two groups. In 2012, many candidates and many parties entered the election, but the SLPP and the APC candidates were the most prominent: Maada Bio for the SLPP and Ernest Bai Koroma, the incumbent, for the APC.

The history of the two parties is tied up with the tumultuous events that took place post-independence. In short, the SLPP party is associated with Milton Margai, the country's first prime minister, while the APC is connected to Siaka Stevens, a critic of Margai who broke off to form the APC and led the country during the 70's and 80's. The relationship between the two parties has never been amicable, persisting to the present day. Once campaigning began in 2012, people seemed wary. Public announcements were periodically aired on the radio in Krio, encouraging people to keep this election peaceful and violence-free.

In a book I happened to be reading at the time, author Aminata Forna recounts living in Sierra Leone as a child during the politically turbulent times of the 60's in the town of Koidu. She writes:

> One afternoon, on the way back to our house from school, with we three children in the car, my mother turned a corner and drove into a pitched battle between several hundred APC and SLPP supporters on the main

street in town. Some people were waving guns, others hitting each other with their fists, sticks, anything they could lay their hands on. My mother pulled up, intending to reverse out. But the people nearby, who were as much engaged in the fighting as anyone else, recognized our car and started to shout for people to clear the road. There was a pause in the battle, like a black and white movie when the music stops, and we drove through the crowd. When we emerged on the other side and looked out of the rear window, the music and fighting had started up again.

– from *The Devil that Danced on Water*

By the 70's, the APC took power and outlawed all opposition parties, including the SLPP, and made the country into a one-party state. During this time, Siaka Stevens was president, essentially making himself into a dictator. In the 90's the country descended into a long period of violence that transcended political parties. The first two elections after the civil war, in 2002 and 2007, were administered by the UN. This election, in 2012, was the first one run by Sierra Leone. No one knew quite what to expect.

The village of Waridala is mostly populated by Maninka people and they traditionally vote SLPP. For this election, the APC was trying to make them switch parties. One man, born in Waridala who had risen to the position of ambassador to Iran, was a staunch APC man and took it upon himself to get his hometown to vote APC. Waridala was quiet until the Muslim holiday of Eid al Ada. On that day the ambassador and various other Maninka APC supporters tried to turn the holiday into a political rally. Campaigning in Sierra Leone does not involve much discussion of politics. Besides the colors and the logos, there did not seem to be any major differences between the two parties. Instead, campaigning seemed to have more in common with a sporting event. People wore red clothes, the more completely red the outfit, the better. During Eid al Ada, impromptu parades moved through town, participants chanting slogans and banging pots. A popular slogan that year was *"O ai e! O sai e!"* No one could explain to me what it meant, although I suspect it was a Themne phrase.

The ambassador put up a huge APC poster on a prominent veranda, featuring a picture of himself and the president. He also sacrificed a young bull in the name of an APC victory. The APC supporters made a few speeches, which mostly seemed to consist of promises—of future prosperity, to build new houses in the village, to construct a health clinic and a community center. In some cases, campaigners simply went around and handed out money to people in order to bolster support. At one point during the day of festivities some SLPP youth came from a neighboring Maninka village, dressed in green and riding motorcycles, showing off their support for the SLPP. Their motorcycles were decorated with green cloth and palm fronds, representing the SLPP palm tree. The youth whooped and hollered and revved their engines, making a few visits to prominent residents before departing.

A few weeks before the election, the president himself made a visit to the nearby village of Karina, another Maninka village with strong SLPP support. I went to see the event with a few of my friends. When I arrived, the normally tranquil town of Karina felt like a party. Music blared. People were in the streets. And everyone was wearing red. It seemed that many of the president's supporters follow him around on the campaign trail because I had never seen the town this full. School children lined up along the road to welcome the president and soon the red-clad revelers lined up along with them. When the president finally arrived, he got out of his vehicle and walked along the road; a cheering crowd of people formed around him and only his baseball cap and silver sideburns were visible at the center of the chaos.

On the day of the election, I was in Kamabai, about ten miles from Waridala. The Peace Corps administration, out of an abundance of caution, had every volunteer in the country move to consolidation points, as they called them, usually volunteers' houses in central locations. Just in case of violence or unrest.

Kamabai was my consolidation point. With my Peace Corps friend who lived in Kamabai, I visited one of the polling centers, a primary school, which, we were told, had been open since five in the morning. Now the sun was up and it was hot. People were in long lines outside of one of the local schools, sweating in the sun as they waited for their turn to vote. As my friend and I are both white, and the fact we were the only visible foreigners around, many assumed that we were observers from the UN. The voting procedure, it seemed, was rather complicated, apparently involving multiple ballot papers for presidential, parliamentary, and regional elections. The process was confusing for some people, especially old people who didn't know how to read. After a person voted, their finger was dipped in purple ink to prevent anyone from voting twice.

Election day passed in Kamabai without much incident, apart from some rumors of SLPP supporters stealing ballot boxes in the nearby city of Makeni. Now it was time to wait. According to the constitution of Sierra Leone, the election results must be announced within ten days of an election. One week after the election, in the evening, Christiana Thorpe, the chair of the NEC, announced the results on the radio: Sierra Leone had elected Ernest Bai Koroma to a second term. Immediately after the announcement, the president was brought to the State House for swearing in. Some fallout occurred after the election: Some cities in the south had to impose curfews and some of the SLPP members of Parliament claimed the elections were fraudulent and threatened to boycott Parliament. However, international observers as well as local people agreed that Sierra Leone held a peaceful election that was free and fair. It was a tremendous accomplishment and a confidence boost for a country still rebuilding from war. An election was occurring almost simultaneously in my own country, the 2012 presidential election, and although I received an absentee ballot, it didn't make it into my hands until after the U.S. election day. I didn't send it back. During that time, I was far more invested in Sierra Leone's election; even though I couldn't vote in it, I felt proud of the country's accomplishment and of all the hard work that people had put in.

The investigation into the murder in Kamabai was put off until after the election results were announced.

One day, not too long after the announcement of the results, I was in Kamabai again. Immediately when I arrived, I noticed a strange, electric atmosphere had settled over the main road through town and people were milling around or standing together knotted in small groups. Something had happened. I saw one of my friends on the street, a teacher—I recognized his trim frame and baseball cap immediately—and I asked him what was going on. He is a local, and a Limba, so he knew everything. But more than that, he had always struck me as a thoughtful and careful man, and I took him to be a reliable source. He said it was about the murder, and in a low voice, he proceeded to tell me the story.

The missing woman's three sons wanted to know what happened to their mother, so they traveled to Kamabai from wherever they were living in order to push for an investigation. At the behest of the brothers, a team of traditional doctors was summoned to locate the body. However, it was not yet possible to begin the investigation. The paramount chief, the highest local authority in Biriwa Chiefdom, was not at his residence in Kamabai. He was away; no one knew quite where he was or when he was coming back. According to what my friend told me, the traditional doctors could not start their work without the permission of the paramount chief. His inconvenient absence made it clear to some people, including my friend, that he had somehow been involved in the woman's disappearance: He didn't want the investigation to go forward. The paramount chief and the other local authorities wanted the matter to be left alone. In the midst of Sierra Leone's peaceful democratic election, it was clear that traditional beliefs about ceremonies and the secret powers of blood still persisted.

The Limbas in Kamabai were divided, according to my friend. Some believed the investigation should go forward and other people did not. The three brothers, however, were not deterred. They wanted the investigation to go forward so they could locate their mother's body. However, apart from the resistance from the paramount chief, there was another obstacle: The brothers needed to pay the traditional doctors for their work, yet all three of them were very poor. Eventually, the brothers somehow found the money to pay the doctors and the doctors claimed that they knew the location of the body, but they still could not move forward as long as the paramount chief withheld permission. As is too often the case around the world, there is no justice for the poor. It takes money and social standing to make things happen, two things which the brothers had very little of.

Just before I arrived in Kamabai that day, my friend continued to explain, an angry mob had gathered outside the paramount chief's house, demanding that the investigation go forward. Some people had begun to throw rocks at the house, breaking a few windows. The mob had since dispersed, but tensions remained high in town—that explained the strange feeling in the air I had noticed immediately upon my arrival. My friend ended his narrative here and we talked of other things. But I couldn't shake a sinking feeling of horror, to hear such a sad tale about the brothers, how little recourse they had. And the whispers of secret ceremonies made me shudder. As a foreigner, I was removed from this conflict, yet at the same time I was close enough to feel it.

A week later, I was shocked to learn that my friend had been taken to jail in Makeni and locked up. He was accused of being among those who stoned the paramount chief's house. My friend had done nothing, as far I could tell; he was simply a bystander in the authorities' attempt to exert control and maintain the status quo. I didn't know what was going to happen to him now. The thought crossed my mind that I would never see him again. He had confided in me about this trouble and I somehow felt implicated; I needed to help, to do something. But I didn't know what, or how. And the whole affair made me uneasy. I did nothing except wait.

When I saw him again, he was at his usual stall at the weekly market in Katana. He had been in jail for fifteen days. It was a relief to see him again, unharmed, and I tried to tell him how glad I was. He acted nonchalant about the whole thing, commenting that he had seen the inside of a prison and seen the kind of life that some people live there and now he was out again. That was all he had to say.

My friend, along with the other people jailed for the alleged vandalism and rioting in Kamabai, had to get a lawyer. The group pooled funds to hire a lawyer from Freetown to come to Makeni to defend them in court. Over the next several weeks, my friend and the others had to take several trips to Makeni to appear in court, but nothing happened because the paramount chief did not show up for the court appointments.

Around that same time, human bones were found in Kamabai, concealed behind a house not too far from where the missing woman used to live. The residents of the house knew nothing about the bones, nor had they seen any animals stripping the bones. No one knew how the bones got there. An expert from Freetown came to collect the bones for analysis, yet once the bones were removed it was said that more were found in the same place.

The investigation stood open, unresolved. Exactly what happened to the missing woman in Kamabai was a mystery. No one could speak out for fear of retribution, so the ball of secrets only tied itself tighter.

Watching the Sierra Leone's election process, I got the sense that democratic elections were somehow foreign to the sensibility of Sierra Leoneans. It seemed at times that they were trying to adhere to an ideal that they didn't quite understand, or even hold themselves. Some people seemed to think that voting against the incumbent president was somehow disrespectful. The president, after all, is the biggest man in the country. Sierra Leoneans have a strong sense of social hierarchy, and people of lower status must always defer to those of higher status and give them respect: Voting runs contrary to that basic social instinct. There were posters and advertisements on the radio urging people that they needed to choose for themselves who to vote for, something that didn't really seem to be happening at all. Instead, the whole idea of voting had been somehow subsumed under ethnic identify, making the label of democratic elections questionable.

And there was the murder. An incident like the one that happened in Kamabai is not unprecedented. People tell stories about similar events happening during past elections—about women or girls missing, kidnapped, or murdered, their bodies used in secret rituals thought to give power to favored candidates and sway elections. But it is impossible to say how widespread it is, how many different traditional doctors were at work during the election. It could have been an isolated incident. But such ceremonies are always hidden and secret, by their very nature, so it is impossible to know for sure.

This election seemed to have two faces. One was the institutional face, of NEC, exhibition centers, polling days, and ink-dipped finger tips. This public, institutional face of the election was widely viewed as a success: Sierra Leone held peaceful elections without the help of the UN, a major milestone in the country's efforts to rebuild after the conflict of the 90's. But another face was there, too, of secrets and rituals. Sierra Leone wears the trappings of democracy uneasily, for it is apparent that deeper, more ancient traditions continue to define people's lives. Some in Sierra Leone still see their president as a traditional chief, who maintains power not through democratic elections but a combination of wisdom, status, and help from traditional doctors.

TOWARDS

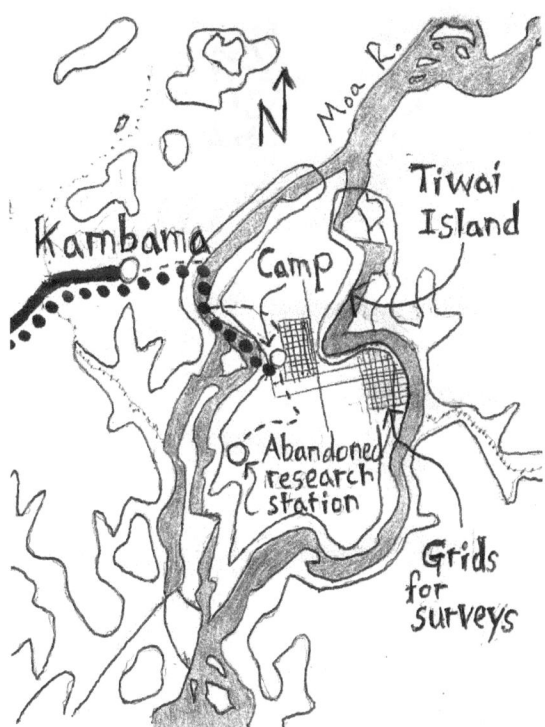

TIWAI

It was my second year of teaching in Sierra Leone, and the December holiday was drawing near, so I decided to travel with some other Peace Corps volunteers to Tiwai Island, a wildlife preserve in the southern part of the country. I wanted to leave Waridala, see some new places, and sketch what I saw. And I wanted to do it by bicycle.

I packed a small bag with some extra clothes, some bicycle tools, and some sketching materials and tied it to the rear rack of my bike. It was a Trek mountain bike, the kind the Peace Corps issued to all of the volunteers, blue, white and black, not fancy but much studier than most of the local bikes. The next morning, I left Waridala at dawn, heading south. As I pedaled, the silhouettes of the hills above Kamabai were sharp against the early morning light. I felt free and light and full of energy.

Kamabai hills at dawn

Soon the sun had climbed up over the horizon, and the harmattan winds had begun to blow, as they do every December. On this day, the harmattan was particular vigorous, shaking the long elephant grass and ruffling the neat symmetry of the palm trees. It was a strange contrast between the heat of the sun and the cool breeze from the north.

Palm trees in the harmattan

I decided to take the scenic route, circling through the town of Bumban. Alongside the primitive rocky road to Bumban, big bluffs rise against the sky, capped by bare rocks. The town of Bumban is located at a cul-de-sac: Here is the end of the road, and the rocky bluffs frame the town on three sides. It was a strange, dreamy town: old concrete buildings with rusting tin roofs tucked away into this forgotten corner of Sierra Leone. The locals, mostly Limba, sat peacefully on their verandas and watched me, some of them inviting me to sit and chat. When the children saw me, they called out, "Father! Father!," for Catholic priests are the light-skinned people they most commonly see. There is a Catholic church in town, run by Spanish missionaries, and since I was there on a Sunday, I could hear the polyrhythms of traditional drumming emanating from the Catholic church, as people prepared for mid-morning mass.

Once upon a time Bumban was located on a trade route that traced its way between these rocky bluffs, an artery for goods being carried between the inner regions of West Africa and the coast. However, the swells of commerce had long since receded from this quiet town. I asked about the back way to Bumbuna, but I was told that there is only a rocky footpath that goes directly over the hills. Reluctantly, I returned the way I came. I almost felt embarrassed for having entered this town for no real reason.

Eventually, I took the main route to the town of Bumbuna, not to be confused with the village of Bumban that I had just visited. Now, I followed the well-traveled gravel road, everything bathed in a layer of orange dust kicked up by mining traffic. The mining at Bumbuna was being carried out by African Minerals, a British company, so many of the vehicles were emblazoned with the company's logo. Bumbuna is well known as the site of a large hydroelectric project, and a large iron mine is in the hills nearby.

Local women walked along the shoulder of this road, many of them barefoot, carrying tubs of laundry or a bundle of firewood on their heads. The menial tasks of rural farmers were a sharp contrast with the industrial power of the large-scale mining project happening up the road. I felt a sense of horror to witness such disparities of wealth like this. Even though I had come to the country to contribute to its improvement and development, the people along this roadside seemed at the whim of forces beyond anyone's control.

Near the junction to Bumbuna

New high-voltage power lines come from Bumbuna Dam, marching through the bush, and at one point I paused at the top of a hill to look at them. A man walking along the road stopped to complain to me. He told me the power lines were installed on his people's land where they make their farms every year, yet they never received any compensation. He was telling me this because I am white and he had a glimmer of hope I might be a person who could do something about it. It felt awkward to consider how much power I was perceived to have, simply due to my skin color, not from something I did or achieved or earned. I politely listened and then excused myself to continue riding. I knew that communal land agreements controlled by word of mouth are no match for large-scale infrastructure projects driven by foreign donations.

Power lines near Bumbuna

    I continued along the dusty road but soon encountered a problem: a flat tire. I was able to fix it easily enough, but the pump I had was not working properly, so I could not inflate the tire. Three old Limba women were nearby, selling palm wine and drinking some of it themselves. I approached them and bought a cup, while I considered my options. The women chatted with each other in Limba and eventually one them summarized the conversation int Krio for me. She pointed at one of her companions and explained, "Na you uman dis beca e yelo lek yu," which is to say, "This is your wife because she has light skin like you." I glanced at the woman, about two shades lighter than her companions, as all the women cackled enthusiastically at the joke. I laughed, too, not quite sure what else to do.
    After the palm wine, I was directed by some helpful people in the village to the local bike mechanic, i.e. the guy with a bag of tools in his house. I had to wait in the shade of a palm leaf hut until the mechanic was summoned from harvesting rice in the bush, a young man named Idrissa. When he returned, he retrieved his bag of tools, patched and pumped the tube and then we had a rousing argument about the price before I went on my way. It wasn't longer before I realized the inner tube was

still leaking and my pump was still not working. I had to resort to pushing my bicycle down the road.

I didn't have to push for long before I came upon three young men gathered around a bicycle in front of a veranda. These men, too, were having repair difficulties. They had a broken bicycle pump and I watched as they attempted to insert the valve stem of an inner tube into a hole in the body of the pump. They showed me their pump and laughed at their pathetic tool. One of the young men introduced himself to me as Amidu, a driver whose *poda poda* had broken down nearby. He told me he'd been stuck in the village for two days waiting for repairs. Helpfully, Amidu removed a few non-essential nuts from his vehicle and somehow used them to help me repair my inner tube.

At last, I sped along the orange gravel road as best I could, the shadows growing long. I felt a growing sense of desperation, for I knew I didn't have anywhere to stay for the night. But at the same time, I welcomed the sense of risk, of uncertainty. It was thrilling to be on my own and on the road. I passed a stream by the side of the road, where a very pregnant woman was washing herself and her small child, both nearly naked, both feeling safe and close to home.

Finally arriving in Bumbuna, a dusty medium-sized town, I asked around for a place to stay. Some people suggested I ask the paramount chief, who received me in the palm leaf hut adjacent to his large and expensive concrete house and told me to talk to the section chief, who is responsible for accommodation of travelers. On my way to the other chief's residence, I happened to run into a man who claimed he had met before in Makeni. He told me he would be happy to accommodate me for the night. Even though I didn't quite remember having met him before, I immediately agreed, given my lack of other options. Again, I felt the risk, I knew it seemed like a bad idea, the kind of decision that feels awkward to explain later, when something has gone wrong. In other words, I really should have known better. But I had no other options at that point, and part of me continued to relish the unknown.

I still visited the section chief, who subjected my new friend, Fada K, to an interview and a lecture. The performance made me feel slightly better. It was a study of contrasts: on the one hand was Section Chief Sulaiman Fona, a middle-aged Muslim man who had just returned from evening prayer, still clad in a prayer cap and gown; on the other hand, was Fada K, leaning against the railing, wearing bright-red jeans and a baseball cap, a pair of headphones over his ears. Fada K listened to the lecture, agreed to be responsible for me for the night and "hold me fine" as they say in Krio. Then I went off with my new friend, through the dimly lit streets, streetlights powered by electricity from the nearby dam.

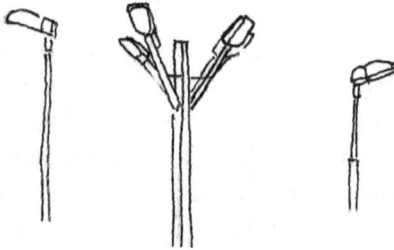

Streetlights in Bumbuna

As we walked, Fada K told me how he was waiting for a job in Bumbuna, how people say that African Minerals will be hiring again in January. He spoke English well and knew some American slang, lacing conversations with the all-purpose "f" word, as in "those fucking bitches are fucking crazy." He told me about his album-release party next month—Fada K is his stage name—and invited me to come.

That night we visited the makeshift shed that served as Bumbuna's bar, where a small group of people danced to the music booming from the speakers with the sort of abandon that I had come to associate with Sierra Leone. My fellow dancers showed me the Azonto, the latest dance craze, which I can only say involves moving your foot in a way that I was unable to make look cool. Later I shared Fada K's small room for some fitful hours of sleep. When morning came, I was relieved and ready to ride again.

Everyone I spoke with that night, it seemed, had come to Bumbuna to look for a job at African Minerals but no one had found work yet. Everyone was still waiting. These masses of unemployed people, like Fada K, received support in the meantime from their friends and families who have jobs. This town of unemployed people ran according to a shadow economy, as people spent money they themselves didn't earn, everyone held up by an invisible network of relationships and responsibilities. While I will never know what it is like to wait in Bumbuna for employment like so many do, I wondered if I had gotten close, coming to town without a place to stay, my life suddenly dependent on the generosity of those around me, unsure of what the next day would bring. Yet the biggest difference was I could so easily leave that town and that life.

In the daylight, it was possible to see a flat area on the top of a hill high above Bumbuna, cut into the orange soil. This was the site of the so-called Nine Hundred Man Camp, the work camp for the employees of African Minerals, where the ones who are lucky enough to secure a job sleep and eat, looking down on the town and those waiting, below.

Flat terrain near Magburaka

The next day, after I said farewell to Fada K, I pedaled along the pothole-littered road until finally I reached the main road and arrived in Magburaka, a regional capital and a much bigger town than Bumbuna, where I stayed with another Peace Corps volunteer for a much-welcome day of rest. It was a relief to have predictable accommodations; it was quiet and safe staying with other Americans, although there was no dancing.

Kono highway

From Magburaka, I headed east, going towards the mountains that blanket the northeastern part of the country. This was on a beautiful paved road, constructed by a German firm a roadside sign told me, all the way to Matatoka. It was market day in Matatoka, when petty traders and customers come together for the weekly market held along the highway. The road was overrun with people, buying dried fish, onions and salt for the day's afternoon meal, shopping for flip flops, or browsing racks of jeans and piles of second-hand clothes from abroad.

Past Matatoka, where steep green hills begin to loom against the sky, the road suddenly began to deteriorate, with patchy pavement interspaced with rough gravel and potholes. During the war, this area of the country was controlled by the rebels and they tore up parts of the road heading to the east, contributing to the dilapidated state of the road. Roads are bad across the country, but this part was spectacularly bad. During the last rainy season, I was told, the road became all but impassable due to mud and it had been impossible for busses and cars to go to Kono. Travelers who were heading out east had had to hire a motorcycle taxi. But this was December, well into the dry season, and the road surface had dried out and firmed up, scars from the rainy season still evident. Memories of the war seem to haunt the entire country, but this damaged road was among the few physical signs I had seen of it.

The road climbed up and wound through the hills, nothing along the highway except the tree-covered slopes and occasional small dust-covered village. I passed through the town of Makali, where I did my best to endure, with a smile, a mock interrogation by a drunk out-of-uniform police officer. Finally, I reached Masingbi, where I planned to meet some other friends in the Peace Corps who were going to ride with me to Tiwai Island. The town is located on the top of a rise, among broad, rolling hills with a covering of yellow grass and a dotting of palm trees. Tall cell phone towers lined the top of the ridge, and later I learned that when they were constructed, they were left ungrounded, leading to spectacular thunderstorms because lighting bounces off the towers in unpredictable directions.

Cell towers near Masingbi

As a Themne enclave, Masingbi is a one-language town. If you are a newcomer to the town and don't speak the language, either you learn Themne, or the town people will drive you out, I was told. People don't even speak Krio very much. *Opoto* is the word yelled by children across the Themne-dominated regions of northern Sierra Leone—and any white person quickly becomes familiar with: Themne for "white person." As we strolled around town looking for dinner, Corey, the volunteer living in Masingbi, helpfully demonstrated just how Themne-centric the town was. A small child asked, "Where is your dog?" –because Corey had adopted a dog, Rafiki, during his stay in Masingbi. He replied in Krio: *"E de pan it pikin,"* that is, "He is eating children." The child did not respond to the joke but stared blankly. Then Corey rephrased it in Themne: *Oi i kakadi an fet.* Only then did the child break out into laughter. So it is in Masignbi: either Themne or nothing at all.

In Masingbi four other volunteers joined me on the ride—a welcome addition to what so far had been lonely pedaling. Two of them, Corey and Madison, were the married couple who were posted to Masingbi, plus the volunteer from Matatoka, Bryan, and another American visiting from the U.S., Bryan's relative. We were quite a sight, I am sure, all of us with our matching blue, black and white Trek mountain bikes from the Peace Corps, pedaling determinedly down the road.

The morning we departed was surprisingly cold. Our breath turned to fog because it was harmattan season and we were at a higher elevation. From Masingbi we turned off the Kono road onto a simple dirt road, heading south towards Boajibu. It appeared possible for four-wheeled vehicles to travel on this road, but it didn't seem to happen very often; most of the traffic we saw was foot traffic with the occasional motorcycle taxi. We passed a few tortuously overloaded trucks, piled high with people and bags, though they were not moving much faster than a walking pace, leaving behind a wafting trail of black exhaust. In the villages along the road, people were warming themselves by small fires in the chilly morning air, everyone bundled up with a random collection of sweatshirts, sweaters, and warm hats. Thick socks worn with flip-flops were a popular accessory.

After about five miles, we crossed into Mende territory. While Themnes are the majority tribe in the north, Mendes are the majority in the south. It was quite easy for us to tell when we had crossed the line: In Mende, the children say *pumoi* when they see a white person. The Mende culture is known to be less aggressive; perhaps this difference was easiest to see in the children. As one of my friends pointed out, when the Themne children say *opoto*, it sounds a little bit like they are swearing at you, but when the Mende children say *pumoi*, it sounds more like a question. I admit I felt a sense of relief to leave behind the shouts of *opoto*. Despite the differences in tone, *pumoi* and *opoto* have the faint vestiges of a common origin: both are corruptions of "Portuguese," the first white people to come to Sierra Leone.

As we headed south, the road became steeper, the ruts deeper and the vegetation thicker. We left behind the grassy hills around Masingbi, and followed the bumpy road into groves of tall, close-set trees and profuse undergrowth. In one small village I bought a bunch of huge yellow bananas that were like a meal.

Above the Sewa River valley

At one point the road came to the brink of a sharp drop in elevation, and I could see for miles over successive lines of forest ridges, each one crested by rows of palm trees. It was a beautiful vista, raw and elemental, and looking out across those green hills, I felt I could glimpse some secret shining future for Sierra Leone, someday, somehow. Then the road dropped down hundreds of feet in elevation into the Sewa River valley below, and we navigated ruts that were three feet deep. At the bottom of the descent was the town of Conta. When we arrived it was Friday, just after two o'clock, and people were in the streets in their prayer clothes, walking home from Friday prayer at the mosque. Two called out to me in French – *Ce va?* – and it turned out they were from neighboring Guinea, where French is the language of the white people. Oddly, I was able to converse with them more in Maninka – their native language and the language of Waridala – than in French. They told me they were involved in diamond work in the area – buying, appraising, and selling. As I continued onwards, the men told me *"Merci! Merci!"* and shook hands with me warmly.

From Conta we continued on towards Boajibu, following the relatively flat terrain along the Sewa River. Along the road we passed rubber tree plantations, each tree bearing an inverted triangle of machete scars, with a small metal cup collecting sap slowly dripping from the disturbed bark. At Gendema the road crosses the Sewa River; here it was necessary to take a ferry, which was little more than a dock connected by pulleys to a pair of cables that run across the river. The vessel, if you could call it that, was capable of carrying vehicles across but there were only foot passengers on that day.

Ferry equipment

We pushed our bikes onto the ferry along with the handful of other passengers. It was the task of three men to move the ferry across the river. Each man had a club-shaped piece of wood with a notch in it. He fitted the notch onto the cable that stretches across the river and pulled on the piece of wood, pulling the ferry forward. Then he unhooked the piece of wood and repeated the process. With three men doing this, the ferry soon was across the river. The ferrymen's movements were quick and efficient, but the set-up of the vessel, dangling in the current, seemed unbelievably precarious.

After we crossed the Sewa, it was a short distance to the town of Boajibu, where we stayed for the night at another Peace Corps friend's house. The memories of war were particularly visible in this town. I was told that Boajibu once had electricity, provided by a small hydroelectric dam nearby, but not anymore as the wires were destroyed during the war. And I noticed the power poles, lines broken and hanging limply from the poles. It is said that this road, which passes through Boajibu, was one of the routes the rebels often took during the war, and the area was particularly hard hit. Even though I was only a traveler passing through, I distinctly felt a twinge of loss, at what once had been, and at what the town could have been had the conflict never happened. I could only imagine the toll it had taken on those who lived through it.

Broken power lines in Boajibu

The next section of road was a relatively smooth and flat ride on a gravel road south to the town of Blama. Compared to the isolated bush villages we had been traveling through, Blama seemed luxurious, a junction town on the Bo-Kenema highway with copious amounts and types of food for sale on the streets and vehicles passing through. We stayed the night at another volunteer's residence here. I saw on the map what seemed like a short route to Tiwai Island directly from Blama on back roads. I couldn't convince my riding partners to go along, so I pedaled down this road to try it out, with a plan to meet them at Tiwai. I was disappointed and felt a little bit anxious to be alone again, but I also somehow felt freer.

Forest south of Blama

At first, the gravel road was in good condition, broad and mostly flat. People were out walking, many seemed to be families going to work on the farm, father, mother and a few trailing children walking together, carrying buckets and bundles on their heads. At one point I passed a pair of mud and grass houses along the road, set off by themselves in the bush. When I stopped to look, I realized it was a school, a junior secondary school in fact. The name of each form – JSSI, JSSII, JSSII – was labeled above the appropriate door in chalk. I also passed a sign for Tobanda Refugee Camp that was slowly disappearing into the encroaching brush, a reminder of the civil war that was over but not yet gone.

Junior secondary school building

Mosque at Boajibu

A young rubber tree on a plantation

In the village of Sendeima I stopped to ask directions. When I told people that I was going to Tiwai Island, they gave me some vague directions, though I got the sense that maybe they didn't really know what I was talking about and made up something to tell me so as not to let me down.

As I approached a fork in the road, I saw four men on one motorcycle, stopped by the side of the road. I again asked directions, and the four men had an animated discussion. A few farmers who were passing by joined in the debate. They reached a consensus: both forks go to Tiwai, but they suggested that I go right, on the well-traveled road. Once all my would-be guides left me and continued on to their destinations, however, I chose the less traveled road, in the interest of adventure if nothing else.

Soon the road became overgrown, and the only tracks were from motorcycles, which had worn a narrow one-track path into the gravel. Strangely enough, I spotted traffic signs on this road, half swallowed by brush, announcing the speed limit, or the presence of upcoming steep hills or narrow bridges. It was surreal, given the lack of traffic on this road, and I couldn't imagine why they had been installed or who had installed them.

I passed through the village of Menima, a peaceful town where only a few of the houses had tin roofs; all the others were made entirely from palm thatch and mud and sticks. When I saw houses like these next to a dusty gravel road with heavy mining traffic, they seemed impoverished compared to Bumbuna, but on this isolated road, the architecture of these mud-and-palm leaf houses was simple and graceful. I asked directions again to Tiwai Island and in this village they seemed to understand more what I was talking about. One woman even told me, "That place is our home."

I came to the next village, Joi, where I met an old man sharpening a machete on a rock on the ground. He joked with me, claiming he was the police in town and that I needed to pay him Le 2,000. Then he abruptly walked off, perhaps going to the bush to work, not waiting for me to answer him.

House along the road

After Joi, the road became even more overgrown, and the road signs disappeared. At one point, the track passed through a grove of huge bamboo plants, fifty feet tall or more, growing in huge clusters and curving cathedral-like over the road. My feeling of traveling through a dream only deepened.

In the little village of Kamasu, the village carpenter who introduced himself as Mohamed Sheriff was at work near the road, busy making a bed frame. After greeting me he launched into a rant about how Africans are not honest – "Black man, he bad o!" – and how everyone turns white when they go to heaven. Then he told a story about a white man he knew who had a motorcycle with two engines that could fly. He seemed a little bit crazy, but he did express a widespread sentiment in Sierra Leone: a deep-seated ideology that favors white people.

In the same village, I passed a group of men putting palm leaf roofing onto a new house. They stopped work to watch me pass. I greeted them, and a man, who called himself Samuel, said that he was fine, *"pass dis yagba we de pan wi,"* that is, "except for this hassle we are facing," suggesting the exhausting work of roofing the house. Then an older man, who was balancing at the very top of the new roof, began making exaggerated gestures in my direction, including puffing motions.

Village of Serabu

    Another one of the men working on the house traced a numeral "two" in the air with his finger. Finally, I understood that they wanted me to buy them 2,000 leones worth of weed. No doubt it would help pass the long workday in the sun. Despite the pervasive racial ideologies, regarding wealth and the lack thereof, that hung over this chance encounter, I gave them the 2,000 leones that they asked for.

    In the village of Serabu, I stopped to rest of a while and of course all the children gathered around to stare and the men asked me every questions they could think of, about where I was going and where I was coming from. After Serabu, the road became a dirt footpath through the bush, though it was well maintained. Small trails veered off towards farms in the bush and I passed a few people heading to their destinations on foot. I made good progress all the way to the main gravel road, where it was a short ride to the village of Kambama. This village is on the shore of the Moa River, right across from Tiwai Island. Finally, after five days of riding, I had arrived.

The road south of Joi

When I reached Kambama, something changed and I was suddenly a tourist. The change was abrupt and weird. In most of the villages I had passed through the people didn't know how to respond to a white person except to stare or ask me for weed money. Here in Kambama they were all set up to take white people's money in a more systematic way. I spoke with a man in a blue vest and a clipboard—oddly formal—then I left my bike in a locked shed, where the other volunteers' bicycles had already been stashed, and another man took me out into the river in a small motorboat. A motorboat! The luxury of it was surprising. Tiwai Island is in the middle of the Moa River; Tiwai, in fact, means "big" in Mende. The boat sped down the blue-gray waters of the Moa, quick and noisy through the wide and slow river, the thick green vegetation spilling into the water on both sides. I felt for a moment that the man driving the boat could take me anywhere he wanted, and no one would ever know where I had gone.

Suddenly the driver pulled the boat into a small sandy inlet among the palm trees and brush. After a short walk, we came to a clearing with a few pavilions and buildings made of concrete, the main camping area. My momentary vision of being kidnapped suddenly seemed silly. I was reunited with the other volunteers here, who were glad to see that I had successfully found my way to the island. The staff at the camp provided us with tents and also cooked for us. We were many black, broken only by the light from a few bare bulbs, and the forest. incessant buzz of the insects in the miles from the nearest town and soon the night came, thick and

The next morning, we woke up early to go on a walk with a guide. Through gaps in the foliage, we could look up into the canopy, where the treetops were framed by the early morning mist, washed by the light of the rising sun. At first I couldn't discern anything, only the hum and howl of the insects and the insatiable greenery. Then I realized they were all around us. We peered into the treetops and we saw them: The monkeys were everywhere. Some were black and white, others were a bright-red orange color.

Black and white colobus monkey

Only later I learned their names: the black, white and red Diana monkey (Mende: *kelli*), the red colobus monkey (Mende: *kuaa gboi*), and the black and white colobus monkey (Mende: *tuwei*). We saw a mother monkey and her baby high in a tree, nibling on bunches of flowers. They were not exactly discrete.

When they moved, it sounded like large branches plummeting from the treetops. Then a trickle of debris would fall from the heights, broken twigs and leaves. The guide knew the different kinds of calls that the monkeys made, and he told us the purpose of the calls and occasionally let off a few of his own monkey calls in response. They are skittish creatures and when they saw us they would quickly escape into another secret pocket of the treetops, though sometimes they would stop to peer at us with an eerie human-like gaze. It was creepy, the stuff of visions and nightmares, a face that watches you from the heart of the forest.

Bamboo on Tiwai

The island seemed to be full of termites; they were spilling out of holes in the ground everywhere, as they consumed the copious amounts of dead plant material on the island. If footsteps interrupted their labors, the little insects would vibrate their bodies, giving off a distinctive rattling sound. We were told that chimpanzees and rare pygmy hippopotamus live on the island, though we did not see either. We did see the site where researchers had documented tool use by the chimps. Our guide pointed out the place where the chimps use sticks and rocks to open seed pods.

The trees on the island were impressive: Many of the species have buttress roots. The top half of the roots rises out of the ground forming series of long narrow ridges that run out

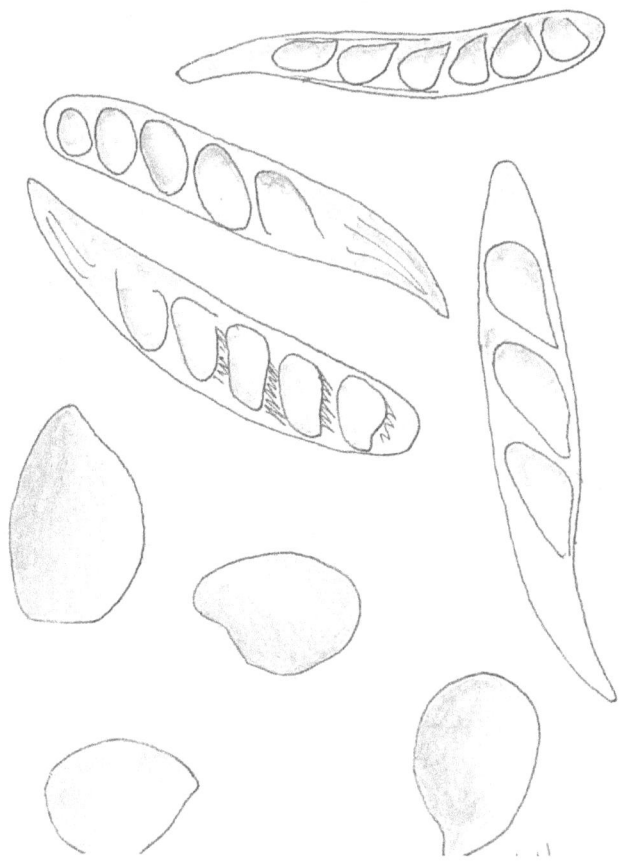

Pentaclethra Macrophilla seed pods

radially from the trunk of the tree, providing support. Big seed pods were scattered everywhere on the ground, the fruit of the tree *Pentaclethra Macrophilla*. December is the season when the seeds ripen and fall off the trees. They called them *fa wuii* in Mende and locals use the seeds and pods to make oil and soap.

One morning we went for a ride in the boat to the upstream tip of the island, where a small beach is located, a good spot for a swim we were told. As the boatload of white people went up the river, we passed a woman doing laundry in the river, and children on the bank who called out "*pumoi*!" At one point, we saw a monkey moving through the trees on the bank, so the driver, a Mende name Mamudu, stopped the boat so we could watch. The monkey began making a series of repetitive calls and Mamudu started imitating them. "*Nyahu! Nyahu! Nyahu!*" he shouted. Then he said to us, "The monkey speaks Mende!" He explained that in Mende "*nyahu*" means "stone me." The driver then interpreted the monkey call. "The monkey wants us to stone him with food, but we won't do that. We can't feed the monkeys!" We laughed at the joke, though it was unclear whom he was making fun of. The monkey? Or foreigners like us and our strange fascination with monkeys?

Buttress roots in Tiwai

We celebrated Christmas on the island, a small group of Americans far away from home and deep in the forest. The Christmas music we played on a portable speaker seemed out of place with the surroundings, yet strangely familiar. That night another volunteer and I went on a hike at night. The full moon was shining brightly, so we turned off our flashlights and crept along the trail to see what we would find. The gray light from the moon made the forest at once brilliant and opaque with shadows. Despite the bright moonlight, we found nothing except the din of the insects and the sound of our own cautious breathing.

I wanted to make a phone call home for Christmas, but, as the island had no cell service, I had to go back to Kambama. One of the guides volunteered to take me in the canoe. The paddle dipped into the water, and the hard plastic canoe slipped out into the river, the water glittering in the sun. The guide easily propelled the canoe upstream and, on the way, he told me a story, speaking in careful, precise English.

The guide said that many years ago a white man named John Oates came to Kambama because he wanted to do research. He was an American man, a professor at Hunter College. The man said he was looking for a monkey, the olive colobus monkey, he called it in his own language. He had traveled through Liberia and he found the monkeys and studied them. Now he was looking in Sierra Leone and he wanted to look on Tiwai Island. This man came to the chief at Kambama, they reached an agreement, and the chief permitted him to begin research.

Spiny trunk of a young cotton tree

Tiwai Island was where the people in Kambama made farms, especially rice. The soil of the land is fertile because of flooding during the rainy season, and they were famous for the rice grown on the island. Once John Oates came, the community was able to work together with him, and farming continued as it had before. However, all research ended during the war. The research site had to be abandoned and the Kambama people fled from their village. The rebels took everything on Tiwai Island, the generators, outboard motors, solar equipment. They even poached the monkeys on the island.

After the war, the people of Kambama returned home and began farming on Tiwai Island again. However, a different man came, a Sierra Leonean, and he wanted to establish a wildlife reserve on Tiwai Island and begin to cater to researchers and tourists again. The arrangement that this new man brought was not as beneficial to the local community as had been with John Oates. Under the arrangement with John Oates, if a guide took visitors on a tour of the island, the visitors would pay the guide directly. If the cook made food for the visitors, the visitors would pay the cook directly. People liked this arrangement, according to the guide. But it no longer worked like this anymore. The money went to the people in charge, while the cook and the guide and the other people who work on the island only received a small amount. It was enough to live on. The problem is, Kambama does not have enough land for farming. Without farming on Tiwai Island, a large section of Kambama's traditional land was lost. The land on the shore is not enough to grow sufficient food to feed everyone. The farmers can't make a living farming, but they also can't make a living working on the island for the tourists.

Cacao seedling

We had reached the shore at Kambama, and the guide continued his narrative. He told me that he is starting to grow cacao, one bag worth 30,000 leones, about eight dollars at the time. He showed me his cacao seedlings near the riverbank, grouped in squares of a hundred plants, each seedling planted in a small, black plastic bag. After five years, the plants will begin to produce. He said he has to think about the future, he has to think about his children. Once the cacao plants begin to produce, he said he hopes to stop working as a guide and focus on farming.

I was saddened to hear his tale, despite its hopeful ending. It was sobering to consider that the cost of protecting a place like Tiwai Island may be the loss of livelihoods for vulnerable people. Even well-meaning tourists or researchers, coming only to watch and observe, impact local communities in unexpected ways. This was my white privilege, I realized: to assume the world was built for me, to expect to move through it unhampered. The worst aspect of white privilege is that those who benefit from it are so often unaware of it. Although it perhaps was not his intention, the guide helped me recognize the impact of my presence, my appearance, my skin color. Even if I don't choose to oppress or disenfranchise others, I participate in patterns and institutions that do.

I eventually was able to make my Christmas phone call home. Even in Kambama, cell reception was not widely available, and someone had to show me the spot, a short walk out of the village, where you can stand and get cell service. A small parade of children followed me as I walked down the road. The man who helped me pointed to a stone in the center of a small, scuffed circle on the ground. This is where cell reception was. The signal was intermittent, and it was necessary to hold the phone up in the air just right. The children stood and watched me as I placed a few calls, then turned to go back.

At last, it was time to go back home, although now that I knew the route, I anticipated that the journey would go more quickly. I went back the way I came, through Blama and then to Boajibu. From Boajibu, I decided to take the back way to visit another Peace Corps friend, Dan, in the village of Jopawahun. I followed a narrow single-track west, going directly up and down a series of steep rocky hills. I stopped to rest in one small village, nothing more than a cluster of red mud homes, and the people there fed me rice and gave me a big bag of oranges. I felt I owed them something in return, but all I could do was thank them and continue on my way.

As I began to pedal up a particularly steep hill, my bike gave a sudden jerk and the something tarted grinding. Upon inspection, I saw that an inside component to the rear freewheel had broken and now it turned freely in both directions. Useless. I pushed the bike for perhaps four miles, coasting down the hills when I was able to, until I reached the town of Njala ("waterside" in Mende). Njala was a surprisingly big town for such an isolated area, with big concrete houses and a large school. Once again I had to find the local mechanic. Unfortunately, there were no new freewheels available in town, although the mechanic did find several broken, worn-out possibilities. Finally, a young man showed up with a broken wheel that had a freewheel attached, which just so happened to fit my bicycle.

In the meantime, two men on a nearby veranda invited me to eat rice. I agreed and we ate hot rice and potato leaf sauce from the same plate. Since this was holiday time, the sauce had big chunks of beef. After eating, one of the men, Kallon, told me in Krio: "You never knew that people even lived here in this little corner of the world until you came here and found the town of Njala!" I thanked them for the meal and, buoyed by the generosity of strangers, I continued my ride.

After another flat, I kept riding late into the evening, the sun sinking orange into the haze on the horizon. Outside of the village of Nengewa, I passed the Seventh Day Adventist Primary School, founded in 1931, the English-style education having come to the Mendes in southern Sierra Leone much before it arrived in the north. I completed the last leg of the journey to Jopawahun by flashlight.

Jopawahun is a small Mende village of farmers, though, as the Peace Corps volunteer, Dan, told me, it was experiencing a small diamond rush. A handful of people had been digging in the nearby stream, and it was rumored that someone found a diamond. As word spread, the population of the village began to swell as more hopeful people can to look for diamonds in the stream. One afternoon during my stay, a group of women gathered at the veranda, clapping and singing. One old woman moved to the center of the circle of dancers, and performed a shuffling dance routine that was unexpectedly spry for her advanced years. I think they expected me to dance with them, but, unsure of the protocol in this unfamiliar village, I remained on the veranda and soon the women moved on. Later Dan told me the women were part of the Bundu society, the secret society for women, and during the dry season they begin initiation ceremonies for young girls. That evening the sound of drumming, clapping and women's voices filled the air until late at night. Although these sounds were not menacing, they weren't happy either, but strange and eerie. I was grateful to be inside a house with four sturdy walls.

The next day I left early for Waridala. On the dusty gravel road, I passed through Yele, where I crossed over into Themne territory and the children began yelling *opoto* again. In Yele I saw a European style church – St. Michael's Church a sign told me -- with architecture that was incongruous with the surroundings, complete with a bas-relief sculpture of St Michael battling a dragon.

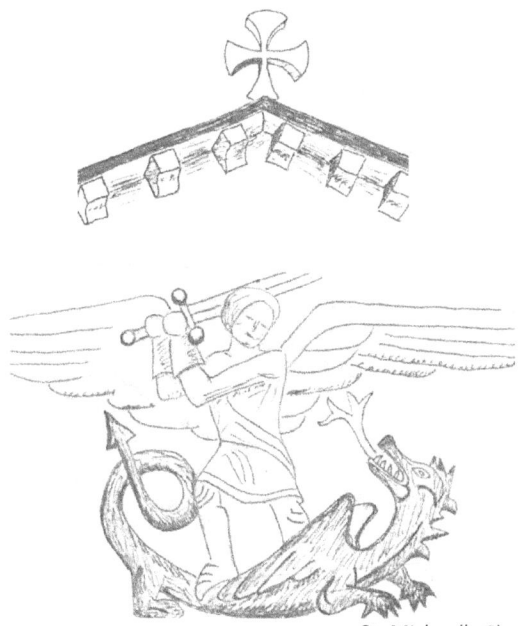

St. Michael's Church in Yele

I went through Matatoka again and Magburaka, then to Makeni, where I turned north. As I neared Bumban again and the Limbas, the children began to say "Father!" again, until finally some began to recognize me: they no longer called me *pumoi, opoto,* or fada, but Alie Fofana, my local Sierra Leone name. It was an unexpectedly comforting feeling. It felt like coming home.

On the trip to Tiwai, I saw a cross section of Sierra Leone. I saw different landscapes, heard different languages, and met different people. Yet everywhere I went, people were fascinated with white foreigners like myself. The children yelled at me, the adults tried to befriend me, and behind every interaction there seemed to be the assumption that all white people have access to great wealth. I felt like I was able to see two different worlds in Sierra Leone. One was the traditional world of the village, where people farm according to traditional methods. The other is the modern industrial world of foreigners like me. The two worlds co-exist uneasily, like the mining trucks roaring through villages of mud and stick houses, tourists visiting Tiwai island to see wildlife, where not too long ago people grew rice. A few select local people benefit from these foreign projects while everyone else is left out.

This trip I took on a bicycle provided the opportunity to move between these two worlds. From the vantage point of the bicycle it was possible to see the country on its own terms: the fascinating mix of languages, the carefully crafted farms and homes made by hand, the friendly and hospitable people. Sierra Leone will never become the foreign countries it so admires, but that is not a bad thing. The world of Sierra Leone has its own unique strength and beauty. Someday hopefully the country will see prosperity not as something that comes from abroad, but that starts at home.

Afterword

In many ways, my time in the Peace Corps was a transformative experience. I learned to love the tradition of hospitality in the country and the streak of deep, dark humor that everyone in Sierra Leone seems to wield with such effectiveness to mock themselves, their hardships, and the world. I experienced my racial identity in a direct and visceral manner. People thought I was rich because I was white. People wanted to be friends with me because I was white. I came to understand the truth that people of color everywhere are familiar with but white people curiously isolate themselves from: that people treat you differently based on your skin color.

Even though I learned much about myself and the world, I found my time in the Peace Corps to be a deeply ambiguous experience. Perhaps part of this was the teaching – it was an impossible task to navigate the cultural space of the classroom. I know that I made meaningful relationships with my students and other teachers, but at the same time I often felt like a placeholder, assigned to CJSS in Waridala by Sierra Leone government desperate to make good choices in front of the international community. It took me too long to even figure out the cultural expectations surrounding the classrooms. Improving education, it seems, will always be something that everyone can get behind; and it will always be far more difficult than it looks.

My job as a teacher provided a unique perspective and most of all I observed how much young people are the same all over the world. Much of my account here was devoted to cultural differences and my attempts to understand and navigate them. But my students were not yet fully socialized into their world, still just young, vulnerable, resilient and free – like young people everywhere. For example, I found the students in Form I – equivalent to sixth grade – to be enthusiastic and endearing, but after three years they were surly and bored, similar to the process followed by middle schoolers in the U.S. In a way, these observations of commonalities were the most heartbreaking of all. So many of my students were highly intelligent and learned so easily and quickly, yet they were stuck in Sierra Leone, memorizing from ragged exercise books, with dim prospects for their futures. It made me aware of the happenstance of birth, how radically different a person's opportunities might be in life, simply due to where on earth they were born. I was born in the U.S., with education freely available to me, at least through 12th grade, and I had opportunities like joining the Peace Corps and learning about the world; most of my students were simply putting off the life of a farmer for a few more years. The contrasts between our respective circumstances were sad, unfair, and, worst of all, just random.

Yet as the specific details of my experiences fade from my memory, the emotions remain: the wonder and awe at the beautiful landscapes, the friendly greetings and self-deprecating humor, the warmth of generosity. Never have I met people who had so little and yet were so kind and joyful. What I experienced was not always pleasant or comforting but at least it was true and real. I left my small-town Oregon home, went far away and found what I was looking for: new people, far-off locations, and a world so big and complex so to be incomprehensible.

www.ingramcontent.com/pod-product-compliance
Lightning Source LLC
Chambersburg PA
CBHW071110160426
43196CB00013B/2526